T0224677

# Practical Spring LDAP

## Using Enterprise Java-Based LDAP in Spring Data and Spring Framework 6

## Second Edition

**Balaji Varanasi**
**Andres Sacco**

Apress®

*Practical Spring LDAP: Using Enterprise Java-Based LDAP in Spring Data and Spring Framework 6, Second Edition*

Balaji Varanasi
Salt Lake City, UT, USA

Andres Sacco
Buenos Aires, Buenos Aires, Argentina

ISBN-13 (pbk): 979-8-8688-0001-6
https://doi.org/10.1007/979-8-8688-0002-3

ISBN-13 (electronic): 979-8-8688-0002-3

Managing Director, Apress Media LLC: Welmoed Spahr
Acquisitions Editor: Melissa Duffy
Development Editor: James Markham
Coordinating Editor: Gryffin Winkler

Cover designed by eStudioCalamar

Cover image by iulia_cristiana on unsplash (www.unsplash.com/)

Distributed to the book trade worldwide by Apress Media, LLC, 1 New York Plaza, New York, NY 10004, U.S.A. Phone 1-800-SPRINGER, fax (201) 348-4505, e-mail orders-ny@springer-sbm.com, or visit www.springeronline.com. Apress Media, LLC is a California LLC and the sole member (owner) is Springer Science + Business Media Finance Inc (SSBM Finance Inc). SSBM Finance Inc is a **Delaware** corporation.

For information on translations, please e-mail booktranslations@springernature.com; for reprint, paperback, or audio rights, please e-mail bookpermissions@springernature.com.

Apress titles may be purchased in bulk for academic, corporate, or promotional use. eBook versions and licenses are also available for most titles. For more information, reference our Print and eBook Bulk Sales web page at http://www.apress.com/bulk-sales.

Any source code or other supplementary material referenced by the author in this book is available to readers on GitHub (https://github.com/Apress). For more detailed information, please visit https://www.apress.com/gp/services/source-code.

Paper in this product is recyclable

*To my grandparents who taught me the importance of learning new things all the time.*

*To my wife and children for supporting me while writing this book.*

# Table of Contents

# About the Authors

**Balaji Varanasi** is a software development manager and technology entrepreneur. He has over 13 years of experience architecting and developing Java/.NET applications and, more recently, iPhone apps. During this period, he has worked in the areas of security, web accessibility, search, and enterprise portals. He has a master's degree in computer science and serves as adjunct faculty, teaching programming and information system courses. When not programming, he enjoys spending time with his lovely wife in Salt Lake City, Utah.

 **Andres Sacco** has been working as a developer since 2007 in different languages, including Java, PHP, Node.js, Scala, and Kotlin. His background is mostly in Java and the libraries or frameworks associated with this language. At most of the companies he worked for, he researched new technologies to improve the performance, stability, and quality of the applications of each company. In 2017, he started to find new ways to optimize the transference of data between applications to reduce the cost of infrastructure. He suggested some actions, some applicable in all of the manual microservices and others in just a few. All of this work includes creating a series of theoretic-practical projects (available on Manning.com). Recently, he coauthored an Apress book titled *Beginning Scala 3*. He also published a set of theoretic-practical projects about uncommon ways of testing, such as architecture tests and chaos engineering.

# About the Technical Reviewer

**Manuel Jordan** is an autodidactic developer and researcher who enjoys learning new technologies for his own experiments about creating new integrations among them.

Manuel won the 2010 Springy Award – Community Champion and Spring Champion 2013. In his little free time, he reads the Bible and composes music on his bass and guitar.

You can reach him through his Twitter account, @dr_pompeii.

# Acknowledgments

I would like to thank my family members and friends for their encouragement and support during the writing of this book:

- My wife, Gisela, who was always patient when I spent long hours at my computer desk working on this book

- My little daughter, Francesca, who helped me relax while writing each chapter

- My baby, Allegra, who is the new family member and my inspiration to write this book

- My friends, German Canale and Julian Delley, who always trusted me to write a book and supported me during tough times

Specially mentioning Manuel Jordan for guiding me in improving the quality of the book.

My sincere thanks to the beautiful team at Apress for their support during the publication of this book. Thanks to Shonmirin P.A. for providing excellent support. Finally, thanks to Mark Powers and Melissa Duffy for suggesting and allowing me to write a book. Also, I want to mention the great job that Balaji Varanasi did with the first edition of this book which gave the base to write the second edition.

# Introduction

*Practical Spring LDAP* provides complete coverage of Spring LDAP, a framework designed to take the pain out of LDAP programming. This book starts by explaining the fundamental concepts of LDAP and showing the reader how to set up the development environment. It then dives into Spring LDAP, analyzing the problems it is designed to solve. After that, the book focuses on the practical aspects of unit testing and integration testing with LDAP. An in-depth treatment of LDAP controls and Spring LDAP features, such as Object-Directory Mapping and LDIF (LDAP Data Interchange Format) parsing, follows this. Finally, it concludes with discussions on LDAP authentication and connection pooling.

## What the Book Covers

*Chapter 1* starts with an overview of directory servers. It then discusses the basics of LDAP and introduces the four LDAP information models. It finishes with an introduction to the LDIF format used for representing LDAP data.

*Chapter 2* focuses on the Java Naming and Directory Interface (JNDI). In this chapter, you look at creating applications that interact with LDAP using plain JNDI.

*Chapter 3* explains Spring LDAP and why it is an important option in an enterprise developer's repertoire. In this chapter, you set up the development environment to create Spring LDAP applications and other important tools, such as Maven and a test LDAP server. Finally, you implement a basic but complete Spring LDAP application using annotations.

*Chapter 4* covers the fundamentals of unit and integration testing. You then look at setting up an embedded LDAP server for unit testing your application code; alternatively, you will see how to use Testcontainers to run LDAP using a docker image. You also review available tools for generating test data. Finally, you use the Mockito library to mock test LDAP code.

*Chapter 5* introduces the basics of JNDI object factories and uses these factories for creating objects that are more meaningful to the application. You then examine a complete Data Access Object (DAO) layer implementation using Spring LDAP and object factories.

*Chapter 6* covers LDAP search. This chapter begins with the underlying ideas of LDAP search. I then introduce various Spring LDAP filters that make LDAP searching easier. Finally, you look at creating a custom search filter to address situations where the current set is insufficient.

*Chapter 7* provides an in-depth overview of LDAP controls that can be used for extending LDAP server functionality. Then it moves on to sorting and paging LDAP results using sort and page controls.

*Chapter 8* deals with Object-Directory Mapping (ODM), a feature in Spring LDAP. In this chapter, you look at bridging the gap between the domain model and the directory server. You then re-implement the DAO using ODM concepts.

*Chapter 9* introduces the important ideas of transactions and transactional integrity before analyzing the transaction abstractions provided by Spring Framework. Finally, it takes a look at Spring LDAP's compensating transaction support.

*Chapter 10* starts with implementing authentication, the most common operation against LDAP. It then deals with parsing LDIF files using another feature introduced in Spring. I end the chapter by looking at the connection pooling support provided by Spring LDAP.

# Target Audience

*Practical Spring LDAP* is intended for developers interested in building Java/JEE applications using LDAP. It also teaches techniques for creating unit/integration tests for LDAP applications. The book assumes basic familiarity with Spring Framework; prior exposure to LDAP is helpful but optional. Developers already familiar with Spring LDAP will find best practices and examples to help them get the most out of the framework.

# Prerequisites

You should install Java JDK[1] 21 or higher on your machine, Maven[2] 3.8.0 or higher, and some IDE. Some options for the IDE could be Eclipse,[3] IntelliJ IDEA,[4] Visual Studio Code,[5] and others, but you can choose which is the best for you.

To reduce the complexity of installing all LDAP vendors on your machine, I recommend you install Docker[6] and use it to run each LDAP. The use and installation of Docker are outside the scope of this book, but there are some tutorials[7] or cheatsheet[8] with the most common commands.

---

**Note**  If you don't have it installed on your machine, you can check Appendixes A, B, and C, which have information about installing the different tools and loading the information on LDAP.

---

After installing all the tools, you must check if they are correctly installed before reading the different chapters.

In the case of Java, you need to run the following command:

```
% java -version
openjdk 21 2023-09-19
OpenJDK Runtime Environment (build 21+35-2513)
OpenJDK 64-Bit Server VM (build 21+35-2513, mixed mode, sharing)
```

After that, you need to check if the version of Maven is correct using this command:

```
% mvn --version
Apache Maven 3.9.1
Maven home: /usr/share/maven
```

---

[1] https://jdk.java.net/

[2] https://maven.apache.org/

[3] https://www.eclipse.org/downloads

[4] https://www.jetbrains.com/es-es/idea/

[5] https://code.visualstudio.com/

[6] https://www.docker.com/

[7] https://docker-curriculum.com/

[8] https://michaelhaar.dev/my-docker-compose-cheatsheet

Last, if you want to check whether Docker runs correctly on your machine, you can do that using the following command:

```
% docker --version
Docker version 24.0.2, build cb74dfc
```

Remember that I mentioned that Docker is optional. It's only recommended for reducing the complexity of installing LDAP vendors on your machine.

## Downloading Source Code

The source code for the examples in this book can be downloaded from `www.apress.com`. For detailed information about locating this book's source code, visit `www.apress.com/gp/services/source-code`. The code is organized by chapter and can be built using Maven.

## Questions?

If you have any questions or suggestions, contact the author at `sacco.andres@gmail.com`.

## CHAPTER 1

# Introduction to LDAP

We all deal with directories daily. We use a telephone directory to look up phone numbers. When visiting a library, we use the library catalog to look up the books we want to read. We use the file system directory with computers to store our files and documents. Simply put, a directory is a repository of information. The information is usually organized so that it can be retrieved easily.

Directories on a network are typically accessed using the client/server communication model. Applications wanting to read or write data to a directory communicate with specialized servers. The directory server performs a read or write operation on the actual directory. Figure 1-1 shows this client/server interaction.

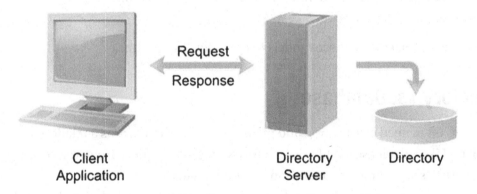

**Figure 1-1.** *Directory server and client interaction*

The communication between the directory server and client applications is usually accomplished using standardized protocols. The Lightweight Directory Access Protocol (LDAP) provides a standard protocol for communicating with a directory. The directory servers that implement the LDAP protocol are usually called LDAP servers. The LDAP

1

© Balaji Varanasi and Andres Sacco 2023
B. Varanasi and A. Sacco, *Practical Spring LDAP*, https://doi.org/10.1007/979-8-8688-0002-3_1

protocol is based on an earlier X.500[1] standard but is significantly simpler (lightweight) and easily extensible. Over the years, the LDAP protocol went through iterations and is currently at version 3.0.

# LDAP Overview

LDAP defines a message protocol used by directory clients and directory servers. LDAP can be better understood by considering the following four models it is based on:

- The Information model determines the structure of information stored in the directory.

- The Naming model defines how information is organized and identified in the directory.

- The Functional model defines the operations performed on the directory.

- The Security model defines how to protect information from unauthorized access.

We will look at each of these models in the following sections.

# Directory vs. Database

Beginners often need clarification and picture an LDAP directory as a relational database. Like a database, an LDAP directory stores information. However, several key characteristics set a directory apart from relational databases.

LDAP directories typically store data that is relatively static. For example, employee information stored in LDAP, such as their phone number or name, does not change daily. However, users and applications look up this information very frequently. Since the data in a directory is accessed more often than updated, LDAP directories follow the WORM principle[2, 3] and are heavily optimized for read performance. Placing data that change quite often in LDAP does not make sense.

---

[1] https://docs.oracle.com/javase/jndi/tutorial/ldap/models/x500.html
[2] https://en.wikipedia.org/wiki/Write_Once_Read_Many
[3] https://www.techtarget.com/searchstorage/definition/WORM-write-once-read-many

Relational databases employ referential integrity and locking techniques to ensure data consistency. The type of data stored in LDAP usually does not warrant such strict consistency requirements. Hence, most of these features need to be present on LDAP servers. Also, transactional semantics to roll back transactions are not defined under LDAP specification.

Relational databases follow normalization principles to avoid data duplication and redundancy. On the other hand, LDAP directories are organized in a hierarchical, object-oriented way. This organization violates some of the normalization principles. Also, there needs to be a concept of table joins in LDAP.

Even though directories lack several of the RDBMS[4] features mentioned earlier, many modern LDAP directories are built on top of relational databases such as DB2,[5] MySQL,[6] and PostgreSQL.[7]

At some point, LDAP has similar characteristics to nonrelational databases like Cassandra,[8] MongoDB,[9] and many others where the performance of the write/read, high availability, and scalability are more relevant than the consistency.

# Information Model

The basic unit of information stored in LDAP is an entry. Entries hold information about real-world objects such as employees, servers, printers, and organizations. Each entry in an LDAP directory comprises zero or more attributes. Attributes are key-value pairs that hold information about the object the entry represents. The key portion of an attribute is also called the attribute type and describes the information that can be stored in the attribute. The value portion of the attribute contains the actual information. Table 1-1 shows a portion of an entry representing an employee. The left column in the entry contains the attribute types, and the right column holds the attribute values.

---

[4] https://www.oracle.com/in/database/what-is-a-relational-database/

[5] https://www.ibm.com/products/db2

[6] https://www.mysql.com/

[7] https://www.postgresql.org/

[8] https://cassandra.apache.org/_/index.html

[9] https://www.mongodb.com/

**Table 1-1.** *Employee LDAP Entry*

| Employee Entry | |
| --- | --- |
| objectClass | inetOrgPerson |
| givenName | John |
| surname | Smith |
| mail | john@inflix.com |
| | jsmith@inflix.com |
| mobile | +1 801 100 1000 |

**Note**    Attribute names, by default, are case-insensitive. However, it is recommended to use camel case format in LDAP operations.

You will notice that the mail attribute has two values. Attributes that are allowed to hold multiple values are called multivalued attributes. Single-valued attributes, on the other hand, can only hold a single value. The LDAP specification does not guarantee the order of the values in a multivalued attribute.

Each attribute type is associated with a syntax that dictates the format of the data stored as an attribute value. For example, the mobile attribute type has a `telephoneNumber` syntax. This forces the attribute to hold a string value with a length between 1 and 32.

Additionally, the syntax also defines the attribute value behavior during search operations. For example, the `givenName` attribute has the syntax `DirectoryString`. This syntax enforces that only alphanumeric characters are allowed as values. Table 1-2 lists some common attributes and their associated syntax description.

***Table 1-2.*** *Common Entry Attributes*

| Attribute Type | Syntax | Description |
|---|---|---|
| commonName | DirectoryString | Stores the common name of a person. |
| company | DirectoryString | Stores the company's name. |
| employeeNumber | DirectoryString | Stores the employee's identification number in the organization. |
| givenName | DirectoryString | Stores the user's first name. |
| jpegPhoto | Binary | Stores one or more images of the person. |
| mail | IA5 String | Stores a person's SMTP mail address. |
| mobile | TelephoneNumber | Stores a person's mobile number. |
| postalAddress | Postal Address | Stores the user's ZIP or postal code. |
| postalCode | DirectoryString | Stores the user's ZIP or postal code. |
| st | DirectoryString | Stores the state or province name. |
| street | DirectoryString | Stores the street address. |
| surname | DirectoryString | Stores the last name of the person. |
| telephoneNumber | TelephoneNumber | Stores the person's primary telephone number. |
| uid | DirectoryString | Stores the user id. |
| title | DirectoryString | Stores the name of the position or the company's function. |
| wwwhomepage | DirectoryString | Stores the official web page of the company. |

The attributes in Table 1-2 are the most used for the developers and tools. Still, there is a big list of other attributes depending on whether your vendor or the tool supports it or not; for example, on the official web page[10] of Microsoft, all the attributes are supported for the Active Directory.

---

[10] https://learn.microsoft.com/en-us/windows/win32/adschema/attributes-all

# Object Classes

In object-oriented languages, such as Java, we create a class and use it as a blueprint for creating objects. The class defines the attributes/data (and behavior/methods) that these instances can have. Similarly, object classes in LDAP determine the attributes an LDAP entry can have. These object classes also define which attributes are mandatory and which are optional. Every LDAP entry has a special attribute aptly named `objectClass` that holds the object class it belongs to. Looking at the objectClass value in the employee entry in Table 1-1, we can conclude that the entry belongs to the `inetOrgPerson` class. Table 1-3 shows the required and optional attributes in a standard LDAP person object class. The `cn` attribute holds the person's common name, whereas the `sn` attribute holds the person's family name or surname.

***Table 1-3.*** *Person Object Class*

| Required Attributes | Optional Attributes |
| --- | --- |
| sn | description |
|  | telephoneNumber |
| cn | userPassword |
| objectClass | seeAlso |

As in Java, an object class can extend other object classes. This inheritance will allow the child object class to inherit parent class attributes. For example, the person object class defines attributes such as common name and surname. The object class `inetOrgPerson` extends the person class and thus inherits all the person's attributes.

Additionally, `inetOrgPerson` defines attributes required for a person working in an organization, such as `departmentNumber` and `employeeNumber`. One special object class, namely, `top`, does not have any parents. All other object classes are decedents of `top` and inherit all the attributes declared in it. The `top` object class includes the mandatory `objectClass` attribute. Figure 1-2 shows the object inheritance.

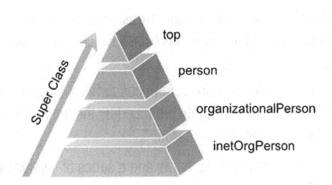

***Figure 1-2.*** *LDAP object inheritance*

Most LDAP implementations come with standard object classes that can be used out of the box. Table 1-4 lists some of these LDAP object classes and their commonly used attributes.

***Table 1-4.*** *Common LDAP Object Classes*

| Object Class | Attributes | Description |
|---|---|---|
| top | objectClass | Defines the root object class. All other object classes must extend this class. |
| organization | o | Represents a company or an organization. The o attribute typically holds the name of the organization. |
| organizationalUnit | ou | Represents a department or similar entity inside an organization. |
| person | sn<br>cn<br>telephoneNumber<br>userPassword | Represents a person in the directory and requires the sn (surname) and cn (common name) attributes. |
| organizationalPerson | registeredAddress<br>postalAddress postalCode | Subclasses that represent a person in an organization. |
| inetOrgPerson | uid departmentNumber<br>employeeNumber<br>givenName manager | It provides additional attributes and can be used to represent a person working in today's Internet- and intranet-based organization. The uid attribute holds the person's username or user id. |

On Oracle's official website,[11] you can find the list of LDAP object classes with information about the Request for Comments (RFC), which added each object class.

---

**Note**   In this book, you will see many references to RFCs. Request for Comments (RFC) is a series of technical documents produced by the Internet Engineering Task Force (IETF)[12] that specify certain standards.

Each RFC has a number as part of the name and a series of sections with the specification. An RFC could become obsolete to many other RFCs because a new specification about certain technology appears, for example, a new version of LDAP.

On the RFC Editor web page,[13] you can find information about RFCs and the publication process of the new one.

---

# Directory Schema

The LDAP directory schema is a set of rules determining the type of information stored in a directory. Schemas can be considered packaging units and contain attribute type definitions and object class definitions. The schema rules are verified before an entry can be stored in LDAP. This schema checking ensures that the entry has all the required attributes and contains no attributes not part of the schema. Figure 1-3 represents a generic LDAP schema.

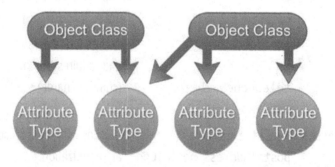

**Figure 1-3.**  *LDAP generic schema*

---

[11] https://docs.oracle.com/cd/E24001_01/oid.1111/e10035/schema_objclass.htm
[12] https://www.ietf.org/
[13] https://www.rfc-editor.org/

Like databases, directory schemas must be well designed to address issues like data redundancy. Before implementing your schema, it is worth looking at publicly available standard schemas. These standard schemas often contain all definitions to store the required data and, more importantly, ensure interoperability across other directories.

## Naming Model

The LDAP Naming model defines how entries are organized in a directory. It also determines how a particular entry can be uniquely identified. The Naming model recommends that entries be stored logically in a hierarchical fashion. This entry tree is often called a directory information tree (DIT). Figure 1-4 provides an example of a generic directory tree.

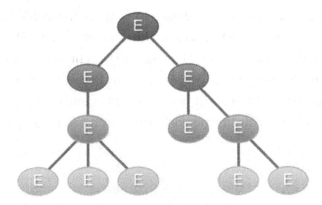

***Figure 1-4.*** *Generic DIT*

The tree's root is usually referred to as the base or suffix of the directory. This entry represents the organization that owns the directory. The format of suffixes can vary from implementation to implementation, but generally, there are three recommended approaches, as listed in Figure 1-5.

***Figure 1-5.*** *Directory suffix naming conventions*

**Note**  DC stands for domain component.

The first recommended technique is to use the organization's domain name as the suffix. For example, if the organization's domain name is example.com, the directory suffix will be o=example.com. The second technique also uses the domain name, but each name component is prepended with "dc=" and joined by commas. So the domain name example.com would result in a suffix dc=example, dc=com. This technique is proposed in RFC 2247[14] and is popular with Microsoft Active Directory. The third technique uses the X.500 model and creates a suffix in the format o=organization name, c=country code. In the United States, the suffix for the organization example would be o=example, c=us.

The naming model also defines naming and uniquely identifying entries in a directory. Entries with a common immediate parent are uniquely identified via their relative distinguished name (RDN), also called distinguished name (DN). The RDN is computed using one or more attribute/value pairs of the entry. In its simplest case, RDN is usually of the form attribute-name = attribute value. Figure 1-6 provides a simplified representation of an organization directory. Each person entry under ou=employees has a unique uid. So the RDN for the first person entry would be uid=emp1, where emp1 is the employee's user id.

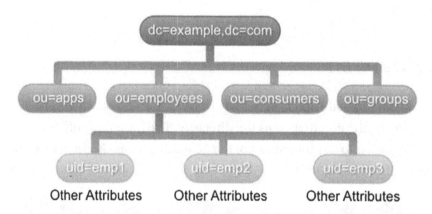

***Figure 1-6.*** *Example of an organization directory*

[14] https://www.ietf.org/rfc/rfc2247.txt

---

**Note**   The distinguished name is not an actual attribute in the entry. It is a logical name associated with the entry.

---

It is important to remember that RDN cannot be used to uniquely identify the entry in the entire tree. However, this can be easily done by combining the RDNs of all the entries in the path from the top of the tree to the entry. The result of this combination is referred to as distinguished name (DN). In Figure 1-6, the DN for person 1 would be uid=emp1, ou=employees, dc=example, dc=com. Since the DN is made by combining RDNs, if an entry's RDN changes, the DNs of that entry and all its child entries also change.

There can be situations where a set of entries does not have a unique attribute. In those scenarios, one option is to combine multiple attributes to create uniqueness. For example, we can use the consumer's common name and email address in the previous directory as an RDN. Multivalued RDNs are represented by separating each attribute pair with a +, like so:

```
cn = Balaji  Varanasi +            mail=balaji@inflinx.com
```

Some special characters on the RDN must be escaped to prevent different problems. The special characters are + (plus), = (equals), < (less than), > (greater than), ; (semicolon), , (comma), \ (backslash), # (number sign), and ".

There are different approaches to escape the characters, like adding the backslash ("\" ASCII 92) before the special character; this approach is the most commonly used. The other replaces the special characters with a backslash and hexadecimal digit, and the last one surrounds the attribute's value with quotation marks ("").

---

**Note**   Multivalued RDNs are usually discouraged. Creating a unique sequence attribute is recommended in those scenarios to ensure uniqueness.

---

# Functional Model

The LDAP Functional model describes the access and modification operations that can be performed on the directory using the LDAP protocol. These operations fall into three categories: query, update, and authentication.

The query operations are used to search and retrieve information from a directory. So whenever some information needs to be read, a search query must be constructed and executed against LDAP. The search operation takes a starting point within DIT, the search depth, and the attributes an entry must have for a match. In Chapter 6, you'll delve deep into searching and look at all the available options.

The update operations add, modify, delete, and rename directory entries. As the name suggests, the add operation adds a new entry to the directory. This operation requires the DN of the entry to be created and a set of attributes that constitute the entry. The delete operation takes a fully qualified DN of the entry and deletes it from the directory. The LDAP protocol allows only the leaf entries to be deleted. The modified operation updates an existing entry. This operation takes the entry's DN and a set of modifications, such as adding a new attribute, updating a new one, or removing an existing one. The rename operation can rename or move entries in a directory.

The authentication operations are used for connecting and ending sessions between the client and the LDAP server. A bind operation initiates an LDAP session between the client and server. Typically, this would result in an anonymous session. The client can provide a DN and credentials to authenticate and create an authenticated session. On the other hand, the unbind operation can be used to terminate an existing session and disconnect from the server.

LDAP V3 introduced a framework for extending existing operations and adding new ones without changing the protocol. You will take a look at these operations in Chapter 7.

# Security Model

The LDAP Security model protects LDAP directory information from unauthorized access. The model specifies which clients can access which parts of the directory and what kinds of operations (search vs. update) are allowed.

The LDAP Security model is based on the client authenticating to the server. As discussed earlier, this authentication process or bind operation involves the client supplying a DN identifying itself and a password. An anonymous session is established if the client does not provide a DN and password. RFC 2829[15] defines a

---

[15] https://www.ietf.org/rfc/rfc2829.txt

set of authentication methods that LDAP V3 servers must support. After successful authentication, the access control models are consulted to determine whether the client has sufficient privileges to do what is requested. Unfortunately, no standards exist for access control models, and each vendor provides their implementations.

# LDIF Format

The LDAP Data Interchange Format (LDIF) is a standard text-based format for representing directory content and update requests. The LDIF format is defined in RFC 2849.[16] LDIF files are typically used to export data from one directory server and import it into another. It is also popular for archiving directory data and applying bulk updates to a directory. You will use LDIF files to store your test data and refresh the directory server between unit tests.

The basic format of an entry represented in LDIF is as follows:

```
#comment
dn: <distinguished name>
objectClass:  <object class>
objectClass:  <object class>
...
...
<attribute  type>: <attribute  value>
<attribute  type>: <attribute  value>
...
```

Lines in the LDIF file starting with a # character are considered comments. The dn and at least one objectClass entry definition are considered required. Attributes are represented as name/value pairs separated by a colon. Multiple attribute values are specified in separate lines and will have the same attribute type. Since LDIF files are purely text based, binary data needs to be Base64 encoded before it is stored as part of the LDIF file.

---

[16] https://www.ietf.org/rfc/rfc2849.txt

Blank lines separate multiple entries in the same LDIF file. Listing 1-1 shows an LDIF file with three employee entries. Notice that the cn attribute is multivalued and is represented twice for each employee.

***Listing 1-1.*** LDIF file with three employee entries

```
#  Barbara's Entry
dn: cn=Barbara J Jensen,  dc=example, dc=com
#  multi valued attribute
cn: Barbara J Jensen
cn:  Babs Jensen
objectClass:  personsn: Jensen
#  Bjorn's  Entry
dn: cn=Bjorn J Jensen,  dc=example, dc=com
cn: Bjorn J Jensen
cn:  Bjorn Jensen
objectClass:  person
sn: Jensen
#  Base64 encoded  JPEG  photo
jpegPhoto:: /9j/4AAQSkZJRgABAAAAAQABAAD/2wBDABALD
A4MChAODQ4SERATGCgaGBYWGDEjJROoOjM9PDkzODdASFxOQ ERXRTc4UG1RV19iZ2hnPk1xeXB
keFxlZ2P/2wBDARESEhgVG
#  Jennifer's  Entry
dn: cn=Jennifer  J Jensen,  dc=example, dc=com
cn: Jennifer J Jensen
cn: Jennifer  Jensen
objectClass: person
sn: Jensen
```

# LDAP History

LDAP was developed by Tim Howes, Steve Kille, and Wengyik Yeong to create a network protocol to get data out. In 1993 appeared the first draft of the RFC 1487,[17] which contained the specification of LDAP based on the access of X.500.

---

[17] https://datatracker.ietf.org/doc/html/rfc1487

The first version acts as a proxy or gateway to X.500 directories, a comprehensive directory service developed in the 1980s.

Tim Howes, with his colleagues, created the *Open Source University of Michigan LDAP Implementation*, which became the reference for all the LDAP servers. The project's website is active[18] and accessible only for historical reference.

The second version, the first to be operative (LDAPv2), was released in 1993 as an Internet Engineering Task Force (IETF) Proposed Standard with basic operations like searching and modifying information. This version offers limited functionality and has some problems related to the security mechanisms.

The third version, the latest available, was released in 1997, including many improvements related to security, like Transport Layer Security (TLS) and the possibility of supporting referrals. It was based on RFCs like RFC 2251[19] and RFC 4519,[20] which explain the protocol and the supported data models. This version became the de facto standard for directory services, and many applications have support to integrate and use LDAP to obtain certain information.

## LDAP Vendors

LDAP gained wide support from various vendors. There has also been a strong open source movement to produce LDAP servers. Table 1-5 outlines some of the popular directory servers and include the information about which is the docker image to run each of them with a small configuration.

---

[18] www.umich.edu/~dirsvcs/ldap/ldap.html
[19] https://datatracker.ietf.org/doc/html/rfc2251
[20] https://datatracker.ietf.org/doc/html/rfc4519

**Table 1-5.** *LDAP Vendors*

| Directory Name | Vendor | Open Source? | URL | Docker Image |
|---|---|---|---|---|
| Apache DS | Apache | Yes | https://directory.apache.org/apacheds/ | https://hub.docker.com/r/openmicroscopy/apacheds |
| OpenLDAP | OpenLDAP | Yes | https://www.openldap.org/ | https://hub.docker.com/r/bitnami/openldap |
| Tivoli Directory Server | IBM | No | https://www.ibm.com/docs/en/i/7.5?topic=services-tivoli-directory-server-i-ldap | No existing official image; you need to create one manually. |
| Active Directory | Microsoft | No | https://learn.microsoft.com/en-us/windows/win32/adsi/so-what-is-active-directory?redirectedfrom=MSDN | No existing official image; you need to create one manually. |
| eDirectory | Novell | No | https://www.microfocus.com/en-us/cyberres/identity-access-management/edirectory | No existing official image; you must create one manually. |
| Oracle Directory Server Enterprise Edition (ODSEE) | Oracle (formerly Sun) | No | https://www.oracle.com/security/identity-management/technologies/directory-server-enterprise-edition | No existing official image; you need to create one manually. |
| Oracle Internet Directory (OID) | | No | https://www.oracle.com/middleware/technologies/internet-directory.html | No existing official image; you need to create one manually. |
| OpenDJ | ForgeRock | Yes | https://github.com/OpenIdentityPlatform/OpenDJ | https://hub.docker.com/r/openidentityplatform/opendj |

ApacheDS and OpenDJ are pure Java implementations of LDAP directories. You will be using these two servers for unit and integration testing of the code throughout this book.

# Sample Application

Throughout this book, you will be working with a directory for a hypothetical book library. I have chosen the library because the concept is universal and easy to grasp. A library usually stores books and other multimedia that patrons can borrow. Libraries also employ people to take care of daily library operations. To keep things manageable, the directory will not store book information. A relational database is suitable for recording book information. Figure 1-7 shows the LDAP directory tree for our library application.

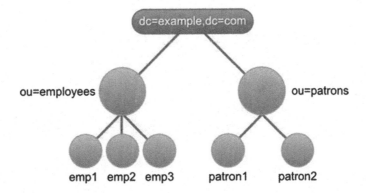

***Figure 1-7.***  *Library DIT*

I have used the RFC 2247[14] convention in this directory tree to name the base entry. The base entry has two organizational unit entries that hold the employees' and patrons' information. The ou=employees part of the tree will hold all the library employee entries. The ou=patrons part of the tree will hold the library patron entries. Both library employee and patron entries are of the type `inetOrgPerson objectClass`. Both employees and patrons access library applications using their unique login id. Thus, the `uid` attribute will be used as the RDN for entries.

# Summary

LDAP and applications that interact with LDAP have become a key part of every enterprise today. This chapter covered the basics of the LDAP directory. You learned that LDAP stores information as entries. Each entry is made up of attributes that are simply key-value pairs. These entries can be accessed via their distinguished names. You also saw that LDAP directories have schemas that determine the type of information that can be stored.

The next chapter will look at communicating with an LDAP directory using Java Naming and Directory Interface (JNDI). In the chapters following Chapter 2, you will focus on using Spring LDAP for developing LDAP applications.

# CHAPTER 2

# Java Support for LDAP

As the name suggests, the Java Naming and Directory Interface (JNDI) provides a standardized programming interface for accessing naming and directory services. It is a generic Application Programming Interface (API) that can access various systems, including file systems, Enterprise Java Beans (EJB),[1] Common Object Request Broker Architecture (CORBA),[2] and directory services such as the Network Information Service and LDAP. JNDI's abstractions to directory services can be viewed as similar to Java Database Connectivity (JDBC)'s abstractions to relational databases.

The JNDI architecture consists of an Application Programming Interface or API and a Service Provider Interface or SPI. Developers program their Java applications using the JNDI API to access directory/naming services. Vendors implement the SPI with details that deal with actual communication to their particular service/product. Such implementations are referred to as service providers. Figure 2-1 shows the JNDI architecture and a few naming and directory service providers. This pluggable architecture provides a consistent programming model and prevents the need to learn a separate API for each product.

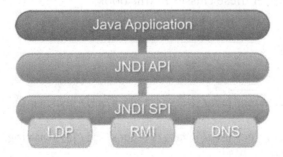

***Figure 2-1.*** *JNDI architecture*

---

[1] https://en.wikipedia.org/wiki/Jakarta_Enterprise_Beans

[2] https://www.ibm.com/docs/en/sdk-java-technology/8?topic=orb-corba

© Balaji Varanasi and Andres Sacco 2023

B. Varanasi and A. Sacco, *Practical Spring LDAP*, https://doi.org/10.1007/979-8-8688-0002-3_2

The JNDI has been part of the standard JDK distribution since Java version 1.3 and has not moved to Jakarta like other packages. The API itself is spread across five packages:

- The **javax.naming**[3] package contains classes and interfaces for looking up and accessing objects in a naming service.

- The **javax.naming.directory**[4] package contains classes and interfaces that extend the core javax.naming package. These classes can access directory services and perform advanced operations such as filtered searching.

- The **javax.naming.event**[5] package has functionality for event notification when accessing naming and directory services.

- The **javax.naming.ldap**[6] package contains classes and interfaces that support the LDAP Version 3 controls and operations. Later chapters will examine controls and operations.

- The **javax.naming.ldap.spi**[7] package contains classes to support defining custom DNS for LDAP. The support of this feature has appeared since Java 12.

- The **javax.naming.spi**[8] package contains the SPI interfaces and classes. As mentioned earlier, service providers implement SPI, and we will not cover these classes in this book.

---

[3] https://docs.oracle.com/en/java/javase/21/docs/api/java.naming/javax/naming/package-summary.html

[4] https://docs.oracle.com/en/java/javase/21/docs/api/java.naming/javax/naming/directory/package-summary.html

[5] https://docs.oracle.com/en/java/javase/21/docs/api/java.naming/javax/naming/event/package-summary.html

[6] https://docs.oracle.com/en/java/javase/21/docs/api/java.naming/javax/naming/ldap/package-summary.html

[7] https://docs.oracle.com/en/java/javase/21/docs/api/java.naming/javax/naming/ldap/spi/package-summary.html

[8] https://docs.oracle.com/en/java/javase/21/docs/api/java.naming/javax/naming/spi/package-summary.html

# LDAP Using JNDI

While JNDI allows access to a directory service, it is essential to remember that JNDI is not a directory or a naming service. Thus, we need a running LDAP directory server to access LDAP using JNDI.

Accessing LDAP using JNDI usually involves three steps:

- Connect to LDAP

- Perform LDAP operations

- Close the resources

---

**Note**   Check if you have installed the correct version of Java on your machine. To do this, look at Appendix A, which explains how to do it.

If you don't have a test LDAP server available, please refer to the steps in Appendix B for installing a local LDAP server or running it using Docker. The explanation about how to install Docker and check if everything is okay appears in Appendix A.

This chapter aims to show how you can do different operations on LDAP using Java without any framework. With this approach, you will see the complexity of doing certain operations and writing many lines of code to do something simple with the assistance of some framework like Spring LDAP.

---

# Connect to LDAP

All the naming and directory operations using JNDI are performed relative to a context. So the first step in using JNDI is to create a context that acts as a starting point on the LDAP server. Such a context is referred to as an initial context. Once an initial context is established, it can look up other contexts or add new objects.

The **Context** interface and **InitialContext** class in the **javax.naming** package can be used for creating an initial naming context. Since we are dealing with a directory here, we will use a more specific **DirContext** interface and its implementation **InitialDirContext**. Both **DirContext** and **InitialDirContext** are available inside the **javax.naming.directory** package. The directory context instances can be configured with properties that provide information about the LDAP server. The code in Listing 2-1 creates a context for an LDAP server running locally on port 1389.

***Listing 2-1.*** How to create a basic connection with LDAP

```
Properties environment =  new  Properties();
environment.setProperty(DirContext.INITIAL_CONTEXT_FACTORY, "com.sun.jndi.
ldap.LdapCtxFactory");
environment.setProperty(DirContext.PROVIDER_URL, "ldap://localhost:11389");
DirContext context  =  new  InitialDirContext(environment);
```

---

**Note**    In the following parts of the chapter, I will explain in detail the most relevant parts to connect and execute some operations to LDAP.

By the end of this chapter, you will see the different outputs of the execution of the different methods.

---

In Listing 2-1, we have used the ***INITIAL_CONTEXT_FACTORY*** constant to specify the service provider class that needs to be used. Here, we use the sun provider ***com. sun.jndi.ldap.LdapCtxFactory***, which is part of the standard JDK distribution. The PROVIDER_URL is used to specify the fully qualified URL of the LDAP server. The URL includes the protocol (LDAP for nonsecure or LDAPs for secure connections), the server hostname, and the port.

---

**Note**    The declaration of the type on a variable has been optional since Java 14, so you don't need to declare that the variable ***environment*** has the type ***Properties***; you can replace the keyword ***var***, and the compiler will infer the correct type.

This change does not add any feature related to the performance, so I decided to keep the code simple.

---

Once a connection to the LDAP server is established, the application can identify itself by providing authentication information. Contexts like the one created in Listing 2-1, where authentication information is not provided, are called anonymous contexts. LDAP servers usually have ACLs (access list controls) that restrict operations and information to certain accounts. So it is very common in enterprise applications to create and use authenticated contexts. Listing 2-2 provides an example of creating an authenticated context. Notice that we have used three additional properties to provide the binding credentials. The **SECURITY_AUTHENTICATION** property is set to simple, indicating that we will use a plain text username and password for authentication.

***Listing 2-2.*** How to connect on LDAP using the credentials

```
Properties environment =  new  Properties();
environment.setProperty(DirContext.INITIAL_CONTEXT_FACTORY, "com.sun.jndi.
ldap.LdapCtxFactory");
environment.setProperty(DirContext.PROVIDER_URL, "ldap://localhost:11389");
environment.setProperty(DirContext.SECURITY_AUTHENTICATION, "simple");
environment.setProperty(DirContext.SECURITY_PRINCIPAL, "Directory
Manager");
environment.setProperty(DirContext.SECURITY_CREDENTIALS, "secret");
DirContext context  =  new  InitialDirContext(environment);
```

---

**Note**   On the declaration of the different properties, you can see the class **DirContext** appear many times, which is not the best approach, so if you want to reduce the duplicates, you can simplify using static imports. For example, you can declare the static import like this: ***import static javax.naming.directory. DirContext.INITIAL_CONTEXT_FACTORY***, and on the declaration of the variable, just use ***PROVIDER_URL***.

---

Any problems occurring during the context creation will be reported as instances of *javax.naming.NamingException*. *NamingException* is the superclass of all the exceptions thrown by the JNDI API. This is a checked exception and must be handled properly for the code to compile. Table 2-1 lists common exceptions we will likely encounter during JNDI development.

***Table 2-1.*** *Common LDAP Exceptions*

| Exception | Description |
|---|---|
| AttributeInUseException | Thrown when an operation tries to add an existing attribute. |
| AttributeModificationException | Thrown when an operation tries to add/remove/update an attribute and violates the attribute's schema or state. For example, adding two values to a single-valued attribute would result in this exception. |
| CommunicationException | Thrown when an application fails to communicate (network problems) with the LDAP server. |
| InvalidAttributesException | Thrown when an operation tries to add or modify an attribute set that has been specified incompletely or incorrectly. For example, adding a new entry without specifying all the required attributes would result in this exception. |
| InvalidAttributeValueException | Thrown when an operation tries to add or modify a value of an attribute that enters a conflict with the schema definition. |
| InvalidSearchFilterException | Thrown when a search operation is given a malformed search filter. |
| LimitExceededException | Thrown when a search operation abruptly terminates as a user- or system-specified result limit is reached. |
| NameAlreadyBoundException | Thrown to indicate that an entry cannot be added as the associated name is already bound to a different object. |
| NotContextException | Thrown when an operation process until the context is required to continue. |
| OperationNotSupportedException | Thrown when a context implementation does not support a specific operation when invoked. |
| PartialResultException | Thrown to indicate that only a portion of the expected results is returned and the operation cannot be completed. |
| SizeLimitExceededException | Thrown when a method produces a result that exceeds a size-related limit. |
| TimeLimitExceededException | Thrown when a method produces a result that exceeds a time-related limit. |

# LDAP Operations

Once we obtain an initial context, we can perform various operations on LDAP using the context. These operations can involve looking up another context, creating a new one, and updating or removing an existing one. Here is an example of looking up another context with DN uid=emp1,ou=employees,dc=inflinx,dc=com:

```
DirContext anotherContext  =  context.lookup("uid=emp1,ou=employees,dc=
                               inflinx,dc=com");
```

We will closely examine each of these operations in the coming section.

# Closing Resources

After completing all desired LDAP operations, it is important to close the context and any other associated resources properly. Closing a JNDI resource simply involves calling the close method on it. Listing 2-3 shows the code associated with closing a **DirContext**. The code shows that the close method also throws a **NamingException** that needs to be properly handled.

**Listing 2-3.** How to close the connection with LDAP

```
try {
    context.close();
} catch  (NamingException e)  {
    //Do something with the exception, like log the error.
}
```

---

**Note**   The previous block does not use "try-with-resources" because DirContext does not implement the auto closeable.

---

# Creating a New Entry

Consider the case where a new employee starts with our hypothetical library, and we are asked to add their information to LDAP. As we have seen earlier, before an entry can be added to LDAP, it is necessary to obtain an InitialDirContext. Listing 2-4 defines a reusable method for doing this.

***Listing 2-4.*** Create a method to connect with LDAP

```
private  DirContext getContext() throws NamingException{
    Properties environment = new  Properties();
    environment.setProperty(DirContext.INITIAL_CONTEXT_FACTORY, "com.sun.
    jndi.ldap.LdapCtxFactory");
    environment.setProperty(DirContext.PROVIDER_URL, "ldap://
    localhost:1389");
    environment.setProperty(DirContext.SECURITY_PRINCIPAL, "cn=Directory
    Manager");
    environment.setProperty(DirContext.SECURITY_CREDENTIALS, "secret");
    return  new InitialDirContext(environment);
}
```

Once we have the initial context, adding the new employee information is straightforward, as shown in Listing 2-5.

***Listing 2-5.*** Add a new entry on LDAP

```
public  void addEmployee(Employee employee)  {
    DirContext context  =  null;
    try  {
        context =  getContext();
        // Populate the attributes
        Attributes attributes  =  new  BasicAttributes();
        attributes.put(new  BasicAttribute("objectClass", "inetOrgPerson"));
        attributes.put(new BasicAttribute("uid", employee.getUid()));
        attributes.put(new BasicAttribute("givenName", employee.
        getFirstName()));
        attributes.put(new BasicAttribute("surname", employee.
        getLastName()));
        attributes.put(new BasicAttribute("commonName", employee.
        getCommonName()));
```

```
    attributes.put(new BasicAttribute("departmentNumber", employee.
    getDepartmentNumber()));
    attributes.put(new  BasicAttribute("mail", employee.getEmail()));
    attributes.put(new BasicAttribute("employeeNumber", employee.
    getEmployeeNumber()));
    Attribute  phoneAttribute =
    new  BasicAttribute("telephoneNumber");
    for(String phone : employee.getPhone())  {
       phoneAttribute.add(phone);
    }
    attributes.put(phoneAttribute);
     // Get the fully   qualified DN
    String dn   =  "uid="+employee.getUid() +  "," +  BASE_PATH;
     // Add  the entry
    context.createSubcontext("dn", attributes);
  } catch(NamingException e)  {
     // Handle the exception and show the description of the problem
  } finally  {
      closeContext(context);
     }
}
```

As you can see, the first step in the process is to create a set of attributes that needs to be added to the entry. JNDI provides the *javax.naming.directory.Attributes* interface and its implementation *javax.naming.directory.BasicAttributes* to abstract an attribute collection. We then add the employee's attributes one at a time to the collection using JNDI's *javax.naming.directory.BasicAttribute* class. Notice that we have taken two approaches in creating the BasicAttribute class. In the first approach, we added the single-valued attributes by passing the attribute name and value to BasicAttribute's constructor. To handle the multivalued attribute telephone, we first created the BasicAttribute instance by just passing in the name. Then, we individually added the telephone values to the attribute. Once all the attributes are added, we invoked the createSubcontext method on the initial context to add the entry. The createSubcontext method requires the fully qualified DN of the entry to be added.

Notice that we have delegated the closing of the context to a separate method closeContext. Listing 2-6 shows its implementation.

***Listing 2-6.*** How to close the connection with LDAP

```
private void closeContext(DirContext context) {
    try {
        if (null != context) {
            context.close();
        }
    } catch (NamingException e) {
        // Handle the exception and show the description of the problem
    }
}
```

# Updating an Entry

Modifying an existing LDAP entry can involve any of the following operations:

- Add a new attribute and value(s) or add a new value to an existing multivalued attribute.

- Replace an existing attribute value(s).

- Remove an attribute and its value(s).

To allow modification of the entries, JNDI provides an aptly named ***javax.naming.directory.ModificationItem*** class.

A ModificationItem consists of the type of modification to be made and the attribute under modification. The following code creates a modification item for adding a new telephone number:

```
Attribute telephoneAttribute =  new  BasicAttribute("telephone",
                          "80181001000");
ModificationItem modificationItem  =  new  ModificationItem(DirContext.
                          ADD_ATTRIBUTE,  telephoneAttribute);
```

Notice that in the preceding code, we have used the constant ADD_ATTRIBUTE to indicate that we want an add operation. Table 2-2 provides the supported modification types along with their descriptions.

*Table 2-2.* *LDAP Modification Types*

| Modification Type | Description |
| --- | --- |
| ADD_ATTRIBUTE | Adds the attribute with the supplied value or values to the entry. If the attribute does not exist, then it will be created. If the attribute is multivalued, this operation adds the specified value(s) to the existing list. However, this operation on an existing single-valued attribute will result in the AttributeInUseException. |
| REPLACE_ATTRIBUTE | Replaces existing attribute values of an entry with the supplied values. If the attribute does not exist, then it will be created. If the attribute already exists, all its values will be replaced. |
| REMOVE_ATTRIBUTE | Removes the specified value from the existing attribute. If no value is specified, the entire attribute will be removed. If the specified value does not exist in the attribute, the operation will throw a NamingException. If the value to be removed is the only value of the attribute, then the attribute is also removed. |

The code for updating an entry is provided in Listing 2-7. The modifyAttributes method takes the entry's fully qualified DN and an array of modification items.

*Listing 2-7.* How to update an entry

```
public void update(String dn, ModificationItem[] items) {
    DirContext context = null;
    try {
        context = getContext();
        context.modifyAttributes(dn, items);
    } catch (NamingException e) {
        // Handle the exception and show the description of the problem
    } finally {
        closeContext(context);
    }
}
```

# Removing an Entry

Removing an entry using JNDI is a straightforward process shown in Listing 2-8. The destroySubcontext method takes the fully qualified DN of the entry that needs to be deleted.

**Listing 2-8.**  How to remove an entry

```
public void remove(String dn) {
    DirContext context = null;
    try {
        context = getContext();
        context.destroySubcontext(dn);
    } catch (NamingException e) {
        // Handle the exception and show the description of the problem
    } finally {
        closeContext(context);
    }
}
```

Many LDAP servers don't allow an entry to be deleted if it has child entries. In those servers, deleting a non-leaf entry would require traversing the subtree and deleting all the child entries. Then the non-leaf entry can be deleted. Listing 2-9 shows the code involved in deleting a subtree.

**Listing 2-9.**  How to remove a subtree of elements

```
public void removeSubtree(DirContext ctx, String root) throws
NamingException {
    NamingEnumeration enumeration = null;
    try {
        enumeration = ctx.listBindings(root);
        while (enumeration.hasMore()) {
            Binding childEntry = (Binding) enumeration.next();
            LdapName childName = new LdapName(root);
            childName.add(childEntry.getName());

            try {
                ctx.destroySubcontext(childName);
```

```
        } catch (ContextNotEmptyException e) {
            removeSubtree(ctx, childName.toString());
            ctx.destroySubcontext(childName);
        }
    }
} catch (NamingException e) {
        // Handle the exception and show the description of the problem
} finally {
    try {
        enumeration.close();
    } catch (Exception e) {
        // Handle the exception and show the description of the problem
    }
    }
}
}
```

---

**Note**   The OpenDJ LDAP server supports a special subtree delete control that can cause the server to delete the non-leaf entry and all its child entries when attached to a delete request. We will look at using LDAP controls in Chapter 7.

---

# Searching Entries

Searching for information is usually the most common operation against an LDAP server. To perform a search, we need to provide information such as the scope of the search, what we are looking for, and what attributes need to be returned. In JNDI, this search metadata is provided using the SearchControls class. Listing 2-10 provides an example of a search control with subtree scope and returns the ***givenName*** and ***telephoneNumber*** attributes. The subtree scope indicates that the search should start from the given base entry and should search all its subtree entries. We will look at the different scopes available in detail in Chapter 6.

***Listing 2-10.*** The attributes to return for each entry

```
SearchControls searchControls  =  new  SearchControls();
searchControls.setSearchScope(SearchControls.SUBTREE_SCOPE);
searchControls.setReturningAttributes(new String[]{"givenName",
"telephoneNumber"});
```

Once the search controls are defined, the next step is invoking one of the many search methods in the ***DirContext*** instance. Listing 2-11 provides the code that searches all the employees and prints their first name and telephone number.

***Listing 2-11.*** How to search elements

```
public void search() {
    DirContext context = null;
    NamingEnumeration<SearchResult> searchResults = null;
    try {
        context = getContext();
        // Setup Search meta data
        SearchControls searchControls = new SearchControls();

        searchControls.setSearchScope(SearchControls.SUBTREE_SCOPE);
        searchControls.setReturningAttributes(new String[] { "givenName",
        "telephoneNumber" });
        searchResults = context.search("dc=inflinx,dc=com",
        "(objectClass=inetOrgPerson)", searchControls);

        while (searchResults.hasMore()) {
            SearchResult result = searchResults.next();
            Attributes attributes = result.getAttributes();
            String firstName = (String) attributes.get("givenName").get();

            // Read the multi-valued attribute
            Attribute phoneAttribute = attributes.get("telephoneNumber");
            String[] phone = new String[phoneAttribute.size()];
            NamingEnumeration phoneValues = phoneAttribute.getAll();

            for (int i = 0; phoneValues.hasMore(); i++) {
                phone[i] = (String) phoneValues.next();
```

```
        }
        //You can use logback or system.out
        logger.info(firstName + "> " + Arrays.toString(phone));
    }
} catch (NamingException e) {
    // Handle the exception and show the description of the problem
} finally {
    try {
        if (null != searchResults) {
            searchResults.close();
        }
        closeContext(context);
    } catch (NamingException e) {
        // Handle the exception and show the description of the problem
    }
}
}
```

Here, we used the search method with three parameters: a base that determines the search's starting point, a filter that narrows down the results, and a search control. The search method returns an enumeration of SearchResults. Each search result holds the LDAP entry's attributes. Hence, we loop through the search results and read the attribute values. Notice that we obtain another enumeration instance for multivalued attributes and read its values one at a time. In the final part of the code, we close the result enumeration and the context resources.

# Check How the Operations Work

After that, reading all the source code of the different operations could be a good idea to check if everything works fine or not. To do this, a possible approach is to create a class that invokes the different methods of accessing LDAP using JNDI.

Listing 2-12 shows you a class App that creates an instance of a class *JndiLdapDaoImpl*, which contains all the methods of the different operations you see from Listings 2-4 to 2-11. In the case of Listing 2-12, you only will execute one operation because it's more simple to analyze the logs.

**Listing 2-12.** A class that invokes the method search

```
public class App {
    public static void main(String[] args) {
        JndiLdapDaoImpl jli = new JndiLdapDaoImpl();
        //Search
        jli.search();
    }
}
```

If you run the application with the previous block of code, you will see something like Listing 2-13.

**Listing 2-13.** The result of obtaining all the employees from LDAP

```
12:23:40.978 [main] INFO com.apress.book.ldap.dao.impl.JndiLdapDaoImpl -
Chie> [+1 622 858 9026]
12:23:40.978 [main] INFO com.apress.book.ldap.dao.impl.JndiLdapDaoImpl -
Chin> [+1 191 452 7983]
12:23:40.978 [main] INFO com.apress.book.ldap.dao.impl.JndiLdapDaoImpl -
ChinFui> [+1 439 500 8383]
12:23:40.978 [main] INFO com.apress.book.ldap.dao.impl.JndiLdapDaoImpl -
Ching-Long> [+1 407 407 2419]
12:13:14.186 [main] INFO com.apress.book.ldap.dao.impl.JndiLdapDaoImpl -
Chip> [+1 833 470 1660]
```

The next step is to add an employee and obtain all the employees to check whether the operations were okay. Let's make some little modifications to the class App, like Listing 2-14.

**Listing 2-14.** A class that invokes the methods add and search

```
public class App {
    public static void main(String[] args) {
        JndiLdapDaoImpl jli = new JndiLdapDaoImpl();

        //Add and search
        jli.addEmployee(getEmployee());
        jli.search();
```

```java
    }

    private static Employee getEmployee() {
        Employee employee = new Employee();
        employee.setEmployeeNumber("50001");
        employee.setFirstName("Andres");
        employee.setLastName("Sacco");
        employee.setEmail("sacco.andres@gmail.com");

        employee.setUid("employee30");
        employee.setPhone(new String[] { "+54 9 1161484" });
        employee.setCommonName("Andres");
        return employee;
    }
}
```

If you run the application with the previous block of code, you will see something like Listing 2-15. Check that a new employee appears at the end of the logs with the name "Andres."

***Listing 2-15.*** The result of adding an employee and obtaining all the employees from LDAP

```
12:23:40.978 [main] INFO com.apress.book.ldap.dao.impl.JndiLdapDaoImpl -
Chie> [+1 622 858 9026]
12:23:40.978 [main] INFO com.apress.book.ldap.dao.impl.JndiLdapDaoImpl -
Chin> [+1 191 452 7983]
12:23:40.978 [main] INFO com.apress.book.ldap.dao.impl.JndiLdapDaoImpl -
ChinFui> [+1 439 500 8383]
12:23:40.978 [main] INFO com.apress.book.ldap.dao.impl.JndiLdapDaoImpl -
Ching-Long> [+1 407 407 2419]
12:13:14.186 [main] INFO com.apress.book.ldap.dao.impl.JndiLdapDaoImpl -
Chip> [+1 833 470 1660]
12:13:14.187 [main] INFO com.apress.book.ldap.dao.impl.JndiLdapDaoImpl -
Andres> [+54 9 1161484]
```

After you add a new employee, the next operation to check is the deletion of an entry from LDAP. You must send the dn like this: **uid=employee29,ou=employees,dc=inflinx, dc=com** to remove the employee29. Let's make some little modifications to the class App, like Listing 2-16.

*Listing 2-16.* A class that invokes the methods remove and search

```
public class App {
    public static void main(String[] args) {
        JndiLdapDaoImpl jli = new JndiLdapDaoImpl();

        //Remove and search
    jli.remove("uid=employee29,ou=employees,dc=inflinx,dc=com");
        jli.search();
    }
}
```

If you run the application with the previous block of code, you will see something like Listing 2-17. If you compare the output of this execution with Listing 2-16, you will see that from the list of employees, the previous one to "Andres," which is employee number 29 with the name "Chip" was removed.

*Listing 2-17.* The result of removing an employee and obtaining all the employees from LDAP

```
12:23:40.978 [main] INFO com.apress.book.ldap.dao.impl.JndiLdapDaoImpl -
Chie> [+1 622 858 9026]
12:23:40.978 [main] INFO com.apress.book.ldap.dao.impl.JndiLdapDaoImpl -
Chin> [+1 191 452 7983]
12:23:40.978 [main] INFO com.apress.book.ldap.dao.impl.JndiLdapDaoImpl -
ChinFui> [+1 439 500 8383]
12:23:40.978 [main] INFO com.apress.book.ldap.dao.impl.JndiLdapDaoImpl -
Ching-Long> [+1 407 407 2419]
12:13:14.187 [main] INFO com.apress.book.ldap.dao.impl.JndiLdapDaoImpl -
Andres> [+54 9 1161484]
```

The last operation to check how it works is to update an existing entry on LDAP. To make this more interesting, you will update the ***givenName*** of the employee you added to Listing 2-14. Let's modify your application's main class to call the update method, as shown in Listing 2-18.

***Listing 2-18.*** A class that invokes the methods update and search

```
public class App {
    public static void main(String[] args) {
        JndiLdapDaoImpl jli = new JndiLdapDaoImpl();

        //Update and search
        BasicAttribute attribute = new BasicAttribute("givenName", "Andy");
        ModificationItem[] items = {new ModificationItem(DirContext.
        REPLACE_ATTRIBUTE, attribute)};
        jli.update("uid=employee30,ou=employees,dc=inflinx,dc=com", items);
        jli.search();
    }
}
```

If you run the application with the previous block of code, you will see something like Listing 2-19. Check that the last entry changed the ***givenName*** attribute from "Andres" to "Andy."

***Listing 2-19.*** The result of updating an attribute for an employee and obtaining all the employees from LDAP

```
12:23:40.978 [main] INFO com.apress.book.ldap.dao.impl.JndiLdapDaoImpl -
Chie> [+1 622 858 9026]
12:23:40.978 [main] INFO com.apress.book.ldap.dao.impl.JndiLdapDaoImpl -
Chin> [+1 191 452 7983]
12:23:40.978 [main] INFO com.apress.book.ldap.dao.impl.JndiLdapDaoImpl -
ChinFui> [+1 439 500 8383]
12:23:40.978 [main] INFO com.apress.book.ldap.dao.impl.JndiLdapDaoImpl -
Ching-Long> [+1 407 407 2419]
12:13:14.187 [main] INFO com.apress.book.ldap.dao.impl.JndiLdapDaoImpl -
Andy> [+54 9 1161484]
```

As you can see from the different examples of the results of the operations, all of them work fine and give the information you requested. Still, suppose something bad happens during the execution of the operation. In that case, the NamingException will give you some information about the reason for the exception, so try to use a mechanism to save the logs in a place accessible to anyone.

# JNDI Drawbacks

Though JNDI provides a nice abstraction for accessing directory services, it suffers from several drawbacks:

- Explicit Resource Management

  The developer is responsible for closing all the resources. This is very error-prone and can result in memory leaks.

- Plumbing Code

  The preceding methods have much plumbing code that can be easily abstracted and reused. This plumbing code makes testing harder, and the developer must learn the API's nitty-gritty.

- Checked Exceptions

  The usage of checked exceptions, especially in irrecoverable situations, is questionable. Having to explicitly handle NamingException in those scenarios usually results in empty try-catch blocks.

# Summary

Java offers you a set of interfaces and classes to access and execute different operations on LDAP simply if you do not need to do complex operations.

The next chapter will look at how to do some operations using Spring LDAP, as you've seen in this chapter. The idea is to show you how Spring LDAP reduces the complexity of certain operations like Spring Data does with the applications that need to access a database.

# CHAPTER 3

# Introducing Spring LDAP

Spring LDAP[1] provides simple, clean, and comprehensive support for LDAP programming in Java. This project started on SourceForge in 2006 under the name LdapTemplate to simplify access to LDAP using JNDI. The project later became part of the Spring Framework portfolio and has come a long way. Figure 3-1 depicts the architecture of a Spring LDAP–based application.

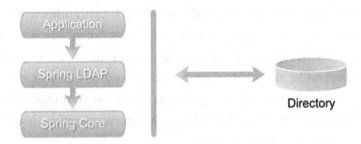

***Figure 3-1.*** *Spring LDAP architecture directory*

The application code uses the Spring LDAP API to perform LDAP server operations. The Spring LDAP framework contains all of the LDAP-specific code and abstractions. Spring LDAP, however, will rely on the Spring Framework for some of its infrastructural needs.

The Spring Framework has become today's standard for developing Java-based enterprise applications. Among many other things, it provides a dependency injection–based lightweight alternative to the JEE programming model. The Spring Framework is the base for Spring LDAP and all other Spring portfolio projects, such as Spring MVC and Spring Security.

---

[1] https://spring.io/projects/spring-ldap

© Balaji Varanasi and Andres Sacco 2023
B. Varanasi and A. Sacco, *Practical Spring LDAP*, https://doi.org/10.1007/979-8-8688-0002-3_3

# Motivation

In the previous chapter, we discussed the shortcomings of the JNDI API. A notable drawback of JNDI is that it is very lengthy; almost all of the code in Chapter 2 has to do with plumbing and very little with application logic. Spring LDAP addresses this problem by providing template and utility classes that take care of the plumbing code so the developer can focus on business logic.

Another notable issue with JNDI is that it requires the developer to explicitly manage resources such as LDAP contexts. This can be very error-prone. Forgetting to close resources can result in leaks and can quickly bring down an application under heavy load. Spring LDAP manages these resources on your behalf and automatically closes them when you no longer need them. It also provides the ability to pool LDAP contexts, which can improve performance.

Any problems that arise during the execution of JNDI operations will be reported as instances of NamingException or its subclasses. NamingException is a checked exception, and thus the developer is forced to handle it. Data access exceptions are usually not recoverable, and most often, only a little can be done to catch these exceptions. To address this, Spring LDAP provides a consistent unchecked exception hierarchy that mimics NamingException. This allows the application designer to choose when and where to handle these exceptions.

Finally, plain JNDI programming is hard and daunting for new developers. Spring LDAP, with its abstractions, makes working with JNDI more enjoyable. Additionally, it provides various features such as Object-Directory Mapping and transaction support, making it an important tool for any enterprise LDAP developer.

# Documentation and Source Code Spring LDAP

Spring Framework portfolio projects can be checked in the documentation from the official website.[2] A direct link is available on the Spring LDAP website,[3] or you can check the source code at the GitHub repository.[4]

---

[2] https://spring.io/projects
[3] https://docs.spring.io/spring-ldap/docs/current/reference/
[4] https://github.com/spring-projects/spring-ldap

Spring LDAP source code can provide valuable insights into the framework architecture. It also includes a rich test suite that can serve as additional documentation and help you understand the framework. You should download and look at the source code. The Git repository also holds a sandbox folder that contains several experimental features that may or may not make it into the framework.

# Spring LDAP Packaging

Now that you can access the Spring LDAP framework's documentation and source code, let's delve into the different components. The LDAP framework is packaged into six components, and Table 3-1 briefly describes each component.

***Table 3-1.***  *Spring LDAP Distribution Modules*

| Component | Description |
|---|---|
| spring-ldap-core | It contains all the classes necessary for using the LDAP framework. This jar is required in all applications. |
| spring-ldap-core-tiger | It contains classes and extensions that are specific to Java 5 and higher. Applications running under Java 5 should not use this jar. |
| spring-ldap-test | It contains classes and utilities that make testing easier. It also includes classes for starting and stopping in-memory instances of the ApacheDS LDAP server. |
| spring-ldap-ldif-core | It contains classes for parsing ldif format files. |
| spring-ldap-ldif-batch | It contains classes necessary to integrate ldif parser with Spring Batch Framework. |
| spring-ldap-odm | It contains classes for enabling and creating Object-Directory Mappings. |

Along with Spring Framework, you need additional jar files for compiling and running applications using Spring LDAP. Table 3-2 lists some of these dependent jar files and describes why they are used.

***Table 3-2.*** *Spring LDAP*

| Library | Description |
| --- | --- |
| slf4j[5] | Logging is used internally by Spring LDAP and Spring Framework. This is a required jar to be included in applications. |
| spring-core | Spring library that contains core utilities used internally by Spring LDAP. This is a required library for using Spring LDAP. |
| spring-beans | Spring Framework library used for creating and managing Spring Beans. Spring LDAP requires another library. |
| spring-context | Spring library that is responsible for dependency injection. This is required when using Spring LDAP inside a Spring application. |
| spring-tx | Spring Framework library that provides transaction abstractions. This is required when using Spring LDAP transaction support. |
| spring-jdbc | The library simplifies access to the database using JDBC under the covers. This is an optional library and should be used for transaction support. |
| commons-pool[6] | Apache Commons Pool library provides support for pooling. This should be included when using Spring LDAP pooling support. |

# Installing Spring LDAP Using Maven

Before you can install and start using Spring LDAP, it is important to ensure that the Java Development Kit (JDK) is installed on your machine; you find the explanation about how to do it in Appendix A. The latest Spring LDAP 3.1.0 version requires JDK 17 and higher and Spring 6.0 or higher. Just remember that we will use JDK 21 to use the latest LTS available.

Apache Maven is an open source, standards-based project management framework that makes building, testing, reporting, and packaging projects easier. If you are new to Maven and are wondering about the tool, the Maven website[7] provides information on its features and many helpful links. Here are some advantages of adopting Maven:

---

[5] https://www.slf4j.org/

[6] https://commons.apache.org/proper/commons-pool/

[7] https://maven.apache.org

- *Standardized directory structure*: Maven standardizes the layout and organization of a project. Every time a new project starts, considerable time is spent on decisions such as where the source code should go or where the configuration files should be placed. Also, these decisions can vary vastly between projects and teams. Maven's standardized directory structure makes adoption easy across developers and even IDEs.

- *Declarative dependency management*: With Maven, you declare your project dependencies in a separate pom.xml file. Maven then automatically downloads those dependencies from repositories and uses them during the build process. Maven also smartly resolves and downloads transitive dependencies (dependencies of dependencies).

- *Archetypes*: Maven archetypes are project templates that can be used to quickly generate new projects. These archetypes are a great way to share best practices and enforce consistency beyond Maven's standard directory structure.

- *Plug-ins*: Maven follows a plug-in-based architecture that makes adding or customizing functionality easy. Hundreds of plug-ins can perform various tasks, from compiling code to creating project documentation. Activating and using a plug-in simply involves declaring a reference to the plug-in in the pom.xml file.

- *Tools support*: All major IDEs today provide tooling support for Maven. This includes wizards for generating projects, creating IDE-specific files, and graphical tools for analyzing dependencies.

# Spring LDAP Archetypes

To jump-start Spring LDAP development, this book uses the following two archetypes, which you can find in the repository of this book:

- **practical-ldap-empty-archetype**: This archetype can create an empty Java project with all the required LDAP dependencies.

- **practical-ldap-archetype**: Similar to the preceding archetype, this archetype creates a Java project with all the required LDAP dependencies. It also includes Spring LDAP configuration files, sample code, and dependencies to run an in-memory LDAP server for testing purposes.

Before you can use the archetypes to create a project, you need to install them. If you still need to do so, download the accompanying source/download files from Apress. In the downloaded distribution, you will find ***practical-ldap-empty-archetype-1.0.0.jar*** and ***practical-ldap-archetype-1.0.0.jar*** archetypes. Once you have the jar files downloaded, run the following command to install on your local repository the first archetype:

```
$ mvn  install:install-file \
    -DgroupId=com.apress.book.ldap \
    -DartifactId=practical-ldap-empty-archetype \
    -Dversion=1.0.0 \
    -Dpackaging=jar  \
    -DgeneratePom=true  \
    -Dfile=<JAR_LOCATION_DOWNLOAD >/practical-ldap-empty-
    archetype-1.0.0.jar
```

If you run the command and everything works fine, you will see something similar to the following logs:

```
[INFO] Scanning for projects...
[INFO]
[INFO] ------------------< org.apache.maven:standalone-pom >-------------------
[INFO] Building Maven Stub Project (No POM) 1
[INFO] --------------------------------[ pom ]---------------------------------
[INFO]
[INFO] --- install:3.1.0:install-file (default-cli) @ standalone-pom ---
[INFO] Installing /home/asacco/Code/practical-spring-ldap/archetypes/
practical-ldap-empty-archetype-1.0.0.jar to /home/asacco/.m2/repository/
com/apress/book/ldap/practical-ldap-empty-archetype/1.0.0/practical-ldap-
empty-archetype-1.0.0.jar
```

```
[INFO] Installing /tmp/mvninstall53656511567513002254.pom to /home/asacco/.
m2/repository/com/apress/book/ldap/practical-ldap-empty-archetype/1.0.0/
practical-ldap-empty-archetype-1.0.0.pom
[INFO] ------------------------------------------------------------------------
[INFO] BUILD SUCCESS
[INFO] ------------------------------------------------------------------------
[INFO] Total time:  0.103 s
[INFO] Finished at: 2023-08-01T11:32:00-03:00
[INFO] ------------------------------------------------------------------------
```

Now repeat the procedure with the next archetype to install in your local repository using the following command:

```
$ mvn  install:install-file \
    -DgroupId=com.apress.book.ldap \
    -DartifactId=practical-ldap-archetype \
    -Dversion=1.0.0 \
    -Dpackaging=jar  \
    -DgeneratePom=true  \
    -Dfile=<JAR_LOCATION_DOWNLOAD >/practical-ldap-archetype-1.0.0.jar
```

These maven install commands will install the two archetypes in your local maven repository. Creating a project using one of these archetypes simply involves running the following command:

```
$ mvn archetype:generate \
-DarchetypeGroupId=com.apress.book.ldap \
-DarchetypeArtifactId=practical-ldap-empty-archetype \
-DarchetypeVersion=1.0.0 \
-DgroupId=com.apress.book.ldap \
-DartifactId=chapter3 \
-DinteractiveMode=false
```

After you execute the command, you will see the following output:

```
[INFO] Scanning for projects...
[INFO]
[INFO] ------------------< org.apache.maven:standalone-pom >--------------
```

```
[INFO] Building Maven Stub Project (No POM) 1
[INFO] ------------------------------[ pom ]----------------------------
[INFO]
[INFO] >>> archetype:3.2.0:generate (default-cli) > generate-sources @
standalone-pom >>>
[INFO]
[INFO] <<< archetype:3.2.0:generate (default-cli) < generate-sources @
standalone-pom <<<
[INFO]
[INFO]
[INFO] --- archetype:3.2.0:generate (default-cli) @ standalone-pom ---
[WARNING] Parameter 'localRepository' is deprecated core expression; Avoid
use of ArtifactRepository type. If you need access to local repository,
switch to '${repositorySystemSession}' expression and get LRM from it
instead.
[INFO] Generating project in Batch mode
[WARNING] Archetype not found in any catalog. Falling back to central
repository.
[WARNING] Add a repository with id 'archetype' in your settings.xml if
archetype's repository is elsewhere.
[INFO] -----------------------------------------------------------------
[INFO] Using following parameters for creating project from Archetype:
practical-ldap-empty-archetype:1.0.0
[INFO] -----------------------------------------------------------------
[INFO] Parameter: groupId, Value: com.apress.book.ldap
[INFO] Parameter: artifactId, Value: chapter3
[INFO] Parameter: version, Value: 1.0-SNAPSHOT
[INFO] Parameter: package, Value: com.apress.book.ldap
[INFO] Parameter: packageInPathFormat, Value: com/apress/book/ldap
[INFO] Parameter: package, Value: com.apress.book.ldap
[INFO] Parameter: groupId, Value: com.apress.book.ldap
[INFO] Parameter: artifactId, Value: chapter3
[INFO] Parameter: version, Value: 1.0-SNAPSHOT
[INFO] Project created from Archetype in dir: /home/asacco/practical-
spring-ldap/code/chapter3
```

```
[INFO] -------------------------------------------------------------
[INFO] BUILD SUCCESS
[INFO] -------------------------------------------------------------
[INFO] Total time:  2.142 s
[INFO] Finished at: 2023-08-03T11:46:08-03:00
[INFO] -------------------------------------------------------------
```

Notice that this command is executed inside the directory `practical-spring-ldap/code`. The command instructs Maven to use the archetype practical-ldap-empty-archetype and generate a project named Chapter 3. The generated project directory structure is shown in Figure 3-2.

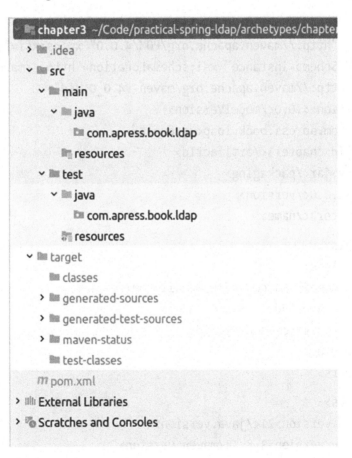

*Figure 3-2.* *Maven-generated project structure*

This directory structure has a src folder with all the code and associated resources, such as XML files. The target folder contains the generated classes and builds artifacts. The main folder under src usually holds the code that eventually reaches production. The test folder contains the related test code. Each of these two folders contains Java and resources subfolders. As the name suggests, the java folder contains Java code, and the resources folder usually contains configuration XML files.

The pom.xml file in the root folder holds the configuration information Maven needs. For example, it contains information about all the dependent jar files required for compiling the code (see Listing 3-1).

***Listing 3-1.*** All the dependencies required to use LDAP

```
<?xml version="1.0" encoding="UTF-8"?>
<project xmlns="http://maven.apache.org/POM/4.0.0" xmlns:xsi="http://www.
w3.org/2001/XMLSchema-instance" xsi:schemaLocation="http://maven.apache.
org/POM/4.0.0 http://maven.apache.org/maven-v4_0_0.xsd">
    <modelVersion>4.0.0</modelVersion>
    <groupId>com.apress.book.ldap</groupId>
    <artifactId>chapter3</artifactId>
    <packaging>jar</packaging>
    <version>1.0.0</version>
    <name>chapter3</name>

    <developers>
        <developer>
            <email>sacco.andres@gmail.com</email>
            <name>Andres Sacco</name>
            <id>sacco.andres</id>
        </developer>
    </developers>

    <properties>
        <java.version>21</java.version>
        <maven.version>3.8.1</maven.version>
        <project.build.sourceEncoding>UTF-8</project.build.
        sourceEncoding>
        <project.reporting.outputEncoding>UTF-8</project.reporting.
        outputEncoding>
```

```xml
    <!-- Dependencies -->
    <org.springframework.version>6.0.11</org.springframework.version>
    <org.springframework.ldap.version>3.1.1</org.springframework.ldap.version>
    <org.slf4j.version>2.0.7</org.slf4j.version>
    <logback.version>1.3.5</logback.version>
    <junit-jupiter-engine.version>5.9.2</junit-jupiter-engine.version>
    <unboundid-ldapsdk.version>3.1.1</unboundid-ldapsdk.version>
    <commons-io.version>2.13.0</commons-io.version>
    <commons-lang.version>2.6</commons-lang.version>

    <!-- Plugins -->
    <formatter-maven-plugin.version>2.8.1</formatter-maven-plugin.version>
    <maven-compiler-plugin.version>3.11.0</maven-compiler-plugin.version>
    <maven-enforcer-plugin.version>3.3.0</maven-enforcer-plugin.version>
</properties>

<dependencies>
    <!-- Spring LDAP Dependencies Start -->
    <dependency>
        <groupId>org.springframework.ldap</groupId>
        <artifactId>spring-ldap-core</artifactId>
        <version>${org.springframework.ldap.version}</version>
        <exclusions>
            <exclusion>
                <artifactId>commons-logging</artifactId>
                <groupId>commons-logging</groupId>
            </exclusion>

            <exclusion>
                <groupId>org.slf4j</groupId>
                <artifactId>slf4j-api</artifactId>
            </exclusion>
        </exclusions>
```

```
            </dependency>

            <dependency>
                <groupId>org.springframework.ldap</groupId>
                <artifactId>spring-ldap-odm</artifactId>
                <version>${org.springframework.ldap.version}</version>
                <exclusions>
                    <exclusion>
                        <artifactId>commons-logging</artifactId>
                        <groupId>commons-logging</groupId>
                    </exclusion>
                </exclusions>
            </dependency>

            <dependency>
                <groupId>org.springframework.ldap</groupId>
                <artifactId>spring-ldap-ldif-core</artifactId>
                <version>${org.springframework.ldap.version}</version>
                <exclusions>
                    <exclusion>
                        <artifactId>commons-logging</artifactId>
                        <groupId>commons-logging</groupId>
                    </exclusion>
                </exclusions>
            </dependency>
            <!-- Spring LDAP Dependencies End -->
            <!-- Spring Dependencies Start -->
            <dependency>
                <groupId>org.springframework</groupId>
                <artifactId>spring-core</artifactId>
                <version>${org.springframework.version}</version>
                <scope>compile</scope>
            </dependency>

            <dependency>
                <groupId>org.springframework</groupId>
                <artifactId>spring-beans</artifactId>
                <version>${org.springframework.version}</version>
```

```xml
        <scope>compile</scope>
</dependency>

<dependency>
        <groupId>org.springframework</groupId>
        <artifactId>spring-expression</artifactId>
        <version>${org.springframework.version}</version>
        <scope>compile</scope>
</dependency>

<dependency>
        <groupId>org.springframework</groupId>
        <artifactId>spring-aop</artifactId>
        <version>${org.springframework.version}</version>
        <scope>compile</scope>
</dependency>

<dependency>
        <groupId>org.springframework</groupId>
        <artifactId>spring-context</artifactId>
        <version>${org.springframework.version}</version>
        <scope>compile</scope>
        <exclusions>
                <!-- Exclude Commons Logging in favor of SLF4j -->
                <exclusion>
                        <groupId>commons-logging</groupId>
                        <artifactId>commons-logging</artifactId>
                </exclusion>
        </exclusions>
</dependency>

<dependency>
        <groupId>org.springframework</groupId>
        <artifactId>spring-context-support</artifactId>
        <version>${org.springframework.version}</version>
        <scope>compile</scope>
</dependency>
```

```
<dependency>
    <groupId>org.springframework</groupId>
    <artifactId>spring-tx</artifactId>
    <version>${org.springframework.version}</version>
    <scope>compile</scope>
</dependency>

<dependency>
    <groupId>org.slf4j</groupId>
    <artifactId>slf4j-api</artifactId>
    <version>${org.slf4j.version}</version>
</dependency>

<dependency>
    <groupId>org.slf4j</groupId>
    <artifactId>jcl-over-slf4j</artifactId>
    <version>${org.slf4j.version}</version>
</dependency>
<!-- Spring Dependencies End -->

<dependency>
    <groupId>ch.qos.logback</groupId>
    <artifactId>logback-core</artifactId>
    <version>${logback.version}</version>
</dependency>

<dependency>
    <groupId>ch.qos.logback</groupId>
    <artifactId>logback-classic</artifactId>
    <version>${logback.version}</version>
    <exclusions>
        <exclusion>
            <groupId>org.slf4j</groupId>
            <artifactId>slf4j-api</artifactId>
        </exclusion>
    </exclusions>
</dependency>

<!-- Test Dependencies Start -->
```

```xml
<dependency>
    <groupId>org.junit.jupiter</groupId>
    <artifactId>junit-jupiter-engine</artifactId>
    <version>${junit-jupiter-engine.version}</version>
    <scope>test</scope>
</dependency>

<dependency>
    <groupId>org.springframework</groupId>
    <artifactId>spring-test</artifactId>
    <version>${org.springframework.version}</version>
    <scope>test</scope>
</dependency>

<dependency>
    <groupId>org.springframework.ldap</groupId>
    <artifactId>spring-ldap-test</artifactId>
    <version>${org.springframework.ldap.version}</version>
    <scope>test</scope>
</dependency>

<dependency>
    <groupId>com.unboundid</groupId>
    <artifactId>unboundid-ldapsdk</artifactId>
    <version>${unboundid-ldapsdk.version}</version>
    <scope>test</scope>
</dependency>

<dependency>
    <groupId>commons-io</groupId>
    <artifactId>commons-io</artifactId>
    <version>${commons-io.version}</version>
    <scope>test</scope>
</dependency>

<dependency>
    <groupId>commons-lang</groupId>
    <artifactId>commons-lang</artifactId>
    <version>${commons-lang.version}</version>
```

```
        <scope>test</scope>
    </dependency>

    <!-- Test Dependencies End -->
  </dependencies>

</project>
```

The `pom.xml` snippet in Listing 3-1 indicates the project will need the `spring-ldap-core.jar` file during compilation.

Maven requires a group id and artifact id to uniquely identify a dependency. A group id is usually unique to a project or organization and is similar to the concept of a Java package. The artifact id is typically the name of the project or a generated component of the project. The scope determines the phase during which the dependency should be included in the classpath. Here are a few possible values:

- *Test*: A test scope indicates that the dependency should be included in the classpath only during the testing. JUnit is an example of such dependency.

- *Provided*: The provided scope indicates that the artifact should be included in the classpath during compilation only. Provided scope dependencies are usually available at runtime via JDK or application container.

- *Compile*: A compile scope indicates that the dependency should always be included in the classpath.

An additional section in the `pom.xml` file contains information about the plug-ins Maven can use to compile and build the code. One such plug-in declaration is displayed in Listing 3-2. It indicates to Maven to use the plug-in named 'maven-compiler-plugin' with version 3.11.0 to compile Java code, consider that in Listing 3-2 appears references to properties that are declared in Listing 3-1. The `finalName` indicates the name of the generated artifact. In this case, it would be `chapter3.jar`. Also, there are two other plug-ins to format all the source code following the standard and another one to check if there is any conflict on the dependencies of your project.

***Listing 3-2.*** Plug-ins used on the project

```
<build>
    <plugins>
        <plugin>
```

```xml
      <groupId>org.apache.maven.plugins</groupId>
      <artifactId>maven-compiler-plugin</artifactId>
      <version>${maven-compiler-plugin.version}</version>
      <configuration>
         <source>${java.version}</source>
         <target>${java.version}</target>
         <compilerArgs>--enable-preview</compilerArgs>
      </configuration>
   </plugin>

   <plugin>
      <groupId>org.apache.maven.plugins</groupId>
      <artifactId>maven-enforcer-plugin</artifactId>
      <version>${maven-enforcer-plugin.version}</version>
      <executions>
         <execution>
            <id>enforce-versions</id>
            <goals>
               <goal>enforce</goal>
            </goals>
            <configuration>
               <rules>
                  <dependencyConvergence/>
                  <requireMavenVersion>
                     <version>${maven.version}</version>
                  </requireMavenVersion>
                  <requireJavaVersion>
                     <version>${java.version}</version>
                  </requireJavaVersion>
               </rules>
            </configuration>
         </execution>
      </executions>
   </plugin>

   <plugin>
      <groupId>net.revelc.code.formatter</groupId>
```

```xml
        <artifactId>formatter-maven-plugin</artifactId>
        <version>${formatter-maven-plugin.version}</version>
        <configuration>
            <encoding>${project.build.sourceEncoding}</encoding>
        </configuration>
        <executions>
            <execution>
                <goals>
                    <goal>format</goal>
                </goals>
                <configuration>
                    <includes>
                        <include>**/*.java</include>
                    </includes>
                </configuration>
            </execution>
        </executions>
    </plugin>
  </plugins>
</build>
```

Run the following command from the command line to build this generated application. This command cleans the target folder, compiles the source files, and generates a jar file inside the target folder:

```
$ mvn  clean  compile package
```

After the execution of the preceding command, the console will show the following output:

```
[INFO] Scanning for projects...
[INFO]
[INFO] ------------------< com.apress.book.ldap:chapter3 >----------------
[INFO] Building chapter3 1.0-SNAPSHOT
[INFO]    from pom.xml
[INFO] -----------------------------[ jar ]-----------------------------
[INFO]
```

```
[INFO] --- clean:3.2.0:clean (default-clean) @ chapter3 ---
[INFO] Deleting /home/asacco/Code/practical-spring-ldap/archetypes/
chapter3/target
[INFO]
[INFO] --- enforcer:3.3.0:enforce (enforce-versions) @ chapter3 ---
[INFO] Rule 0: org.apache.maven.enforcer.rules.dependency.
DependencyConvergence passed
[INFO] Rule 1: org.apache.maven.enforcer.rules.version.
RequireMavenVersion passed
[INFO] Rule 2: org.apache.maven.enforcer.rules.version.
RequireJavaVersion passed
[INFO]
[INFO] --- formatter:2.8.1:format (default) @ chapter3 ---
[INFO] Using 'UTF-8' encoding to format source files.
[INFO] Number of files to be formatted: 0
[INFO]
[INFO] --- resources:3.3.0:resources (default-resources) @ chapter3 ---
[INFO] Copying 0 resource
[INFO]
[INFO] --- compiler:3.11.0:compile (default-compile) @ chapter3 ---
[INFO] Nothing to compile - all classes are up to date
[INFO]
[INFO] --- enforcer:3.3.0:enforce (enforce-versions) @ chapter3 ---
[INFO] Rule 0: org.apache.maven.enforcer.rules.dependency.
DependencyConvergence passed
[INFO]
[INFO] --- formatter:2.8.1:format (default) @ chapter3 ---
[INFO] Using 'UTF-8' encoding to format source files.
[INFO] Number of files to be formatted: 0
[INFO]
[INFO] --- resources:3.3.0:resources (default-resources) @ chapter3 ---
[INFO] Copying 0 resource
[INFO]
[INFO] --- compiler:3.11.0:compile (default-compile) @ chapter3 ---
[INFO] Nothing to compile - all classes are up to date
```

```
[INFO]
[INFO] --- resources:3.3.0:testResources (default-testResources) @
chapter3 ---
[INFO] Copying 0 resource
[INFO]
[INFO] --- compiler:3.11.0:testCompile (default-testCompile) @ chapter3 ---
[INFO] Nothing to compile - all classes are up to date
[INFO]
[INFO] --- surefire:3.0.0:test (default-test) @ chapter3 ---
[INFO]
[INFO] --- jar:3.3.0:jar (default-jar) @ chapter3 ---
[INFO] Building jar: /home/asacco/Code/practical-spring-ldap/archetypes/
chapter3/target/chapter3.jar
[INFO] ------------------------------------------------------------------
[INFO] BUILD SUCCESS
[INFO] ------------------------------------------------------------------
[INFO] Total time:  0.705 s
[INFO] Finished at: 2023-08-03T12:52:12-03:00
[INFO] ------------------------------------------------------------------
```

This setup, along with a text editor, is enough to start developing and packaging Java-based LDAP applications. However, it is a no-brainer that you can be more productive developing and debugging applications using a graphical IDE. There are several IDEs, with Eclipse, NetBeans, and IntelliJ IDEA being the most popular. For this book, you will be using IntelliJ.

# Creating Projects Using IntelliJ

In the earlier "Spring LDAP Archetypes" section, you used the practical-ldap-empty-archetype archetype to generate a project from the command line. Now let's look at generating the same project using IntelliJ.

1. From the File menu, select New ➤ Project. It will launch the New Project wizard (see Figure 3-3). Select the Maven Archetype, and the version of the JDK for this book is 17. Also, write "chapter3" as the name of the project.

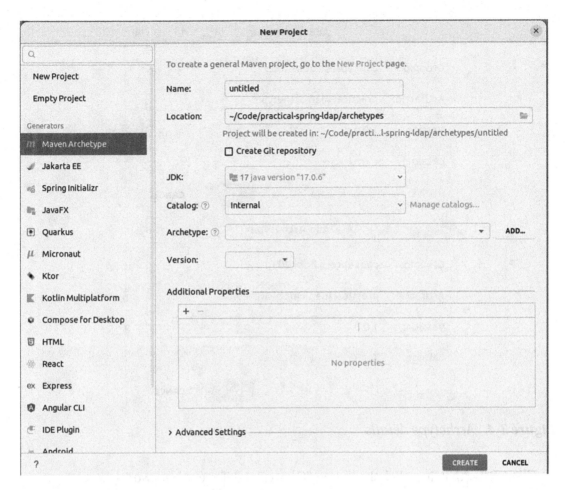

***Figure 3-3.*** *New project*

2.  On the Archetype combo (see Figure 3-4), click "Add." This
    step assumes that you have already installed the archetype, as
    mentioned earlier. Fill the Add Archetype dialog with the details in
    Figure 3-4 and click "Add." Do the same for the other archetype.

***Figure 3-4.*** *Archetype details*

3.  After that, just click the button "Create," and if everything works fine, you will see the structure of Figure 3-5 in the case that you choose the archetype "practical-ldap-archetype."

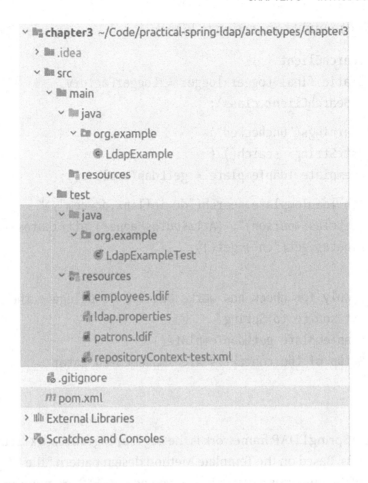

*Figure 3-5.* *Generated project structure*

You can create projects using the command line or your IDE; both approaches generate the same.

# Spring LDAP Hello World

With this information in hand, let's dive into the world of Spring LDAP. You will start by writing a simple search client that reads all the patron names in the ou=patrons LDAP branch. This is similar to the example you looked at in Chapter 2. Listing 3-3 shows the search client code.

***Listing 3-3.*** The manual connection to LDAP

```
public class SearchClient {
    private static final Logger logger = LoggerFactory.
    getLogger(SearchClient.class);

    @SuppressWarnings("unchecked")
    public List<String> search() {
        LdapTemplate ldapTemplate = getLdapTemplate();

        return ldapTemplate.search("dc=inflinx,dc=com", "
        (objectclass=person)", (AttributesMapper) attributes -> (String)
        attributes.get("cn").get());
    }

    //Do this only for check how works but try to delegate the creation of
    the context source to Spring
    private LdapTemplate getLdapTemplate() {
        // Setup of the context - Are implemented later
    }
}
```

Central to the Spring LDAP framework is the org.springframework.ldap.core.
LdapTemplate class. Based on the Template Method design pattern,[8] the LdapTemplate
class takes care of the unnecessary plumbing involved in LDAP programming. It
provides several overloaded search, lookup, bind, authenticate, and unbind methods
that make LDAP development a breeze. The LdapTemplate is threadsafe, and concurrent
threads can use the same instance.

---

**Note**   Spring LDAP version 1.3 introduced a variation of LdapTemplate called
SimpleLdapTemplate. This is a Java 5–based convenience wrapper for the
classic LdapTemplate. The SimpleLdapTemplate adds Java 5 Generics
support to lookup and search methods. These methods now take implementations

---

[8] https://en.wikipedia.org/wiki/Template_method_pattern

of `ParameterizedContextMapper<T>` as parameters, allowing the search and lookup methods to return typed objects.

The `SimpleLdapTemplate` exposes only a subset of operations available in `LdapTemplate`. These operations, however, are the most commonly used ones, and hence `SpringLdapTemplate` would be sufficient in many situations. The `SimpleLdapTemplate` also provides the `getLdapOperations()` method that exposes the wrapped `LdapOperations` instance and can invoke the less commonly used template methods.

---

With the release 3.0.0 of Spring LDAP, the class `SpringLdapTemplate` disappeared to keep the code simple, and the only available option is to use `LdapTemplate` for that reason, if you find any block of code on an application knows that is using an old version of Spring LDAP.

You start the search method implementation by obtaining an instance of the `LdapTemplate` class. Then you invoke a variation of the `LdapTemplate`'s search method. The first parameter of the search method is the LDAP base, and the second parameter is the search filter. The search method uses the base and filter to perform a search, and each `javax.naming.directory.SearchResult` obtained is supplied to an implementation of `org.springframework.ldap.core.AttributesMapper` that is provided as the third parameter. In Listing 3-3, the `AttributesMapper` implementation is achieved by creating an anonymous class that reads each `SearchResult` entry and returns the common name of the entry.

In Listing 3-3, the `getLdapTemplate` method is empty. Now let's look at implementing this method. For `LdapTemplate` to properly execute the search, it needs an initial context on the LDAP server. Spring LDAP provides `org.springframework.ldap.core.ContextSource` interface abstraction and its implementation `org.springframework.ldap.core.support.LdapContextSource` for configuring and creating context instances. Listing 3-4 shows the complete method for `getLdapTemplate` implementation.

***Listing 3-4.*** The configuration of the LDAPTemplate

```
private LdapTemplate getLdapTemplate() {
    LdapContextSource contextSource = new LdapContextSource();
    contextSource.setUrl("ldap://localhost:11389");
```

```
        contextSource.setUserDn("cn=Directory Manager");
        contextSource.setPassword("secret");
        try {
            contextSource.afterPropertiesSet();
        } catch(Exception e) {
            logger.error(e.getClass() + ": " + e.getMessage());
        }

        LdapTemplate ldapTemplate = new LdapTemplate();
        ldapTemplate.setContextSource(contextSource);
        return ldapTemplate;
}
```

You start the method implementation by creating a new LdapContextSource and populating it with information about the LDAP server, such as the server URL and binding credentials. You then invoke the afterPropertiesSet method on the context source that allows Spring LDAP to perform housekeeping operations. Finally, you create a new LdapTemplate instance and pass in the newly created context source.

This completes your search client example. Listing 3-5 shows the main method that invokes the search operation and prints the names to the console.

*Listing 3-5.* The main method to run the application and do the search operation

```
public static void main(String[] args) {
    SearchClient client = new SearchClient();
    List<String> names = client.search();

    for(String name: names) {
        System.out.println(name);
    }
}
```

This search client implementation uses the Spring LDAP API without any Spring Framework–specific paradigms. In the coming sections, you will look at springifying this application. But before you do that, let's quickly look at Spring ApplicationContext.

# Spring ApplicationContext

Central to every Spring Framework application is the notion of ApplicationContext. Implementations of this interface are responsible for creating and configuring Spring beans. The application context also acts as an IoC container and is responsible for performing the dependency injection. A Spring bean is simply a standard POJO with metadata needed to run inside the Spring container.

In a standard Spring application, the ApplicationContext is configured via an XML file, Java annotations, and JavaConfig. Listing 3-6 shows a sample application context file with one bean declaration. The bean myBean is of type com.apress.book.ldap. SimplePojo. When the application loads the context, Spring creates an instance of SimplePojo and manages it.

***Listing 3-6.*** Configuration of a simple POJO

```
<?xml version="1.0"  encoding="UTF-8"?>
<beans xmlns="http://www.springframework.org/schema/beans"
       xmlns:xsi="http://www.w3.org/2001/XMLSchema-instance"
       xmlns:context="http://www.springframework.org/schema/context"
       xsi:schemaLocation="http://www.springframework.org/schema/
beans http://www.springframework.org/schema/beans/spring-beans.xsd
       http://www.springframework.org/schema/context
http://www.springframework.org/schema/context/spring-context.xsd">
       <bean  id="myBean" class="com.apress.book.ldap.SimplePojo"/>
</beans>
```

# Spring-Powered Search Client

Our conversion of the search client implementation begins with the applicationContext.xml file, as shown in Listing 3-7.

***Listing 3-7.*** Configuration of the application

```
<?xml version="1.0" encoding="UTF-8"?>
<beans xmlns="http://www.springframework.org/schema/beans"
       xmlns:xsi="http://www.w3.org/2001/XMLSchema-instance"
       xmlns:context="http://www.springframework.org/schema/context"
```

```
xsi:schemaLocation="http://www.springframework.org/schema/beans
http://www.springframework.org/schema/beans/spring-beans.xsd
http://www.springframework.org/schema/context http://www.
springframework.org/schema/context/spring-context.xsd">
<context:component-scan base-package="com.apress.book.ldap" />

<bean id="contextSource" class="org.springframework.ldap.core.
support.LdapContextSource">
    <property name="url" value="ldap://localhost:11389" />
    <property name="userDn" value="cn=Directory Manager" />
      <property name="password" value="secret" />
</bean>

<bean id="ldapTemplate" class="org.springframework.ldap.core.
LdapTemplate">
        <constructor-arg ref="contextSource"  />
</bean>
</beans>
```

In the context file, you declare a `contextSource` bean to manage connections to the LDAP server. For `LdapContextSource` to properly create instances of `DirContext`, you need to provide it with information about the LDAP server. The `url` property takes the fully qualified URL (`ldap://server:port format`) to the LDAP server. The base property can be used to specify the root suffix for all LDAP operations. The `userDn` and `password` properties are used to provide authentication information. Next, you configure a new `LdapTemplate` bean and inject the `contextSource` bean.

With all your dependencies declared in the context file, you can re-implement the search client, as shown in Listing 3-8. Consider that Listing 3-8 have some improvements compared with the examples that you see in Chapter 2 because this one uses directly the context of Spring.

***Listing 3-8.*** Another way to obtain the information is without configuring the context.

```
package com.apress.book.ldap;

import java.util.List;

import javax.naming.NamingException;
```

```java
import javax.naming.directory.Attributes;

import org.springframework.beans.factory.annotation.Autowired;
import org.springframework.beans.factory.annotation.Qualifier;
import org.springframework.context.ApplicationContext;
import org.springframework.context.support.ClassPathXmlApplicationContext;
import org.springframework.ldap.core.AttributesMapper;
import org.springframework.ldap.core.LdapTemplate;
import org.springframework.stereotype.Component;

@Component
public class SpringSearchClient {

            private LdapTemplate ldapTemplate;
    @Autowired
    public SpringSearchClient(@Qualifier("ldapTemplate") LdapTemplate
    ldapTemplate) {
        this.ldapTemplate = ldapTemplate;
    }

    @SuppressWarnings("unchecked")
    public List<String> search() {

        return ldapTemplate.search("dc=inflinx,dc=com",
        "(objectclass=person)",
                new AttributesMapper() {
                    @Override
                    public Object mapFromAttributes(Attributes
                    attributes) throws NamingException {
                        return (String)attributes.get("cn").get();
                    } });

    }
}
```

You will notice that this code is no different from the SearchClient code you saw in Listing 3-4. You just extracted the creation of LdapTemplate to an external configuration file. The @Autowired annotation instructs Spring to inject the ldapTemplate dependency. This simplifies the search client class and helps you focus on the search logic.

The code to run the new search client is shown in Listing 3-9. You start by creating a new instance of ClassPathXmlApplicationContext. The ClassPathXmlApplication Context takes the applicationContext.xml file as its parameter. Then you retrieve an instance of SpringSearchClient from the context and invoke the search method.

***Listing 3-9.*** The main of the application

```
public static void main(String[] args) {
    ApplicationContext context = new ClassPathXmlApplicationContext("class
path:applicationContext.xml");
    SpringSearchClient client = context.getBean(SpringSearchClient.class);
    List<String> names = client.search();

    for(String name: names) {
        System.out.println(name);
    }
}
```

If you run the previous class, you will obtain the same results as the previous way to connect with LDAP and iterate the objectClass person.

```
00:13:54.161 [main] DEBUG o.s.c.s.ClassPathXmlApplicationContext -
Refreshing org.springframework.context.support.ClassPathXmlApplicationConte
xt@64d7f7e0
00:13:54.234 [main] DEBUG o.s.c.a.ClassPathBeanDefinitionScann
er - Identified candidate component class: file [/home/asacco/Code/
practical-spring-ldap/chapter3/target/classes/com/apress/book/ldap/
LdapOperationsClient.class]
00:13:54.235 [main] DEBUG o.s.c.a.ClassPathBeanDefinitionScann
er - Identified candidate component class: file [/home/asacco/Code/
practical-spring-ldap/chapter3/target/classes/com/apress/book/ldap/
SearchClient.class]
00:13:54.235 [main] DEBUG o.s.c.a.ClassPathBeanDefinitionScann
er - Identified candidate component class: file [/home/asacco/Code/
practical-spring-ldap/chapter3/target/classes/com/apress/book/ldap/
SpringSearchClient.class]
00:13:54.245 [main] DEBUG o.s.b.f.xml.XmlBeanDefinitionReader - Loaded 9
bean definitions from class path resource [applicationContext.xml]
```

```
00:13:54.252 [main] DEBUG o.s.b.f.s.DefaultListableBeanFactory - Creating
shared instance of singleton bean 'org.springframework.context.annotation.
internalConfigurationAnnotationProcessor'
00:13:54.265 [main] DEBUG o.s.b.f.s.DefaultListableBeanFactory - Creating
shared instance of singleton bean 'org.springframework.context.event.
internalEventListenerProcessor'
00:13:54.265 [main] DEBUG o.s.b.f.s.DefaultListableBeanFactory - Creating
shared instance of singleton bean 'org.springframework.context.event.
internalEventListenerFactory'
00:13:54.266 [main] DEBUG o.s.b.f.s.DefaultListableBeanFactory - Creating
shared instance of singleton bean 'org.springframework.context.annotation.
internalAutowiredAnnotationProcessor'
00:13:54.268 [main] DEBUG o.s.b.f.s.DefaultListableBeanFactory - Creating
shared instance of singleton bean 'ldapOperationsClient'
00:13:54.274 [main] DEBUG o.s.b.f.s.DefaultListableBeanFactory - Creating
shared instance of singleton bean 'ldapTemplate'
00:13:54.277 [main] DEBUG o.s.b.f.s.DefaultListableBeanFactory - Creating
shared instance of singleton bean 'contextSource'
00:13:54.287 [main] DEBUG o.s.l.c.s.AbstractContextSource -
AuthenticationSource not set - using default implementation
00:13:54.287 [main] DEBUG o.s.l.c.s.AbstractContextSource - Not using
LDAP pooling
00:13:54.288 [main] DEBUG o.s.l.c.s.AbstractContextSource - Trying provider
Urls: ldap://localhost:11389
00:13:54.296 [main] DEBUG o.s.b.f.s.DefaultListableBeanFactory - Creating
shared instance of singleton bean 'searchClient'
00:13:54.296 [main] DEBUG o.s.b.f.s.DefaultListableBeanFactory - Creating
shared instance of singleton bean 'springSearchClient'
00:13:54.308 [main] DEBUG o.s.l.c.s.AbstractContextSource - Got Ldap
context on server 'ldap://localhost:11389'
Cherise Andric
Cherish Andros
Cherlyn Andrukat
Cherri Andrusiak
```

........................................

# Spring LdapTemplate Operations

In the previous section, you utilized `LdapTemplate` to implement search. Now, let's look at using `LdapTemplate` for adding, removing, and modifying information in LDAP.

# Add Operation

The `LdapTemplate` class provides several bind methods that allow you to create new LDAP entries. The simplest among those methods is as follows:

```
public void bind(String dn, Object obj,  Attributes  attributes)
```

The first parameter to this method is the unique distinguished name of the object that needs to be bound. The second parameter is the object to be bound and is usually an implementation of the `DirContext` interface. The third parameter is the attribute of the object to be bound. Among the three, only the first parameter is required, and you can pass a null for the rest of the two.

Listing 3-10 shows the code involved in creating a new patron entry with a minimal set of information. You start the method implementation by creating a new instance of the `BasicAttributes` class to hold the patron attributes. Single-valued attributes are added by passing the attribute name and value to the put method. To add the multivalued attribute objectclass, you create a new instance of `BasicAttribute`. You then add the entry's objectClass values to the `objectClassAttribute`, and add it to the attributes list. Finally, you invoke the bind method on the `LdapTemplate` with the patron information and the patron's fully qualified DN. This adds the patron entry to the LDAP server.

***Listing 3-10.*** Add patron operation

```
public void addPatron() {
    // Set the Patron attributes
    Attributes attributes = new BasicAttributes();
    attributes.put("sn", "Patron999");
    attributes.put("cn", "New Patron999");

    // Add the multi-valued attribute
    BasicAttribute objectClassAttribute = new BasicAttribute("objectclass");
    objectClassAttribute.add("top");
```

```
    objectClassAttribute.add("person");
    objectClassAttribute.add("organizationalperson");
    objectClassAttribute.add("inetorgperson");
    attributes.put(objectClassAttribute);

    ldapTemplate.bind("uid=patron999,ou=patrons,dc=inflinx,dc=com", null,
    attributes);
}
```

# Modify Operation

Consider the scenario where you want to add a telephone number to the newly added patron. To do that, `LdapTemplate` provides a convenient `modifyAttributes` method with the following signature:

```
public void modifyAttributes(String dn, ModificationItem[]  mods)
```

This variation of `modifyAttributes` method takes the fully qualified unique DN of the entry to be modified as its first parameter. The second parameter takes an array of `ModificationItems` where each modification item holds the attribute information that needs modification. Listing 3-11 shows an example of *modifyattributes*, such as adding a new telephone to a patron.

***Listing 3-11.*** Add a new telephone number to the patron

```
public void addTelephoneNumber() {
    Attribute attribute = new BasicAttribute("telephoneNumber", "801
    100 1000");
    ModificationItem item = new ModificationItem(DirContext.ADD_ATTRIBUTE,
    attribute);
    ldapTemplate.modifyAttributes("uid=patron999,ou=patrons,dc=inflinx,
    dc=com", new ModificationItem[] {item});
}
```

In this implementation, you simply create a new `BasicAttribute` with telephone information. Then you create a new `ModificationItem` and pass in the `ADD_ATTRIBUTE` code, indicating that you add an attribute. Finally, you invoke the `modifyAttributes` method with the patron DN and the modification item. The DirContext has a REPLACE_ATTRIBUTE code that, when used, will replace an attribute's value. Similarly, the REMOVE_ATTRIBUTE code will remove the specified value from the attribute.

# Deleting Operation

Similar to addition and modification, LdapTemplate makes it easy to remove an entry with the unbind method. Listing 3-12 provides the code that implements the unbind method and removes a patron. As you can see, the unbind method takes the DN for the entry that needs to be removed.

***Listing 3-12.***  Remove one element

```
public void removePatron() {     ldapTemplate.unbind("uid=patron999,ou=patrons,
dc=inflinx,dc=com");
}
```

A good way to check all the operations is to create a class that contains all these methods with the name LdapOperationsClient and create a main class that checks if all of them work. Listing 3-13 shows the main method of the class, which invokes all the operations.

***Listing 3-13.***  Main method invoking all the operations

```
@Component
public class LdapOperationsClient {

    private LdapTemplate ldapTemplate;
    @Autowired

    public LdapOperationsClient(@Qualifier("ldapTemplate") LdapTemplate
    ldapTemplate) {
        this.ldapTemplate = ldapTemplate;
    }

    //Methods that appears on the previous Listing

    public static void main(String[] args) {
        ApplicationContext context = new ClassPathXmlApplicationContext
        ("classpath:applicationContext.xml");
```

```
    LdapOperationsClient client = context.
    getBean(LdapOperationsClient.class);
    client.addPatron();
    client.addTelephoneNumber();
    client.removePatron();
    }
}
```

When you run all the methods together, you will see the following output on the console:

```
00:36:41.457 [main] DEBUG o.s.c.s.ClassPathXmlApplicationContext -
Refreshing org.springframework.context.support.ClassPathXmlApplication
Context@1c72da34
00:36:41.535 [main] DEBUG o.s.c.a.ClassPathBeanDefinitionScanner -
Identified candidate component class: file [/home/asacco/Code/practical-
spring-ldap/code/chapters/chapter3/target/classes/com/apress/book/ldap/
LdapOperationsClient.class]
00:36:41.536 [main] DEBUG o.s.c.a.ClassPathBeanDefinitionScanner -
Identified candidate component class: file [/home/asacco/Code/practical-
spring-ldap/code/chapters/chapter3/target/classes/com/apress/book/ldap/
SearchClient.class]
00:36:41.536 [main] DEBUG o.s.c.a.ClassPathBeanDefinitionScanner -
Identified candidate component class: file [/home/asacco/Code/practical-
spring-ldap/code/chapters/chapter3/target/classes/com/apress/book/ldap/
SpringSearchClient.class]
00:36:41.546 [main] DEBUG o.s.b.f.xml.XmlBeanDefinitionReader - Loaded 9
bean definitions from class path resource [applicationContext.xml]
00:36:41.553 [main] DEBUG o.s.b.f.s.DefaultListableBeanFactory - Creating
shared instance of singleton bean 'org.springframework.context.annotation.
internalConfigurationAnnotationProcessor'
00:36:41.567 [main] DEBUG o.s.b.f.s.DefaultListableBeanFactory - Creating
shared instance of singleton bean 'org.springframework.context.event.
internalEventListenerProcessor'
```

```
00:36:41.568 [main] DEBUG o.s.b.f.s.DefaultListableBeanFactory - Creating
shared instance of singleton bean 'org.springframework.context.event.
internalEventListenerFactory'
00:36:41.569 [main] DEBUG o.s.b.f.s.DefaultListableBeanFactory - Creating
shared instance of singleton bean 'org.springframework.context.annotation.
internalAutowiredAnnotationProcessor'
00:36:41.570 [main] DEBUG o.s.b.f.s.DefaultListableBeanFactory - Creating
shared instance of singleton bean 'ldapOperationsClient'
00:36:41.578 [main] DEBUG o.s.b.f.s.DefaultListableBeanFactory - Creating
shared instance of singleton bean 'ldapTemplate'
00:36:41.582 [main] DEBUG o.s.b.f.s.DefaultListableBeanFactory - Creating
shared instance of singleton bean 'contextSource'
00:36:41.598 [main] DEBUG o.s.l.c.s.AbstractContextSource -
AuthenticationSource not set - using default implementation
00:36:41.599 [main] DEBUG o.s.l.c.s.AbstractContextSource - Not using
LDAP pooling
00:36:41.599 [main] DEBUG o.s.l.c.s.AbstractContextSource - Trying provider
Urls: ldap://localhost:11389
00:36:41.612 [main] DEBUG o.s.b.f.s.DefaultListableBeanFactory - Creating
shared instance of singleton bean 'searchClient'
00:36:41.612 [main] DEBUG o.s.b.f.s.DefaultListableBeanFactory - Creating
shared instance of singleton bean 'springSearchClient'
00:36:41.644 [main] DEBUG o.s.l.c.s.AbstractContextSource - Got Ldap
context on server 'ldap://localhost:11389'
00:36:41.653 [main] DEBUG o.s.l.c.s.AbstractContextSource - Got Ldap
context on server 'ldap://localhost:11389'
00:36:41.657 [main] DEBUG o.s.l.c.s.AbstractContextSource - Got Ldap
context on server 'ldap://localhost:11389'
```

As you can see, there is no reference to what happens with the operations because nothing appears on the console. The best way to check if the different operations work or not is to test each operation alone and check on the tool to see if the information on LDAP works or not.

# Summary

The Spring LDAP framework aims at simplifying LDAP programming in Java. In this chapter, you got a high-level overview of Spring LDAP and some of the concepts associated with Spring Framework. You also looked at the setup needed to get up and running with Spring LDAP. In the next chapter, you will focus on testing Spring LDAP applications.

# CHAPTER 4

# Testing LDAP Code

Testing is an essential aspect of any software development process. As well as detecting bugs, it also helps to verify that all requirements are met and that the software works as expected. Today, formally or informally, testing is included in almost every phase of the software development process. Depending on what is being tested and the purpose behind the test, we end up with several different types of testing. The most common testing done by developers is unit testing, which ensures that individual units work as expected. Integration testing usually follows unit testing and focuses on the interaction between previously tested components. Developers are usually involved in creating automated integration tests, especially tests that deal with databases and directories. Next is system testing, where the complete, integrated system is evaluated to ensure all requirements are met. Nonfunctional requirements such as performance and efficiency are also tested as part of system testing. Acceptance testing is usually done at the end to ensure that the delivered software meets the customer/business user's needs.

---

**Note**    Consider this chapter only to cover the essential aspects of unit and integration testing. To learn more about testing, you can read one of the most recommended testing, Martin Fowler's[1] blog, which tackles topics like BDD, different types of testing, and good practices.

---

## Concepts About Testing

Before going in depth on creating tests that check different operations on the use of LDAP, it is relevant to clarify any doubt about some terms related to testing.

---

[1] https://martinfowler.com/tags/testing.html

© Balaji Varanasi and Andres Sacco 2023
B. Varanasi and A. Sacco, *Practical Spring LDAP*, https://doi.org/10.1007/979-8-8688-0002-3_4

# Unit Testing

Unit testing is a methodology where the smallest parts of the application, referred to as units, are verified and validated individually in isolation. In structural programming, the unit could be an individual method or function. In object-oriented programming (OOP), an object is the smallest executable unit. Interaction between objects is central to any OO design and is usually done by invoking methods. Thus, unit testing in OOP can range from testing individual methods to testing a cluster of objects.

Writing unit tests requires a developer's time and effort. But this investment has been proven to deliver several undeniable benefits.

---

**Note**    It is essential to measure how much of the code is covered by unit tests. To do this, several tools could help you, like Emma,[2] Clover,[3] and Jacoco.[4] The most used of the tools is Jacoco, which allows you to upload the metrics to Sonar5 to centralize all the information about the coverage of all your applications and give you the possibility to define quality gates which indicates the minimum coverage your company accepts.

If you want to learn more about what code coverage implies and how the tools generate the percentage of coverage, there is an excellent article on Martin Fowler's blog.[5]

---

The most significant advantage of unit testing is that it can help identify bugs at the early stages of development. Bugs discovered only during QA or in production consume much more debugging time and money. Also, a good set of unit tests acts as a safety net and gives confidence when code is refactored. Unit tests can help improve the design and even serve as documentation.

---

[2] https://emma.sourceforge.net/
[3] https://www.atlassian.com/software/clover
[4] https://www.eclemma.org/jacoco/
[5] https://martinfowler.com/bliki/TestCoverage.html

Good unit tests have the following characteristics:

- Every unit test must be independent of other tests. This atomic nature is essential, and each test must not cause any side effects to other tests. Unit tests should also be order independent.

- A unit test must be repeatable. For a unit test to be of any value, it must produce consistent results. Otherwise, it cannot be used as a sanity check during refactoring.

- Unit tests must be easy to set up and clean up. So they should not rely on external systems such as databases and servers.

- Unit tests must be fast and provide immediate feedback. It would not be productive to wait on long-running tests before you make another change.

- Unit tests must be self-validating. Each test should contain enough information to determine whether a test passes or fails automatically. No manual intervention should be needed to interpret the results.

Enterprise applications often use external systems like databases, directories, and web services. This is especially true in the DAO layer. Unit testing database code, for example, may involve starting a database server, loading it with schema and data, running tests, and shutting down the server. This quickly becomes tricky and complex. One approach is to use mock objects and hide the external dependencies. Where this is not sufficient, it may be necessary to use integration testing and test the code with external dependencies intact.

One of the most used libraries to test a Java application is JUnit,[6] which has many other libraries that add extra features, including Spring Boot Test,[7] which uses the latest version of JUnit to do certain operations. Consider other alternatives to testing in Java, like Spock[8] or TestNG.[9] Still, these are out of the scope of this book, discussing the pros and cons of each possible option because there are many books and articles covering this topic.

---

[6] https://junit.org/junit5/
[7] https://docs.spring.io/spring-boot/docs/current/reference/html/features.html#features.testing
[8] https://spockframework.org/
[9] https://testng.org/doc/

# Mock Testing

The goal of mocks in testing is to use mock objects to simulate real objects in controlled ways. Mock objects implement the same interface as real objects but are scripted to mimic/fake and track their behavior. There is no restriction about using mocks on any type of testing, but in this case, it is applied to the unit tests.

For example, consider a `UserAccountService` that has a method to create new user accounts. Implementing such a service usually involves validating the account information against business rules, storing the newly created account in a database, and sending a confirmation email. Persisting data and emailing information are usually abstracted out to classes in other layers. When writing a unit test to validate the business rules associated with account creation, you might not care about the intricacies of the email notification part. However, you do want to verify that an email was generated. This is precisely where mock objects come in handy. To achieve this, you just need to give the `UserAccountService` a mock implementation of the `EmailService` responsible for sending emails. The mock implementation will mark the email request and return a hardcoded result. Mock objects are a great way to isolate tests from complex dependencies, allowing them to run faster.

---

**Note**   If you want to learn more about mocks, stubs, and other types of fake responses, there is a great article on Martin Fowler's blog.[10] Also, you can read *Effective Software Testing*[11] by Manning, another great resource to learn about mocks and other testing-related topics.

---

Several open source frameworks make working with mock objects easier. Popular ones include Mockito,[12] EasyMock,[13] JMock,[14] and PowerMock.[15] In the case of this book, you will use Mockito, which is one of the most popular options to create mocks, integrates with many other libraries like JUnit, is well documented, and has a big community of users.

---

[10] https://martinfowler.com/articles/mocksArentStubs.html

[11] www.manning.com/books/effective-software-testing

[12] https://site.mockito.org/

[13] https://easymock.org/

[14] https://jmock.org/

[15] https://github.com/powermock/powermock

Some of these frameworks allow the creation of mocks for classes that don't implement any interfaces. Regardless of the framework used, unit testing using mock objects usually involves the following steps:

- Create a new mock instance.

- Set up the mock. This involves instructing the mock what to expect and what to return.

- Run the tests, passing the mock instance to the component under test.

- Verify the results.

---

**Note**    It's not the scope of this book to explain all the possible features, pros, and cons of each framework, so this chapter only covers the most relevant aspects of creating mocks using Mockito. If you want to learn more about this great library, there is the book *Mockito Made Clear*[16] by Ken Kousen.

---

# Integration Testing

Even though mock objects serve as great placeholders, you will soon run into cases where faking will not be enough. This is especially true for DAO layer code, where you must validate SQL query executions and verify modifications to database records. Testing this kind of code falls under the umbrella of integration testing. As mentioned earlier, integration testing focuses on testing interactions between components with their dependencies in place.

It has become common for developers to write automated integration tests using unit testing tools, thereby blurring the distinction between them. However, it is important to remember that integration tests are usually slower and don't run in isolation. Frameworks such as Spring provide container support for writing and executing integration tests easily. The improved availability of embedded databases, directories, and servers enables developers to write faster integration tests.

---

[16] https://pragprog.com/titles/mockito/mockito-made-clear/

In the case of this chapter, you will see two different alternatives to create integration tests. One uses an embedded LDAP, and another uses a Docker container to run an image of the LDAP vendor that you use throughout the different chapters of this book. The following sections will give you more detail about the difference between both alternatives.

# Libraries to Do Tests

In the case of LDAP, there are several libraries to do tests, but in this section, you will see the basics about the most used in the Java community.

## JUnit

It has become the de facto standard for unit testing Java applications. The introduction of annotations in JUnit 4.x made it even easier to create tests and assert test results for expected values. With the release of JUnit 5.x, new features appear to simplify the day-to-day job of developers, like having in one sentence all the possible conditions to check so that in the case that one test fails, you can know all the conditions that fail. JUnit can easily be integrated with build tools like Gradle[17] and Maven.[18] It also has great tooling support available in all popular IDEs.

With JUnit, the standard practice is writing a separate class with test methods. This class is often called a test case, and each test method is intended to test a single unit of work. It is also possible to organize test cases into groups called test suites.

The best way to learn JUnit is to write a test method. Listing 4-1 shows a simple `StringUtils` class with an `isEmpty` method. The method takes a `String` as a parameter and returns true if it is either null or empty.

---

[17] https://gradle.org/
[18] https://maven.apache.org/

***Listing 4-1.*** A simple example of a method to check if a String is empty

```java
public class StringUtils {
    public static boolean isEmpty(String text) {
        return text == null || "".equals(text);
    }
}
```

Let's create a test for Listing 4-1 that checks different conditions; you can see that Listing 4-2 is the JUnit class with a method to test the code.

***Listing 4-2.*** Different tests to check each possible scenario

```java
import org.junit.jupiter.api.Test;

import static org.junit.jupiter.api.Assertions.assertFalse;
import static org.junit.jupiter.api.Assertions.assertTrue;

@DisplayName("String Utils tests cases")
class StringUtilsTest {
    @Test
    @DisplayName("String Utils should return true when the input is null")
    void should_return_true_with_null() {
        assertTrue(StringUtils.isEmpty(null));
    }

    @Test
    @DisplayName("String Utils should return true when the input is empty")
    void should_return_true_with_empty() {
        assertTrue(StringUtils.isEmpty(""));
    }

    @Test
    @DisplayName("String Utils should return false when the input have
    a value")
    void should_return_false_with_text() {
        assertFalse(StringUtils.isEmpty("Practical Spring Ldap"));
    }
}
```

To use the different classes of JUnit, you need to include the dependency in
Listing 4-3. In the case of this chapter, you will use the different archetypes, which
include some dependencies related to testing.

***Listing 4-3.*** JUnit dependency that you must include on the POM file

```
<dependency>
    <groupId>org.junit.jupiter</groupId>
    <artifactId>junit-jupiter-engine</artifactId>
    <version>${junit-jupiter-engine.version}</version>
    <scope>test</scope>
</dependency>
```

Notice that I have followed the convention <Class Under Test>Test for naming the
test class. Before JUnit 4.x, test methods needed to begin with the word "test". With 4.x,
test methods must be marked with annotation @Test. Also, notice that all the tests have
the annotation @DisplayName to provide more information about what the idea of the
test is.

There are two ways to run the tests:

- *Using the command line and Maven*: You need to open a terminal or
  use the IDE and execute the command **mvn test**, which will give the
  following output:

```
➜  ~ mvn test
[INFO] Scanning for projects...
[INFO]
[INFO] ------------------< com.apress.book.ldap:chapter4 >----------------
[INFO] Building chapter4 1.0.0
[INFO]    from pom.xml
[INFO] --------------------------------[ jar ]----------------------------
[INFO]
[INFO] --- enforcer:3.3.0:enforce (enforce-versions) @ chapter4 ---
[INFO] Rule 0: org.apache.maven.enforcer.rules.dependency.
       DependencyConvergence passed
[INFO] Rule 1: org.apache.maven.enforcer.rules.version.
       RequireMavenVersion passed
```

```
[INFO] Rule 2: org.apache.maven.enforcer.rules.version.
        RequireJavaVersion passed
[INFO]
[INFO] --- formatter:2.8.1:format (default) @ chapter4 ---
[INFO] Using 'UTF-8' encoding to format source files.
[INFO] Number of files to be formatted: 7
[INFO] Successfully formatted:         0 file(s)
[INFO] Fail to format:                 0 file(s)
[INFO] Skipped:                        7 file(s)
[INFO] Read only skipped:              0 file(s)
[INFO] Approximate time taken:         0s
[INFO]
[INFO] --- resources:3.3.0:resources (default-resources) @ chapter4 ---
[INFO] Copying 2 resources
[INFO]
[INFO] --- compiler:3.11.0:compile (default-compile) @ chapter4 ---
[INFO] Nothing to compile - all classes are up to date
[INFO]
[INFO] --- resources:3.3.0:testResources (default-testResources)
        @ chapter4 ---
[INFO] Copying 6 resources
[INFO]
[INFO] --- compiler:3.11.0:testCompile (default-testCompile) @ chapter4 ---
[INFO] Changes detected - recompiling the module! :source
[INFO] Compiling 1 source file with javac [debug target 21] to target/
        test-classes
[INFO]
[INFO] --- surefire:3.0.0:test (default-test) @ chapter4 ---
[INFO] Using auto detected provider org.apache.maven.surefire.
        junitplatform.JUnitPlatformProvider
[INFO]
[INFO] -------------------------------------------------------
[INFO]  T E S T S
[INFO] -------------------------------------------------------
[INFO] Running com.apress.book.ldap.test.StringUtilsTest
```

```
[INFO] Tests run: 3, Failures: 0, Errors: 0, Skipped: 0, Time elapsed: 0.02
       s - in com.apress.book.ldap.test.StringUtilsTest
[INFO]
[INFO] Results:
[INFO]
[INFO] Tests run: 3, Failures: 0, Errors: 0, Skipped: 0
[INFO]
[INFO] ------------------------------------------------------------------
---------
[INFO] BUILD SUCCESS
[INFO] ------------------------------------------------------------------
---------
[INFO] Total time:  1.345 s
[INFO] Finished at: 2023-10-14T19:51:24-03:00
[INFO] ------------------------------------------------------------------
---------
```

- *Using the IDE*: This method changes from IDE to IDE, but most
  cases have the same way to run the tests. If you use IntelliJ, you
  have a green but on the class or the method, and if you press and
  indicate that you want to run the test, you will have an output like
  Figure 4-1.

**Figure 4-1.** *Output of the execution of the tests*

Table 4-1 lists some important annotations available in JUnit 5.

**Table 4-1.** *JUnit 5 Annotations*

| Annotation | Description |
|---|---|
| @Test | Annotates a method as a JUnit test method. The method should be of public scope and have a void return type. |
| @BeforeEach | Marks a method to run before every test method. Useful for setting up test fixtures. The @Before method of a superclass is run before the current class. |
| @AfterEach | Marks a method to be run after every test method. Useful for tearing down test fixtures. The @After method of a superclass is run after the current class. |
| @Disabled | Marks a method to be ignored during test runs. This helps avoid the need for commenting on half-baked test methods. |

*(continued)*

***Table 4-1.*** *(continued)*

| Annotation | Description |
| --- | --- |
| @DisplayName | This annotation gives a specific name to a class or method. On this annotation, you can use special characters, numbers, spaces, or emojis. |
| @BeforeAll | Annotates a method to run before any test method is run. For a test case, the method is run only once and can be used to provide class-level setup work. |
| @AfterAll | Annotates a method to run after all the test methods are run. This can be useful for performing any cleanups at a class level. |
| @ExtendWith | Specifies the class extends the test methods for another one. |

Consider that the table only shows the most relevant annotations you need to use on the test; there are many other annotations on the JUnit official website.[19]

# Mockito

Mockito[20] is a mocking framework written in Java that has become one of the most popular options to create and manage mocks because it offers a simple syntax and support with many other test libraries like JUnit. With this library, you can declare different types of responses on the interfaces/classes you mock depending on the situation you want to test, from a specific value to throwing an exception.

Following the same approach as JUnit, the best way to learn Mockito is with a practical example. Let's define two simple classes with a certain level of connection to create the scenario. Listing 4-4 shows a simple service that takes two numbers and executes a sum operation.

***Listing 4-4.*** A simple class that executes a math operation

```
public class MathService {
    public int add(int numberOne, int numberTwo){
        return numberOne + numberTwo;
    }
}
```

---

[19] https://junit.org/junit5/docs/current/user-guide/#writing-tests-annotations
[20] https://site.mockito.org/

The next step is to create another class with the MathService as a dependency, which you will mock. Listing 4-5 shows you a class with a method that invokes the same method of the service.

**Listing 4-5.** A service class that invokes another class

```
public class Calculator {
    private final MathService service;
    public Calculator(MathService service) {
        this.service = service;
    }
    public int add(int numberOne, int numberTwo){
        return service.add(numberOne, numberTwo);
    }
}
```

Before creating any tests and creating the mocks, you must add the dependency compatible with JUnit 5, which is shown in Listing 4-6.

**Listing 4-6.** Mockito dependency that you must include on the POM file

```
<dependency>
    <groupId>org.mockito</groupId>
    <artifactId>mockito-junit-jupiter</artifactId>
    <version>${mockito-junit-jupiter.version}</version>
    <scope>test</scope>
</dependency>
```

The last step is to create a test that mocks the MathService class because you only want to test the behavior of the Calculator class. Listing 4-7 shows you the context definition and a simple test.

**Listing 4-7.** Simple tests using Mockito

```
import org.junit.jupiter.api.BeforeEach;
import org.junit.jupiter.api.DisplayName;
import org.junit.jupiter.api.Test;
```

```java
import static org.junit.jupiter.api.Assertions.assertEquals;
import static org.mockito.Mockito.*;

@DisplayName("Calculator tests cases")
class CalculatorTest {

    private MathService mathService;

    private Calculator calculator;

    @BeforeEach

    public void setUp() {
        mathService = mock(MathService.class); // This class is a mock
        calculator = new Calculator(mathService);
    }

    @Test
    @DisplayName("Check that the sum of two numbers is okay")
    void should_sum_two_numbers() {
        // Given - Creating the mocks
        when(mathService.add(1, 4)).thenReturn(5);

        // When - Execution of the operation
        int result = calculator.add(1, 4);

        // Then - Verify the results and the interactions with the
        mocks class
        verify(mathService).add(1, 4);
        assertEquals(5, result);
    }
}
```

As you can see in Listing 4-7, there are some static methods like when, mock, and verify that are part of the features that introduce Mockito not just to create mocks but with the idea to help validate if the mocks are used or not for your tests.

Table 4-2 lists some important methods available in Mockito.

*Table 4-2.* *Mockito Methods*

| Methods | Description |
|---|---|
| mock | This method creates a mock for a particular class which intercepts all the invocations, and you can change the class's behavior. |
| verify | This method will help you to check if a particular mock with certain parameters was invoked. This is extremely useful to understand if the logic works fine. |
| any | You will use this method to indicate that you want any value that receives the mock, active the new behavior. |
| doThrow | You can use this method to throw a particular exception when the mock is invoked in a specific condition. |
| when/ given | You will use this method to specify the condition that the invocation needs to execute the mock. |

Consider that the table only shows the most relevant annotations you need to use on the test; there are many other annotations on the Mockito official website.[21]

# Testcontainers

Testcontainers[22] is a lightweight and open source library that allows you to run different containers on your application and reuse different test cases. This library supports multiple testing frameworks, like different versions of JUnit and Spock, and you can use it on Java or Kotlin projects.

The containers could be databases or other services that your application requires; for example, if your application needs to use a specific service of AWS, you can use the image of LocalStack.[23] Testcontainers develop a set of modules[24] to reduce the complexity of running a container and configure this particular image; for example, there are modules for the most popular databases and queues.

---

[21] https://javadoc.io/doc/org.mockito/mockito-core/latest/org/mockito/Mockito.html
[22] https://testcontainers.com/
[23] https://github.com/localstack/localstack
[24] https://testcontainers.com/modules/

Behind the scenes, this library uses Docker[25] to download and run the different containers, so before using your project, check the general requirements[26] related to the versions of Docker that the library needs to satisfy. Also, since November 2020, Docker Hub introduced some restrictions on using the different images on the repository, like the number of times you download, but in the case of the open source projects, the restrictions do not apply because the idea is that Docker Hub works as a central repository. Consider that if you use this library in a pipeline, the machine running needs to satisfy the same requirements.

Before creating any test using containers, you must add the dependencies compatible with JUnit 5, which appears in Listing 4-8.

***Listing 4-8.*** Testcontainers dependency that you must include on the POM file

```
<dependency>
    <groupId>org.testcontainers</groupId>
    <artifactId>testcontainers</artifactId>
    <version>${testcontainers.version}</version>
    <scope>test</scope>
</dependency>

<dependency>
    <groupId>org.testcontainers</groupId>
    <artifactId>junit-jupiter</artifactId>
    <version>${testcontainers.version}</version>
    <scope>test</scope>
</dependency>
```

After that, let's create a simple test that only runs a simple hello-world image as shown in Listing 4-9.

***Listing 4-9.*** Declaration of a container to be used on the test

```
import org.junit.jupiter.api.DisplayName;
import org.junit.jupiter.api.Test;
import org.testcontainers.containers.GenericContainer;
import org.testcontainers.junit.jupiter.Container;
import org.testcontainers.junit.jupiter.Testcontainers;
import org.testcontainers.utility.DockerImageName;

@Testcontainers
```

---

[25] https://www.docker.com/

[26] https://java.testcontainers.org/supported_docker_environment/

```
@DisplayName("Hello world container tests cases")
class HelloWorldContainerTest {

    @Container
    public static GenericContainer container = new GenericContainer(Docker
    ImageName.parse("testcontainers/helloworld"));

    @Test
    @DisplayName("Check that the test and the container works fine")
    void should_works_the_container() {

    }
}
```

As you can see, Listing 4-9 includes a new annotation called @**Testcontainers**, which is responsible for managing the life cycle of the containers during the execution of tests. Also, there is another annotation on the tests with the name @Container, which indicates that the variable that you declared needs that Testcontainers run the container. If you run the command **mvn test** in your terminal, you will see on the logs something like this:

```
11:10:21.531 [main] INFO org.testcontainers.DockerClientFactory - Connected
to docker:
  Server Version: 23.0.5
  API Version: 1.42
  Operating System: Docker Desktop
  Total Memory: 7579 MB
11:10:21.539 [main] DEBUG org.testcontainers.utility.RyukResourceReaper -
Ryuk is enabled
11:10:21.541 [main] DEBUG org.testcontainers.utility.
PrefixingImageNameSubstitutor - No prefix is configured
11:10:21.541 [main] DEBUG org.testcontainers.utility.
ImageNameSubstitutor - Did not find a substitute image for testcontainers/
ryuk:0.5.1 (using image substitutor: DefaultImageNameSubstitutor
(composite of 'ConfigurationFileImageNameSubstitutor' and
'PrefixingImageNameSubstitutor'))
```

The previous logs indicates that **Testcontainers** connect with **Docker** to use the image **testcontainers/ryuk** that will contain all the containers that you use on your different tests so with this library you will be running **Docker** in **Docker** for that reason you can share or not the same container of one database between different tests. Figure 4-2 show you how TestContainers works when you execute the tests.

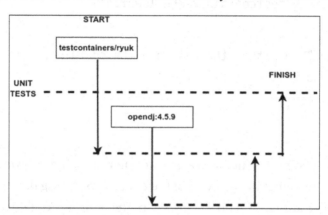

***Figure 4-2.*** *The flow of execution of the containers*

Consider that this approach takes more time than the previous one because you run a real LDAP vendor.

## Creating the Tests

After a brief introduction to different testing concepts, it's time to see in detail the different libraries that will help you to create the different types of tests on a project. To do this, use the same command in Chapter 3 to create a new project named chapter4:

```
$ mvn archetype:generate \
-DarchetypeGroupId=com.apress.book.ldap \
-DarchetypeArtifactId=practical-ldap-empty-archetype \
-DarchetypeVersion=1.0.0 \
-DgroupId=com.apress.book.ldap \
-DartifactId=chapter4 \
-DinteractiveMode=false
```

---

**Note**    In the following chapters, this instruction will be only mentioned with the idea of not duplicating the same sentence in each chapter.

---

Let's create a simple application that accesses LDAP and execute common operations like getting all the elements, adding, removing, or modifying an element. First, you need to create an object which represents a Patron, so create a domain class like Listing 4-10; this class does not contain all the possible attributes that could exist on LDAP, but it's enough to show how to create tests.

***Listing 4-10.*** Domain classes that represent an object on LDAP

```
public class Patron {

    private String uid;
    private String firstName;
    private String lastName;
    private String commonName;
    private String email;

    public Patron() {
    }

    public Patron(String uid, String firstName, String lastName, String
    commonName, String email) {
        this.uid = uid;
        this.firstName = firstName;
        this.lastName = lastName;
        this.commonName = commonName;
        this.email = email;
    }
    // Setters and getters
}
```

The next step is to create the class that contains all the operations more or less similar to the examples in Chapter 3. Still, instead of having everything hardcoded on the different methods, the idea is to create dynamic methods that receive by parameters the values to do certain operations.

***Listing 4-11.*** Domain classes that represent an object on LDAP

```
@Component
public class LdapOperationsClient {
```

```java
    private LdapTemplate ldapTemplate;
    public LdapOperationsClient(@Autowired @Qualifier("ldapTemplate")
    LdapTemplate ldapTemplate) {
        this.ldapTemplate = ldapTemplate;
    }

public void add(String id, Patron patron) {
        // Set the Patron attributes
        Attributes attributes = new BasicAttributes();
        attributes.put("sn", patron.getLastName());
        attributes.put("givenName", patron.getFirstName());
        attributes.put("cn", patron.getCommonName());
        attributes.put("mail", patron.getEmail());

        // Add the multi-valued attribute
        BasicAttribute objectClassAttribute = new
        BasicAttribute("objectclass");
        objectClassAttribute.add("top");
        objectClassAttribute.add("person");
        objectClassAttribute.add("organizationalperson");
        objectClassAttribute.add("inetorgperson");
        attributes.put(objectClassAttribute);

        ldapTemplate.bind("uid=" + id + ",ou=patrons,dc=inflinx,dc=com",
        null, attributes);
    }

public void updateEmail(String uid, String mail) {
        Attribute attribute = new BasicAttribute("mail", mail);
        ModificationItem item = new ModificationItem(DirContext.REPLACE_
        ATTRIBUTE, attribute);
        ldapTemplate.modifyAttributes("uid=" + uid + ",ou=patrons,dc=inflinx,
        dc=com", new ModificationItem[] { item });
    }

public void remove(String uid) {
        ldapTemplate.unbind("uid=" + uid + ",ou=patrons,dc=inflinx,dc=com");
    }
```

```
public List<Patron> search() {
    return ldapTemplate.search("dc=inflinx,dc=com",
    "(objectclass=person)", (AttributesMapper) attributes -> {
        Patron patron = new Patron();
        patron.setUid((String) attributes.get("uid").get());
        patron.setFirstName((String) attributes.
        get("givenName").get());
        patron.setLastName((String) attributes.get("sn").get());
        patron.setEmail((String) attributes.get("mail").get());
        patron.setCommonName((String) attributes.get("cn").get());
        return patron;
    });
}

}
```

Just these two classes are enough to create different scenarios of testing using mocks with Mockito, embedded servers, or Testcontainers.

## Mocking the Templates

This approach is the simplest because it does not imply that you need to run the entire application to test if something works fine. You can think of this type of test as a unit test because you only want to test your class without using or checking what happens with other classes. In the case of Listing 4-11, you need to mock the LdapTemplate and only check your logic. In Listing 4-12, create a mock over the template to simulate any response you want on your tests.

*Listing 4-12.* Test class with mocks

```
import com.apress.book.ldap.domain.Patron;
import org.junit.jupiter.api.BeforeEach;
import org.junit.jupiter.api.DisplayName;
import org.junit.jupiter.api.Test;
import org.springframework.ldap.core.AttributesMapper;
import org.springframework.ldap.core.LdapTemplate;
import javax.naming.directory.Attributes;
import javax.naming.directory.BasicAttributes;
```

```java
import java.util.ArrayList;
import java.util.List;

import static org.junit.jupiter.api.Assertions.*;
import static org.mockito.ArgumentMatchers.*;
import static org.mockito.Mockito.mock;
import static org.mockito.Mockito.when;

@DisplayName("LDAP Operations Test using mocks")
public class LdapOperationsClientMockTest {

    LdapOperationsClient client;
    LdapTemplate ldapTemplate;

    @BeforeEach
    public void setup() {
        ldapTemplate = mock(LdapTemplate.class);
        this.client = new LdapOperationsClient(ldapTemplate);
    }
    //Tests
}
```

---

**Note**    The Mockito library is not part of the archetype, so you need to include it manually.

---

The next step is to create tests that use the mocks of our class and return one element when you try to search LDAP and transform the result into a Patron object. Listing 4-13 shows you how to create tests for certain operations mocking only the access to LDAP.

*Listing 4-13.* Test class with mocks

```java
@Test
@DisplayName("Check that operation search return a patron")
public void should_return_patrons() {
    Attributes attribute = new BasicAttributes();
    attribute.put("sn", "Sacco");
    attribute.put("givenName", "Andres");
```

```
List<Attributes> attributes = new ArrayList<>();
attributes.add(attribute);
//Mock the response
when(ldapTemplate.search(anyString(), anyString(),
any(AttributesMapper.class))).thenReturn(attributes);

List<Patron> patrons = client.search();

assertAll(() -> assertNotNull(patrons), () -> assertEquals(1, patrons.
size()));
}
```

If you run these tests using your IDE or from the console, everything will work. As you can imagine, this approach looks great for checking certain business logic, but as cons, you do not test if everything occurs in the same way that you expected on your LDAP; for that reason, you need to create an integration test using a server.

## Testing Using Embedded Server

ApacheDS,[27] OpenDJ,[28] and UnboundID[29] are open source LDAP directories that can be embedded into Java applications. Embedded directories are part of the application's JVM, making automating tasks such as startup and shutdown easy. They have a small startup time and typically run fast. Embedded directories also eliminate the need for a dedicated, stand-alone LDAP server for each developer or build machine.

Embedding an LDAP server involved in the past creating and starting/stopping the server programmatically, but many years ago, with the new versions of Spring and JUnit, you delegated the responsibility to do it. This approach is the most recommended, but if you want to manage the life cycle of embedding an LDAP server, you can do it by adding all the logic to start and stop it on each test execution.

---

[27] https://directory.apache.org/

[28] https://www.openidentityplatform.org/opendj

[29] https://ldap.com/

[30] https://directory.apache.org/apacheds/

[31] https://ldap.com/unboundid-ldap-sdk-for-java/

In the case of Spring LDAP, you can use two different alternatives of embedded server, which are based on ApacheDS[30] or UnboundID.[31] In the case of this book, you will use the second option because Spring does not have support for the latest versions of ApacheDS, and UnboundID is agnostic to the vendor.

---

**Note**    OpenDJ had an embedded server in the old versions of this vendor but was deprecated some years ago. On the source code, you will see that the classes exist, but just in case, you have a legacy application and need to do some tests.

---

After the introduction of the idea of an embedded server, it's time to modify the pom file and add the dependencies. Listing 4-14 shows the different libraries that you need to include.

***Listing 4-14.***  Dependencies to use an embedded server

```
<dependency>
    <groupId>org.springframework</groupId>
    <artifactId>spring-test</artifactId>
    <version>${org.springframework.version}</version>
    <scope>test</scope>
</dependency>

<dependency>
    <groupId>org.springframework.ldap</groupId>
    <artifactId>spring-ldap-test</artifactId>
    <version>${org.springframework.ldap.version}</version>
    <scope>test</scope>
</dependency>

<dependency>
    <groupId>com.unboundid</groupId>
    <artifactId>unboundid-ldapsdk</artifactId>
    <version>${unboundid-ldapsdk.version}</version>
    <scope>test</scope>
</dependency>
```

After that, you need to create a file containing all the configurations on the **src/test/ resources**. Let's start with the basic configuration shown in Listing 4-15.

***Listing 4-15.*** Configuration of the application

```xml
<?xml version="1.0" encoding="UTF-8"?>
<beans xmlns="http://www.springframework.org/schema/beans"
        xmlns:xsi="http://www.w3.org/2001/XMLSchema-instance"
        xmlns:context="http://www.springframework.org/schema/context"
        xsi:schemaLocation="http://www.springframework.org/schema/beans
        http://www.springframework.org/schema/beans/spring-beans.xsd
        http://www.springframework.org/schema/context http://www.
        springframework.org/schema/context/spring-context.xsd">

        <context:component-scan base-package="com.apress.book.ldap" />

        <bean id="contextSource" class="org.springframework.ldap.core.
        support.LdapContextSource">
            <property name="url" value="ldap://localhost:18880" />
            <property name="userDn" value="uid=admin,ou=system" />
             <property name="password" value="secret" />
        </bean>

        <bean id="ldapTemplate" class="org.springframework.ldap.core.
        LdapTemplate">
            <constructor-arg ref="contextSource"  />
        </bean>
                    </beans>
```

Now you need to add the modifications to create the embedded server and populate with the same information when the server starts. Listing 4-16 sets up the basic configuration and loads the file **patrons.ldif**, which you need to include in the directory **src/test/resources** of your project. All of this is to populate LDAP with a basic set of information to test the different operations.

***Listing 4-16.*** Configuration of the embedded server

```xml
<!-- Populates the LDAP server with initial data -->
<bean class="org.springframework.ldap.test.LdifPopulator" depends-on=
"embeddedLdapServer">
    <property name="contextSource" ref="contextSource" />
```

```xml
        <property name="resource" value="classpath:patrons.ldif" />
        <property name="base" value="dc=inflinx,dc=com" />
        <property name="clean" value="true" />
        <property name="defaultBase" value="dc=inflinx,dc=com" />
</bean>
<bean id="embeddedLdapServer" class="org.springframework.ldap.test.
unboundid.EmbeddedLdapServerFactoryBean">
        <property name="partitionName" value="inflinx"/>
        <property name="partitionSuffix" value="dc=inflinx,dc=com" />
        <property name="port" value="18880" />
</bean>
```

Consider that each time you execute a test, the server will be recreated, so if you do some modifications with the information on LDAP, it will not affect other tests that use the same data.

After you do all the configuration, the last task is to create a simple test that validates that the search method works fine and returns the list of Patrons, as shown in Listing 4-17.

***Listing 4-17.*** A simple test that uses an embedded server

```java
@ExtendWith(SpringExtension.class)
@ContextConfiguration("classpath:repositoryContext-test.xml")
@DisplayName("LDAP Operations Test using an embedded LDAP")
public class LdapOperationsClientEmbbededTest {

    @Autowired
    LdapOperationsClient client;

    @Test
    @DisplayName("Check that operation search return a patron")
    public void should_return_patrons() {
        List<Patron> patrons = client.search();

        assertAll(() -> assertNotNull(patrons), () -> assertEquals(100,
        patrons.size()));
    }
}
```

If you run this test, everything will work fine, and in the case that you create several tests on the same class, each time the tests are executed the server will load the information again.

# Moving to Tests with Testcontainers

After the creation of tests that check using LDAP if the logic of our business is okay or not, the next step is to replace the embedded server with a real one using a container that uses the same version that you used in the previous chapters to run your source code.

As you can see in the previous section, the use of embedded LDAP in tests is simple, so you can think, "Why do I need to use Testcontainers vs. embedded?" The answer to this question is simple, because there are some problems connected with using embedded LDAP:

- Not all vendors have an embedded option so that everything may work fine on your tests, but in a real environment, it could fail your logic.

- Embedded LDAP does not have support for all the versions of some vendors; for example, in the case of ApacheDS, you can't use versions up to 1.5.5, so at some point, this problem looks like the previous one.

Not everything is great with the use of Testcontainers because it implies that the execution of the tests takes some seconds until the container is up and healthy to be used for your tests.

Let's start creating our tests using Testcontainers; in the case of LDAP, no particular module exists that simplifies the process of configuration, but you can run a Docker-compose file as shown in Listing 4-18. Remember to create the file with the name **docker-compose.yml** and include in the folder **src/tests/resources**.

*Listing 4-18.* A simple docker-compose file with the configuration of LDAP

```
version: '3.0'
services:
  opendj:
    image: openidentityplatform/opendj:4.5.9
    ports:
      - 18880:1389
```

```
environment:
    - ROOT_USER_DN=uid=admin,ou=system
    - ROOT_PASSWORD=secret
    - BASE_DN=dc=inflinx,dc=com
```

The next step is to create a copy of the file in Listings 4-15 and 4-16; let's call it *repositoryContext-testcontainers.xml* just to differentiate from the other configuration, removing the part related to the configuration of the embedded server.

```
<bean id="embeddedLdapServer" class="org.springframework.ldap.test.
unboundid.EmbeddedLdapServerFactoryBean">
    <property name="partitionName" value="inflinx"/>
    <property name="partitionSuffix" value=" dc=inflinx,dc=com" />
    <property name="port" value="18880" />
</bean>
```

The last step is to create tests that run the file that you defined in Listing 4-18. To do this, you need to use the class *DockerComposeContainer*, which is part of the library's core. Listing 4-19 shows how to configure the Testcontainers and wait until LDAP is ready to receive requests.

*Listing 4-19.* An example of a test using Testcontainers

```
import com.apress.book.ldap.domain.Patron;
import org.junit.jupiter.api.Test;
import org.junit.jupiter.api.extension.ExtendWith;
import org.springframework.beans.factory.annotation.Autowired;
import org.springframework.test.context.ContextConfiguration;
import org.springframework.test.context.junit.jupiter.SpringExtension;
import org.testcontainers.containers.DockerComposeContainer;
import org.testcontainers.containers.wait.strategy.Wait;
import org.testcontainers.junit.jupiter.Container;
import org.testcontainers.junit.jupiter.Testcontainers;

import java.io.File;
import java.util.List;

import static org.junit.jupiter.api.Assertions.*;
```

```
@Testcontainers
@ExtendWith(SpringExtension.class)
@ContextConfiguration("classpath:repositoryContext-testcontainers.xml")
@DisplayName("LDAP Operations Test using Testcontainers")
public class LdapOperationsClientContainerTest {

    @Container
    public static DockerComposeContainer ldap = new DockerComposeContainer(
            new File("src/test/resources/docker-compose.yml"))
                    .waitingFor("opendj_1", Wait.
                    forLogMessage(".*started*\\n", 1)).
                    withLocalCompose(true);

    @Autowired
    LdapOperationsClient client;

    @Test
    @DisplayName("Check that operation remove works")
    public void should_return_patrons() {
        List<Patron> patrons = client.search();

        assertAll(() -> assertNotNull(patrons), () -> assertEquals(100,
        patrons.size())));
    }
}
```

If you run this particular test, it will take some second until you have the confirmation that everything works fine because the container of LDAP takes some seconds until it's ready. This is a good alternative to check if your code works fine with a specific vendor and version.

## Summary

In this chapter, you took a deep dive into testing LDAP code. You started with an overview of testing concepts. Then you spent time setting up UnboundID for embedded testing. Although embedded testing simplifies things, there are times when you want to test code, minimizing the need for external infrastructure dependencies, but remember that if you want to be sure whether everything on your source code works fine or not, Testcontainers is the best alternative to do it.

In the next chapter, you will look at creating Data Access Objects (DAOs) that interact with LDAP using object factories.

# CHAPTER 5

# Advanced Spring LDAP

## JNDI Object Factories

JNDI provides the notion of object factories, which makes dealing with LDAP information easier. As the name suggests, an object factory transforms directory information into meaningful objects for the application. For example, object factories can have a search operation return object instances like `Patron` or `Employee` instead of plain `javax.naming.NamingEnumeration`.

Figure 5-1 depicts the flow involved when an application performs LDAP operations with an object factory. The flow starts with the application invoking a search or a lookup operation. The JNDI API will execute the requested operation and retrieve entries from LDAP. These results are then passed to the registered object factory, transforming them into objects. These objects are handed over to the application.

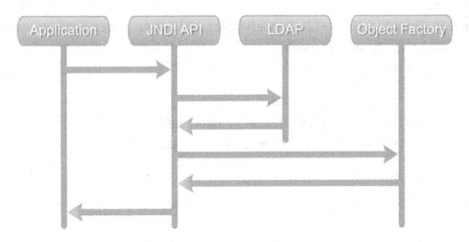

*Figure 5-1.* *JNDI/object factory flow*

© Balaji Varanasi and Andres Sacco 2023
B. Varanasi and A. Sacco, *Practical Spring LDAP*, https://doi.org/10.1007/979-8-8688-0002-3_5

Object factories dealing with LDAP must implement the `javax.naming.spi.DirObjectFactory` interface. Listing 5-1 shows a `Patron` object factory implementation that takes the passed-in information and creates a `Patron` instance. The `obj` parameter to the `getObjectInstance` method holds reference information about the object. The `name` parameter holds the name of the object. The `attrs` parameter contains the attributes associated with the object. In the `getObjectInstance`, you read the required attributes and populate the newly created `Patron` instance.

**Listing 5-1.**  An example of how to map the attributes in an object

```
package com.apress.book.ldap;

import java.util.Hashtable;

import javax.naming.Context;
import javax.naming.Name;
import javax.naming.directory.Attributes;
import javax.naming.directory.BasicAttributes;
import javax.naming.spi.DirObjectFactory;

import com.apress.book.ldap.domain.Patron;

public class PatronObjectFactory implements DirObjectFactory {

    @Override
    public Object getObjectInstance(Object obj, Name name, Context nameCtx,
    Hashtable<?, ?> environment,
            Attributes attrs) {

        Patron patron = new Patron();
        patron.setUid(attrs.get("uid").toString());
        patron.setFullName(attrs.get("cn").toString());

        return patron;
    }

    @Override
    public Object getObjectInstance(Object obj, Name name, Context nameCtx,
    Hashtable<?, ?> environment){
```

```
    return getObjectInstance(obj, name, nameCtx, environment, new
    BasicAttributes());
  }
}
```

Before using this object factory, it must be registered during initial context creation. Listing 5-2 shows an example of using PatronObjectFactory during lookups. You register the PatronObjectFactory class using the DirContext.OBJECT_FACTORIES property. Notice that the context's lookup method now returns a Patron instance.

---

**Note**   Remember that Appendix C provides all the information about configuring the LDAP server.

---

*Listing 5-2.* An example of executing certain operations

```
package com.apress.book.ldap;

import java.util.Properties;

import javax.naming.NamingException;
import javax.naming.directory.DirContext;
import javax.naming.ldap.InitialLdapContext;
import javax.naming.ldap.LdapContext;

import com.apress.book.ldap.domain.Patron;
import org.slf4j.Logger;
import org.slf4j.LoggerFactory;

public class JndiObjectFactoryLookupExample {

    private static final Logger logger = LoggerFactory.getLogger(JndiObject
    FactoryLookupExample.class);

    private LdapContext getContext() throws NamingException {
        Properties environment = new Properties();
        environment.setProperty(DirContext.INITIAL_CONTEXT_FACTORY, "com.
        sun.jndi.ldap.LdapCtxFactory");
        environment.setProperty(DirContext.PROVIDER_URL, "ldap://
        localhost:11389");
```

```
        environment.setProperty(DirContext.SECURITY_PRINCIPAL,
        "cn=Directory Manager");
        environment.setProperty(DirContext.SECURITY_CREDENTIALS, "secret");
        environment.setProperty(DirContext.OBJECT_FACTORIES, "com.apress.
        book.ldap.PatronObjectFactory");

        return new InitialLdapContext(environment, null);
    }

    public Patron lookupPatron(String dn) {
        Patron patron = null;
        try {
            LdapContext context = getContext();
            patron = (Patron) context.lookup(dn);
        } catch (NamingException e) {
            logger.error(e.getClass() + ": " + e.getMessage());
        }
        return patron;
    }

    public static void main(String[] args) {
        JndiObjectFactoryLookupExample jle = new
        JndiObjectFactoryLookupExample();
        Patron p = jle.lookupPatron("uid=patron99,ou=patrons,dc=inflinx,
        dc=com");
          logger.info(p.toString());
    }
}
```

If you run the previous example, you will see the following output:

```
11:53:14.630 [main] INFO  c.a.b.l.JndiObjectFactoryLookupExample - Full
name:cn: Aggie Aguirre
```

Consider that with Spring LDAP, none of the previous examples have this level of complexity.

# Spring and Object Factories

Spring LDAP provides an out-of-the-box implementation of `DirObjectFactory` called `org.springframework.ldap.core.support.DefaultDirObjectFactory`. As you saw in the previous section, the `PatronObjectFactory` creates instances of `Patrons` from the contexts found. Similarly, the `DefaultDirObjectFactory` creates instances of `org.springframework.ldap.core.DirContextAdapter` from found contexts.

The `DirContextAdapter` class is generic and can be viewed as a holder of LDAP entry data. The `DirContextAdapter` class provides a variety of utility methods that greatly simplify getting and setting attributes. As you will see in later sections, when changes are made to attributes, the `DirContextAdapter` automatically keeps track of those changes and simplifies updating LDAP entry data. The simplicity of the `DirContextAdapter`, along with `DefaultDirObjectFactory`, enables you to easily convert LDAP data into domain objects, reducing the need to write and register a lot of object factories.

In the following sections, you will use the `DirContextAdapter` to create an Employee DAO that abstracts read and write access to Employee LDAP entries.

---

**Note**   Most Java and JEE applications today access a persistent store for everyday activities. The persistent stores vary from popular relational databases to LDAP directories to legacy mainframe systems. Depending on the type of persistent store, the mechanism to obtain and manipulate data will vary greatly. This can result in tight coupling between the application and data access code, making it hard to switch between the implementations. This is where a Data Access Object or DAO pattern can help.

The Data Access Object is a popular core JEE pattern that encapsulates access to data sources. Low-level data access logic, such as connecting to the data source and manipulating data, is cleanly abstracted to a separate layer by the DAO. A DAO implementation usually includes

1.  A DAO interface that provides the CRUD method contract

2.  Concrete implementation of the interface using a data source–specific API

3.  Domain objects or transfer objects that the DAO returns

With a DAO in place, the rest of the application need not worry about the underlying data implementation and can focus on high-level business logic.

# DAO Implementation Using Object Factory

Typically, the DAOs you create in Spring applications have an interface that serves as the DAO's contract and an implementation that contains the actual logic to access the data store or directory. Listing 5-3 shows the EmployeeDao interface for the Employee DAO you will implement. The DAO has create, update, and delete methods for modifying employee information. It also has two finder methods, one that retrieves an employee by its id and another that returns all the employees.

*Listing 5-3.* The definition of the DAO with the most relevant methods

```
package com.apress.book.ldap.repository;

import java.util.List;

import com.apress.book.ldap.domain.Employee;

public interface EmployeeDao {

    void create(Employee employee);

    void update(Employee employee);

    void delete(String id);

    Employee find(String id);

    List<Employee> findAll();
}
```

The previous EmployeeDao interface uses an Employee domain object. Listing 5-4 shows this Employee domain object. Employee implementation holds all the essential attributes of a library employee. Notice that instead of using the fully qualified DN, you will use the uid attribute as the object's unique identifier.

**Listing 5-4.** The definition of the Employee class

```
package com.apress.book.ldap.domain;

public class Employee {

    private String uid;
    private String firstName;
    private String lastName;
    private String commonName;
    private String email;
    private String employeeNumber;
    private String[] phone;

    // getters and setters omitted
}
```

You start with a basic implementation of the EmployeeDao, as shown in Listing 5-5.

**Listing 5-5.** The default definition of the implementation of the DAO

```
package com.apress.book.ldap.repository;

import java.util.List;
import org.springframework.beans.factory.annotation.Autowired;
import org.springframework.beans.factory.annotation.Qualifier;
import org.springframework.ldap.core.LdapTemplate;
import com.apress.book.ldap.domain.Employee;

@Repository("employeeDao" )
public class EmployeeDaoLdapImpl implements EmployeeDao {

    private LdapTemplate ldapTemplate;

    public EmployeeDaoLdapImpl(@Autowired @Qualifier("ldapTemplate")
    LdapTemplate ldapTemplate) {
```

```
        this.ldapTemplate = ldapTemplate;
    }

    @Override
    public List<Employee> findAll() { return null; }

    @Override
    public Employee find(String id) { return null; }

    @Override
    public void create(Employee employee) {}

    @Override
    public void delete(String id) {}

    @Override
    public void update(Employee employee) {}
}
```

In this implementation, you are injecting an instance of LdapTemplate. The actual
creation of the LdapTemplate will be done in an external configuration file. Listing 5-6
shows the repositoryContext.xml file, which is located in the folder **src/test/
resources**, with LdapTemplate and associated bean declarations.

***Listing 5-6.*** The default configuration of the application

```
<?xml version="1.0" encoding="UTF-8"?>
<beans xmlns="http://www.springframework.org/schema/beans"
       xmlns:xsi="http://www.w3.org/2001/XMLSchema-instance"
       xmlns:context="http://www.springframework.org/schema/context"
       xsi:schemaLocation="http://www.springframework.org/schema/beans
       http://www.springframework.org/schema/beans/spring-beans.xsd
        http://www.springframework.org/schema/context http://www.
        springframework.org/
        schema/context/spring-context.xsd">

    <context:component-scan base-package="com.apress.book.ldap" />

    <bean id="contextSource" class="org.springframework.ldap.core.support.
    LdapContextSource">
```

```
        <property name="url" value="ldap://localhost:11389" />
        <property name="userDn" value="cn=Directory Manager" />
        <property name="password" value="secret" />
        <property name="base" value="ou=employees,dc=inflinx,dc=com"/>
    </bean>

    <bean id="ldapTemplate" class="org.springframework.ldap.core.
    LdapTemplate">
        <constructor-arg ref="contextSource"  />
    </bean>

</beans>
```

This configuration file is similar to the one you saw in Chapter 3. You provide the LDAP server information to the LdapContextSource to create a contextSource bean. By setting the base to "ou=employees,dc=inflinx,dc=com", you have restricted all the LDAP operations to the employee branch of the LDAP tree. It is important to understand that a search operation on the branch "ou=patrons" will not be possible using the contexts created here. If the requirement is to search all of the branches of the LDAP tree, then the base property needs to be an empty string.

An important property of LdapContextSource is the dirObjectFactory, which can be used to set a DirObjectFactory to use. However, in Listing 5-6, you didn't use this property to specify your intent to use DefaultDirObjectFactory. That is because, by default, LdapContextSource registers the DefaultDirObjectFactory as its DirObjectFactory.

You have the LdapTemplate bean declaration in the configuration file's final portion. You have passed in the LdapContextSource bean as the constructor argument to the LdapTemplate.

# Implementing Finder Methods

Implementing the findAll method of the Employee DAO requires searching LDAP for all the employee entries and creating Employee instances with the returned entries. To do this, you will be using the following method in the LdapTemplate class:

```
public <T> List<T> search(String base, String filter,
ParameterizedContextMapper<T> mapper)
```

Since you are using the `DefaultDirObjectFactory`, every time a search or a lookup is performed, every context found in the LDAP tree will be returned as an instance of `DirContextAdapter`. Like the search method you saw in Listing 3-8, the preceding search method takes `base` and `filter` parameters. Additionally, it takes an instance of `AbstractContextMapper<T>`. The preceding `search` method will pass the returned `DirContextAdapters` to the `ContextMapper<T>` instance for transformation.

Listing 5-7 provides the context mapper implementation for mapping `Employee` instances. As you can see, the `EmployeeContextMapper` extends `AbstractContextMapper`, an abstract class that implements `ContextMapper`.

***Listing 5-7.*** An example of the implementation of a mapper

```
package com.apress.book.ldap.repository.mapper;

import com.apress.book.ldap.domain.Employee;
import org.springframework.ldap.core.DirContextOperations;
import org.springframework.ldap.core.support.AbstractContextMapper;
public class EmployeeContextMapper extends
AbstractContextMapper<Employee> {

    @Override
    protected Employee doMapFromContext(DirContextOperations context) {
        Employee employee = new Employee();

        employee.setUid(context.getStringAttribute("uid"));
        employee.setFirstName(context.getStringAttribute("givenName"));
        employee.setLastName(context.getStringAttribute("sn"));
        employee.setCommonName(context.getStringAttribute("cn"));
        employee.setEmployeeNumber(context.getStringAttribute("employee
        Number"));
        employee.setEmail(context.getStringAttribute("mail"));
        employee.setPhone(context.getStringAttributes("telephoneNumber"));

        return employee;
    }
}
```

In Listing 5-7, the `DirContextOperations` parameter to the `doMapFromContext` method is an interface for `DirContextAdapter`. As you can see, the `doMapFromContext` implementation involves creating a new `Employee` instance and reading the attributes you are interested in from the supplied context.

With the `EmployeeContextMapper` in place, the `findAll` method implementation becomes trivial. Since all the employee entries have the `objectClass inetOrgPerson`, you will use `"(objectClass=inetOrgPerson)"` as the search filter. Listing 5-8 shows the `findAll` implementation.

***Listing 5-8.*** Implementation of finding all the information from LDAP

```
@Override
public List<Employee> findAll() {
    return ldapTemplate.search("", "(objectClass=inetOrgPerson)", new
    EmployeeContextMapper());
}
```

The other finder method can be implemented by searching an LDAP tree with the filter (uid=`<supplied employee id>`) or performing an LDAP lookup with an employee DN. Since search operations with filters are more expensive than looking up a DN, you will implement the `find` method using the lookup. Listing 5-9 shows the `find` method implementation.

***Listing 5-9.*** Implementation of finding one element on LDAP

```
@Override
public Employee find(String id) {
    DistinguishedName dn = new DistinguishedName();
    dn.add("uid", id);
    return ldapTemplate.lookup(dn, new EmployeeContextMapper());
}
```

You start the implementation by constructing a DN for the employee. Since the initial context base is restricted to the employee branch, you have just specified the RDN portion of the employee entry. Then you use the `lookup` method to look up the employee entry and create an `Employee` instance using the `EmployeeContextMapper`.

This concludes the implementation of both finder methods. Let's create a JUnit test class for testing your finder methods. The test case is shown in Listing 5-10.

***Listing 5-10.*** Implementation of tests on the search methods

```
package com.apress.book.ldap.repository;

import java.util.List;

import com.apress.book.ldap.domain.Employee;
import org.springframework.beans.factory.annotation.Autowired;
import org.springframework.beans.factory.annotation.Qualifier;
import org.springframework.ldap.core.DirContextAdapter;
import org.springframework.ldap.core.DirContextOperations;
import org.springframework.ldap.core.DistinguishedName;
import org.springframework.ldap.core.LdapTemplate;
import org.springframework.stereotype.Repository;

import com.apress.book.ldap.repository.mapper.EmployeeContextMapper;

@Repository("employeeDao")
public class EmployeeDaoLdapImpl implements EmployeeDao {

    private LdapTemplate ldapTemplate;

    public EmployeeDaoLdapImpl(@Autowired @Qualifier("ldapTemplate")
    LdapTemplate ldapTemplate) {
        this.ldapTemplate = ldapTemplate;
    }

    @Override
    public List<Employee> findAll() {
        return ldapTemplate.search("", "(objectClass=inetOrgPerson)",
        new EmployeeContextMapper());
    }

    @Override
    public Employee find(String id) {
        DistinguishedName dn = getDistinguishedName(id);
        return ldapTemplate.lookup(dn, new EmployeeContextMapper());
    }

    private DistinguishedName getDistinguishedName(String id) {
        DistinguishedName dn = new DistinguishedName();
```

```
        dn.add("uid", id);
        return dn;
    }

    // the logic will be added on the following pages
    @Override
    public void create(Employee employee) {}

    @Override
    public void delete(String id) {}

    @Override
    public void update(Employee employee) {}
}
```

Notice that you have specified the repositoryContext-test.xml in the ContextConfiguration. This test context file is shown in Listing 5-11. You created an embedded LDAP server to run on port 18880 and populate using employee.ldif file, which needs to be located in the **src/test/resources** folder, containing the test data you will use throughout this book.

***Listing 5-11.*** Configuration of the context

```
<?xml version="1.0" encoding="UTF-8"?>
<beans xmlns="http://www.springframework.org/schema/beans"
    xmlns:xsi="http://www.w3.org/2001/XMLSchema-instance"
    xmlns:ldap="http://www.springframework.org/schema/ldap"
    xmlns:context="http://www.springframework.org/schema/context"
    xsi:schemaLocation="http://www.springframework.org/schema/beans
                    https://www.springframework.org/schema/beans/
                    spring-beans.xsd http://www.springframework.org/
                    schema/ldap https://www.springframework.org/
                    schema/ldap/spring-ldap.xsd
                    http://www.springframework.org/schema/context
                    http://www.springframework.org/schema/context/
                    spring-context.xsd">

    <context:component-scan base-package="com.apress.book.ldap" />
```

```
<ldap:context-source id="contextSource"
                     password="secret"
                     url="ldap://127.0.0.1:18880"
                     username="uid=admin,ou=system"
                     base="ou=employees,dc=inflinx,dc=com"/>

<!-- Populates the LDAP server with initial data -->
<bean class="org.springframework.ldap.test.LdifPopulator" depends-
on="embeddedLdapServer">
    <property name="contextSource" ref="contextSource" />
    <property name="resource" value="classpath:employees.ldif" />
    <property name="base" value="dc=inflinx,dc=com" />
    <property name="clean" value="true" />
    <property name="defaultBase" value="dc=inflinx,dc=com" />
</bean>

<bean id="embeddedLdapServer" class="org.springframework.ldap.test.
unboundid.EmbeddedLdapServerFactoryBean">
    <property name="partitionName" value="inflinx"/>
    <property name="partitionSuffix" value="${ldap.base}" />
    <property name="port" value="18880" />
</bean>

<bean id="ldapTemplate" class="org.springframework.ldap.core.
LdapTemplate">
    <constructor-arg ref="contextSource" />
</bean>
</beans>
```

Remember that each test will clear the database, so you can do a lot of operations without affecting the rest of the tests.

# Create Method

LdapTemplate provides several bind methods for adding entries to LDAP. To create a new Employee, you will use the following bind method variation:

```
public void bind(DirContextOperations ctx)
```

This method takes a DirContextOperations instance as its parameter. The bind method invokes the getDn method on the passed-in DirContextOperations instance and retrieves the fully qualified DN of the entry. It then binds all the attributes to the DN and creates a new entry.

The implementation of the create method in the Employee DAO is shown in Listing 5-12. As you can see, you start by creating a new instance of a DirContextAdapter. Then you populate the context's attributes with employee information. The last line in the method does the actual binding.

**Listing 5-12.** Method to create a new employee on LDAP

```
@Override
public void create(Employee employee) {
    DistinguishedName dn = getDistinguishedName(employee.getUid());

    DirContextAdapter context = new DirContextAdapter();
    context.setDn(dn);
    context.setAttributeValues("objectClass",
            new String[] { "top", "person", "organizationalperson",
            "inetorgperson" });
    context.setAttributeValue("givenName", employee.getFirstName());
    context.setAttributeValue("sn", employee.getLastName());
    context.setAttributeValue("cn", employee.getCommonName());
    context.setAttributeValue("mail", employee.getEmail());
    context.setAttributeValue("employeeNumber", employee.
    getEmployeeNumber());
    context.setAttributeValues("telephoneNumber", employee.getPhone());

    ldapTemplate.bind(context);
}
```

**Note**    Compare the code in Listing 5-12 with the code in Listing 3-10. You can see that DirContextAdapter does a great job simplifying attribute manipulation.

Let's quickly verify the create method's implementation with the JUnit test case in Listing 5-13.

***Listing 5-13.*** Test to validate if the creation method works fine

```
@Test
@DisplayName("Check that operation create one employee")
public void should_create_a_new_employee() {
    String empUid = "employee1000";

    Employee employee = new Employee();
    employee.setUid(empUid);
    employee.setFirstName("Test");
    employee.setLastName("Employee1000");
    employee.setCommonName("Test Employee1000");
    employee.setEmail("employee1000@inflinx.com");
    employee.setEmployeeNumber("45678");
    employee.setPhone(new String[] { "801-100-1200" });

    employeeDao.create(employee);

    employee = employeeDao.find(empUid);
    assertNotNull(employee);
}
```

To simplify the test, only validate if the object is not null, but as a suggestion, try to validate all the fields.

# Update Method

Updating an entry involves adding, replacing, or removing its attributes. The simplest way to achieve this is to remove the entire entry and create it with a new set of attributes. This technique is referred to as rebinding. Deleting and recreating an entry could be more efficient, and it makes more sense to operate on changed values.

In Chapter 3, you used the modifyAttributes and ModificationItem instances for updating LDAP entries. Even though modifyAttributes is a nice approach, it does require a lot of work to manually generate the ModificationItem list. Thankfully, DirContextAdapter automates this and makes updating an entry a breeze. Listing 5-14 shows the update method implementation using DirContextAdapter.

***Listing 5-14.*** Method to update attributes

```
@Override
public void update(Employee employee) {
    DistinguishedName dn = getDistinguishedName(employee.getUid());

    DirContextOperations context = ldapTemplate.lookupContext(dn);

    context.setAttributeValues("objectClass",
            new String[] { "top", "person", "organizationalperson",
            "inetorgperson" });
    context.setAttributeValue("givenName", employee.getFirstName());
    context.setAttributeValue("sn", employee.getLastName());
    context.setAttributeValue("cn", employee.getCommonName());
    context.setAttributeValue("mail", employee.getEmail());
    context.setAttributeValue("employeeNumber", employee.
    getEmployeeNumber());
    context.setAttributeValues("telephoneNumber", employee.getPhone());

    ldapTemplate.modifyAttributes(context);
}
```

In this implementation, you will notice that you first look up the existing context using the employee's DN. Then you set all the attributes as you did in the create method. (The difference is that DirContextAdapter keeps track of value changes made to the entry.) Finally, you pass in the updated context to the modifyAttributes method. The modifyAttributes method will retrieve the modified item list from the DirContextAdapter and perform those modifications on the entry in LDAP. Listing 5-15 shows the associated test case that updates an employee's first name.

***Listing 5-15.*** Test the update method

```
@Test
@DisplayName("Check that operation update one employee")
public void should_update_an_employee() {
    Employee employee = employeeDao.find("employee1");
    employee.setFirstName("Employee New");
    employeeDao.update(employee);
```

```
    employee = employeeDao.find("employee1");
    assertEquals(employee.getFirstName(), "Employee New");
}
```

As a suggestion, when you upload an entire object validate that all the fields have the correct value; in this case, to simplify the scenario, the tests only check one attribute.

# Delete Method

Spring LDAP makes unbinding straightforward with the unbind method in the LdapTemplate. Listing 5-16 shows the code involved in deleting an employee.

*Listing 5-16.* Delete method using the uid

```
@Override
public void delete(String id) {
    DistinguishedName dn = getDistinguishedName(id);
    ldapTemplate.unbind(dn);
}
```

Since your operations are all relative to the initial context with the base "ou=employees, dc=inflinx,dc=com", you create the DN with just uid, the entry's RDN. Invoking the unbind operation will remove the entry and all its associated attributes.

Listing 5-17 shows the associated test case to verify the deletion of the entry. Once an entry is successfully removed, any find operation on that name will result in a NameNotFoundException. The test case validates this assumption.

*Listing 5-17.* Test the delete method using the uid

```
@Test
@DisplayName("Check that operation remove one employee")
public void should_delete_an_employee() {
    String empUid = "employee11";
    employeeDao.delete(empUid);
    assertThrows(NameNotFoundException.class, () -> {
        employeeDao.find(empUid);
    });
}
```

This is the last operation of the DAO, which gives an overview of how to execute the different operations using Spring LDAP.

# Summary

In this chapter, you were introduced to the world of JNDI object factories. You then looked at the `DefaultDirObjectFactory`, Spring LDAP's object factory implementation. You spent the rest of the chapter implementing an Employee DAO using `DirContextAdapter` and `LdapTemplate`.

In the next chapter, you will dive deeply into the world of LDAP search and search filters.

# CHAPTER 6

# Searching LDAP

Searching for information is the most common operation against LDAP. A client application initiates an LDAP search by passing in search criteria, the information that determines where to search and what to search for. Upon receiving the request, the LDAP server executes the search and returns all the entries that match the criteria.

## LDAP Search Criteria

The LDAP search criteria comprise three mandatory parameters – base, scope, and filter – and several optional parameters. Let's look at each of these parameters in detail.

## Base Parameter

The base portion of the search is a distinguished name (DN) that identifies the branch of the tree that will be searched. For example, a base of `"ou=patrons, dc=inflinx, dc=com"` indicates that the search will start in the Patron branch and move downward. It is also possible to specify an empty base, which will result in searching the root DSE entry.

---

**Note** The root DSE or DSA-Specific Entry is a special entry in the LDAP server. It typically holds server-specific data such as the vendor name, vendor version, and different controls and features it supports.

---

© Balaji Varanasi and Andres Sacco 2023
B. Varanasi and A. Sacco, *Practical Spring LDAP*, https://doi.org/10.1007/979-8-8688-0002-3_6

## Scope Parameter

The scope parameter determines how deep, relative to the base, an LDAP search needs to be performed. The LDAP protocol defines three possible search scopes: base, one level, and subtree. Figure 6-1 illustrates the entries evaluated as part of the search with different scopes.

- The base scope restricts the search to the LDAP entry identified by the base parameter. No other entries will be included as part of the search. In your Library application schema, with a base DN dc=inflinx,dc=com and scope of the base, a search would just return the root organization entry, as shown in Figure 6-1.

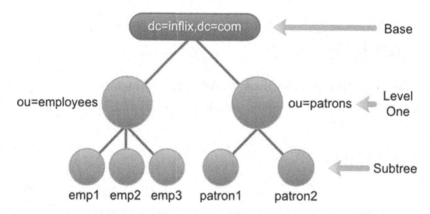

*Figure 6-1.* *Search scopes*

The one-level scope indicates searching all the entries one level directly below the base. The base entry itself is not included in the search. So, with base dc=inflinx,dc=com and the one-level scope, a search for all entries would return *employees* and *patrons* organizational units.

Finally, the subtree scope includes the base entry and all its descendent entries in the search. This is the slowest and most expensive option of the three. In your Library example, a search with this scope and base dc=inflinx, dc=com would return all the entries.

# Filter Parameter

In your Library application LDAP server, let's say you want to find all the patrons that live in the Midvale area. From the LDAP schema, you know patron entries have the `city` attribute that holds their city name. So this requirement essentially boils down to retrieving all entries with the `city` attribute with a value of "Midvale." This is exactly what a search filter does. A search filter defines the characteristics that all the returning entries possess. Logically speaking, the filter applies to each entry in the set identified by base and scope. Only the entries that match the filter become part of the returned search results.

An LDAP search filter comprises three components: an attribute type, an operator, and a value (or range of values) for the attribute. Depending on the operator, the value part can be optional. These components must always be enclosed inside parentheses, like so:

```
Filter = (attributetype operator value)
```

With this information in hand, the search filter to locate all patrons living in Midvale would look like this:

```
(city=Midvale)
```

Now, let's say you want to find all the patrons who live in the Midvale area *and* have an email address so that you can send them news of occasional library events. The resulting search filter combines two filter items: an item that identifies patrons in Midvale and an item that identifies patrons with an email address. You have already seen the first item of the filter. Here is the other portion of the filter:

```
(mail=*)
```

The =* operator indicates the presence of an attribute. So the expression `mail=*` will return all entries with a value in their `mail` attribute. The LDAP specification defines filter operators that can be used to combine multiple filters and create complex filters. Here is the format for combining the filters:

```
Filter = (operator filter1 filter2)
```

Notice the use of prefix notation, where the operator is written before their operands for combining the two filters. Here is the required filter for your use case:

```
(&(city=Midvale)(mail=*))
```

The & in this filter is an *And* operator. The LDAP specification defines a variety of search filter operators. Table 6-1 lists some of the commonly used operators.

***Table 6-1.*** *Search Filter Operators*

| Name | Symbol | Example | Description |
|------|--------|---------|-------------|
| Equality Filter | = | (sn=Smith) | Matches all the entries with the last name Smith. |
| Substring Filter | =, * | (sn=Smi*) | Matches all entries whose last name begins with Smi. |
| Greater Than or Equals Filter | >= | (sn>=S*) | Matches all entries that are alphabetically greater than or equal to S. |
| Less Than or Equals Filter | <= | (sn<=S*) | Matches all entries that are alphabetically lower than or equal to S. |
| Presence Filter | =* | (objectClass=*) | Matches all entries that have the attribute objectClass. This is a popular expression used to retrieve all entries in LDAP. |
| Approximate Filter | ~= | (sn~=Smith) | Matches all entries whose last name is a variation of Smith. So this can return Smith and Snith. |
| And Filter | & | (&(sn=Smith)(zip=84121)) | Returns all Smiths living in the 84121 area. |
| Or Filter | \| | (\|(sn=Smith)(sn=Lee)) | Returns all entries with last name Smith or Lee. |
| Not Filter | ! | (!(sn=Smith)) | Returns all entries whose last name is not Smith. |

# Optional Parameters

Besides the preceding three parameters, including several optional parameters to control search behavior is possible. For example, the timelimit parameter indicates the time to complete the search. Similarly, the sizelimit parameter places an upper bound on the number of entries that can be returned as part of the result.

A very commonly used optional parameter involves providing a list of attribute names. When a search is performed, the LDAP server, by default, returns all the attributes associated with entries found in the search. Sometimes, this might not be desirable. In those scenarios, you can provide a list of attribute names as part of the search, and the LDAP server would return only entries with those attributes. Here is an example of a search method in the LdapTemplate that takes an array of attribute names (ATTR_1, ATTR_2, and ATTR_3):

```
ldapTemplate.search("SEARCH_BASE", "uid=USER_DN", 1, new String[]{"ATTR_1",
"ATTR_2", ATTR_3}, new SomeContextMapperImpl());
```

When this search is performed, the entries returned will only have ATTR_1, ATTR_2, and ATTR_3. This could reduce the data transferred from the server and is useful in high-traffic situations.

Since version 3, LDAP servers can maintain attributes for each entry for purely administrative purposes. These are called operational attributes and are not part of the entry's objectClass. The returned entries will not contain the operational attributes by default when performing an LDAP search. You must list operational attribute names in the search criteria to retrieve operational attributes.

---

**Note**    Examples of operational attributes include createTimeStamp, which holds the time when the entry was created, and pwdAccountLockedTime, which records when a user's account was locked.

---

# LDAP Injection

LDAP injection is a technique where an attacker alters an LDAP query to run arbitrary LDAP statements against the directory server. LDAP injection can result in unauthorized data access or modifications to the LDAP tree. Applications that don't perform proper input validation or sanitize their input are prone to LDAP injection. This technique is similar to the popular SQL injection attack used against databases.

To better understand LDAP injection, consider a web application that uses LDAP for authentication. Such applications usually provide a web page that lets a user enter their username and password. To verify that the username and password match, the application would construct an LDAP search query that looks more or less like this:

```
(&(uid=USER_INPUT_UID)(password=USER_INPUT_PWD))
```

Let's assume that the application simply trusts the user input and doesn't perform any validation. Now if you enter the text jdoe)(&))( as the username and any random text as password, the resulting search query filter would look like this:

```
(&(uid=jdoe)(&))((password=randomstr))
```

If the username jdoe is a valid user id in LDAP, then regardless of the entered password, this query will always evaluate to true. This LDAP injection would allow an attacker to bypass authentication and get into the application. The "LDAP Injection & Blind LDAP Injection" article[1] discusses various LDAP injection techniques in great detail.

Preventing LDAP injection, and any other injection techniques in general, begins with proper input validation. It is essential to sanitize the entered data and properly encode it before it is used in search filters.

# Spring LDAP Filters

In the previous section, you learned that LDAP search filters are essential for narrowing down the search and identifying entries. However, dynamically creating LDAP filters can be tedious, especially when combining multiple filters. Making sure that all the braces are correctly closed can be error-prone. It is also important to escape special characters correctly.

Spring LDAP provides several filter classes that make creating and encoding LDAP filters easy. All these filters implement the Filter interface and are part of the org.springframework.ldap.filter package. Listing 6-1 shows the Filter API interface.

*Listing 6-1.* The Filter interface definition with all the methods

```
package org.springframework.ldap.filter;

public interface Filter {

    String encode();

    StringBuffer encode(StringBuffer buf);
```

---

[1] www.blackhat.com/presentations/bh-europe-08/Alonso-Parada/Whitepaper/bh-eu-08-alonso-parada-WP.pdf

```
    boolean equals(Object o);

    int hashCode();
}
```

The first encode method in this interface returns a string representation of the filter. The second encode method accepts a `StringBuffer` as its parameter and returns the encoded version of the filter as a `StringBuffer`. For your regular development process, you use the first version of the encode method that returns String.

The `Filter` interface hierarchy is shown in Figure 6-2. The hierarchy shows that `AbstractFilter` implements the `Filter` interface and acts as the root class for all other filter implementations. The `BinaryLogicalFilter` is the abstract superclass for binary logical operations such as AND and OR. The `CompareFilter` is the abstract superclass for filters that compare values such as `EqualsFilter` and `LessThanOrEqualsFilter`.

---

**Note**   Most LDAP attribute values, by default, are case-insensitive for searches.

---

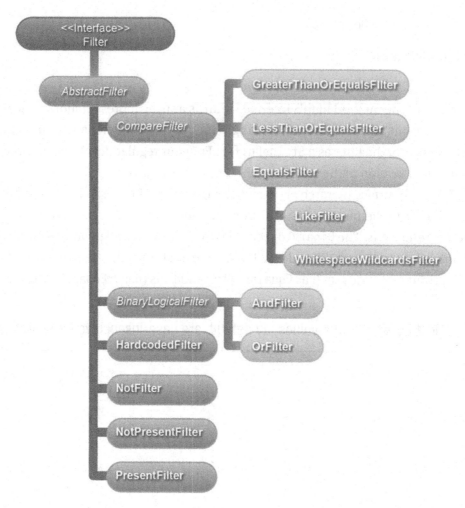

**Figure 6-2.** *Filter hierarchy*

In the coming sections, you will look at each of the filters in Figure 6-2. Before you do that, let's create a reusable method that will help you test your filters. Listing 6-2 shows the searchAndPrintResults method that uses the passed-in Filter implementation parameter and performs a search using it. It then outputs the search results to the console. Notice that you will be searching the Patron branch of the LDAP tree.

**Listing 6-2.** The Search class receives a filter

```
package com.apress.book.ldap.filter;

import java.util.List;

import com.apress.book.ldap.domain.Patron;
```

```
import com.apress.book.ldap.mapper.PatronContextMapper;
import org.slf4j.Logger;
import org.slf4j.LoggerFactory;
import org.springframework.beans.factory.annotation.Autowired;
import org.springframework.beans.factory.annotation.Qualifier;
import org.springframework.ldap.core.LdapTemplate;
import org.springframework.ldap.filter.Filter;
import org.springframework.stereotype.Component;

@Component("searchFilter")
public class SearchFilter {
    private static final Logger logger = LoggerFactory.
    getLogger(SearchFilter.class);

private LdapTemplate ldapTemplate;

    public SearchFilter(@Autowired @Qualifier("ldapTemplate") LdapTemplate
    ldapTemplate) {
        this.ldapTemplate = ldapTemplate;
    }

    public List<Patron> searchAndPrintResults(Filter filter) {
        List<Patron> results = ldapTemplate.search("ou=patrons,dc=inflinx,
        dc=com", filter.encode(), new PatronContextMapper());

        logger.info("Results found in search: " + results.size());
        for (Patron patron : results) {
            logger.info(patron.toString());
        }
        return results;
    }
}
```

The class in Listing 6-2 uses the class **Patron**, which you saw in previous chapters, and a **PatronContextMapper**, which follows the same idea of the previous chapters to define a class that does the transformation from LDAP to a concrete object. Listing 6-3 shows you how the class looks like.

***Listing 6-3.*** The context mapper transforms the attributes on an object

```java
package com.apress.book.ldap.mapper;
import com.apress.book.ldap.domain.Patron;
import org.springframework.ldap.core.DirContextOperations;
import org.springframework.ldap.core.support.AbstractContextMapper;

public class PatronContextMapper extends AbstractContextMapper<Patron> {
    @Override
    protected Patron doMapFromContext(DirContextOperations context) {
        Patron patron = new Patron();

        patron.setUid(context.getStringAttribute("uid"));
        patron.setFirstName(context.getStringAttribute("givenName"));
        patron.setLastName(context.getStringAttribute("sn"));
        patron.setFullName(context.getStringAttribute("cn"));
        patron.setEmail(context.getStringAttribute("mail"));

        return patron;
    }
}
```

There are more attributes on the Patron object, but to keep it simple, the example just appears as the most relevant attribute.

# EqualsFilter

An `EqualsFilter` can be used to retrieve all entries that have the specified attribute and value. Let's say you want to retrieve all patrons with the first name ***Abbi***. To do this, you create a new instance of `EqualsFilter`:

```java
EqualsFilter filter = new EqualsFilter("givenName", "Abbi");
```

The first parameter to the constructor is the attribute name, and the second parameter is the attribute value. Invoking the `encode` method on this filter results in the string (givenName=Abbi).

Listing 6-4 shows the test case invoking the searchAndPrintResults with the preceding EqualsFilter parameter. The console output of the method is also shown in the listing. Notice that the results have patrons with the first name *Abbi*. That is because the sn attribute, like most LDAP attributes, is defined in the schema as case-insensitive.

***Listing 6-4.*** Example of the equals filter

```
@Test
@DisplayName("Check that search operation using equals filter works")
public void should_works_equalsFilter() {
    Filter filter = new EqualsFilter("givenName", "Abbi");
    List<Patron> results = searchFilter.searchAndPrintResults(filter);
    assertAll(
            ()-> assertNotNull(results),
            ()-> assertEquals(1, results.size()),
            ()-> assertEquals("Abbi Abbott", results.get(0).getFullName())
    );
}

Results found in search: 1
Full name: Abbi Abbott
```

# LikeFilter

The LikeFilter is useful for searching LDAP when only a partial value of an attribute is known. The LDAP specification allows the usage of the wildcard * to describe these partial values. Say you want to retrieve all users whose first name begins with "Abb." To do this, you create a new instance of LikeFilter and pass in the wildcard substring as an attribute value:

```
LikeFilter filter = new LikeFilter("givenName", "Abb*");
```

Invoking the encode method on this filter results in the string (givenName=Abb*). Listing 6-5 shows the test case and the results of invoking the searchAndPrintResults method with the LikeFilter.

**Listing 6-5.** Example of a like filter

```
@Test
@DisplayName("Check that search operation using like filter works")
public void should_works_likeFilter() {
    Filter filter = new LikeFilter("givenName", "Abb*");
    List<Patron> results = searchFilter.searchAndPrintResults(filter);
    assertAll(
            ()-> assertNotNull(results),
            ()-> assertEquals(7, results.size())
    );
}
```

```
Results found in search: 7
Full name: Abbey Abbie
Full name: Abbi Abbott
Full name: Abbie Abdalla
Full name: Abby Abdo
Full name: Abbye Abdollahi
Full name: Abbas Abbatantuono
Full name: Abbe Abbate
```

The wildcard * in the substring is used to match zero or more characters. However, it is essential to understand that LDAP search filters do not support regular expressions. Table 6-2 lists some substring examples.

**Table 6-2.** *LDAP Substring Examples*

| LDAP Substring | Description |
| --- | --- |
| (givenName=*son) | Matches all patrons whose first name ends with son. |
| (givenName=J*n) | Matches all patrons whose first name starts with J and ends with n. |
| (givenName=*a*) | Matches all patrons with first name containing the character a. |
| (givenName=J*s*n) | Matches patrons whose first name starts with J, contains character s, and ends with n. |

You might be wondering about the necessity of a `LikeFilter` when you can accomplish the same filter expression by simply using the `EqualsFilter`, like this:

```
EqualsFilter filter = new EqualsFilter("uid", "Ja*");
```

Using `EqualsFilter` in this scenario will not work because the encode method in `EqualsFilter` considers the wildcard * in the Ja* as a special character and properly escapes it. Thus, when used for a search, the preceding filter would result in all entries with a first name starting with Ja*.

# PresentFilter

`PresentFilters` are useful for retrieving LDAP entries with at least one value in a given attribute. Consider the earlier scenario where you wanted to retrieve all the patrons with an email address. To do this, you create a `PresentFilter`, as shown:

```
PresentFilter presentFilter = new PresentFilter("mail");
```

Invoking the encode method on the `presentFilter` instance results in the string (mail=*). Listing 6-6 shows the test code and the result when the `searchAndPrintResults` method is invoked with the preceding `presentFilter`.

***Listing 6-6.*** Example of a present filter

```
@Test
@DisplayName("Check that search operation using present filter works")
public void should_works_presentFilter() {
    Filter filter = new PresentFilter("mail");
    List<Patron> results = searchFilter.searchAndPrintResults(filter);
    assertAll(
            ()-> assertNotNull(results),
            ()-> assertEquals(101, results.size())
    );
}
```

```
Results found in search: 100

Full name: Aaccf Amar
Full name: Aaren Atp
Full name: Abbey Abbie
Full name: Abbi Abbott
Full name: Abbie Abdalla
. . . . . . . . .
. . . . . . . . .
```

# NotPresentFilter

NotPresentFilters are used to retrieve entries that don't have a specified attribute. Attributes that do not have any value in an entry are considered to be not present. Now, let's say you want to retrieve all patrons that don't have an email address. To do this, you create an instance of NotPresentFilter, as shown:

```
NotPresentFilter notPresentFilter = new NotPresentFilter("email");
```

The encoded version of the notPresentFilter results in the expression !(email=*). Running the searchAndPrintResults results in the output shown in Listing 6-7. The first null is for the organizational unit entry "ou=patrons,dc=inflinx,dc=com".

*Listing 6-7.* Example of a not present filter

```java
@Test
@DisplayName("Check that search operation using non present filter works")
public void should_works_notPresentFilter() {
    Filter filter = new NotPresentFilter("email");
    List<Patron> results = searchFilter.searchAndPrintResults(filter);
    assertAll(
            ()-> assertNotNull(results),
            ()-> assertEquals(1, results.size())
    );
}

Results found in search: 1
Full name: Aggy Ahad
```

# Not Filter

A `NotFilter` is helpful for retrieving entries that do not match a given condition. In the "LikeFilter" section, you looked at retrieving all entries that start with Ja. Now let's say you want to retrieve all entries that don't start with **Ade**. This is where a `NotFilter` comes into the picture. Here is the code for accomplishing this requirement:

```
NotFilter notFilter = new NotFilter(new LikeFilter("givenName", "Ade*"));
```

Encoding this filter results in the string `!(givenName=Ade*)`. As you can see, the `NotFilter` adds the negation symbol (`!`) to the filter passed into its constructor. Invoking the `searchAndShowResults` method results in the output shown in Listing 6-8.

***Listing 6-8.*** Example of a not filter

```
@Test
@DisplayName("Check that search operation using non filter works")
public void should_works_notFilter() {
    NotFilter notFilter = new NotFilter(new LikeFilter("givenName",
    "Ade*"));
    List<Patron> results = searchFilter.searchAndPrintResults(notFilter);
    assertAll(
            ()-> assertNotNull(results),
            ()-> assertEquals(86, results.size())
    );
}
```

```
Results found in search: 86

Full name: Aaccf Amar
Full name: Aaren Atp
Full name: Abbey Abbie
Full name: Abbi Abbott
Full name: Abbie Abdalla
.........
.........
```

It is also possible to combine `NotFilter` and `PresentFilter` to create expressions equivalent to `NotPresentFilter`. Here is a new implementation that gets all the entries that don't have an email address:

```
NotFilter notFilter = new NotFilter(new PresentFilter("email"));
```

# GreaterThanOrEqualsFilter

The `GreaterThanOrEqualsFilter` helps match all entries that are lexicographically equal to or higher than the given attribute value. For example, a search expression (`postalCode >= 57018`) can retrieve all entries with a postal code after 58018, in addition to 58018. Listing 6-9 shows this implementation along with the output results.

***Listing 6-9.*** Example of a greater than filter

```
@Test
@DisplayName("Check that search operation using greater than or equals
filter works")
public void should_works_greaterThanOrEqualsFilter() {
    Filter filter = new GreaterThanOrEqualsFilter("postalCode", "57018");
    List<Patron> results = searchFilter.searchAndPrintResults(filter);
    assertAll(
            ()-> assertNotNull(results),
            ()-> assertEquals(46, results.size())
    );
}

Results found in search: 46

Full name: Abbey Abbie
Full name: Aggy Ahad
Full name: Abbie Abdalla
Full name: Abbye Abdollahi
Full name: Abdalla Abdou
.........
.........
```

# LessThanOrEqualsFilter

The `LessThanOrEqualsFilter` can be used to match entries lexicographically equal or lower than the given attribute. So, the search expression (`postalCode<=57018`) will return all entries with the postal code lower or equal to 57018. Listing 6-10 shows the test code that invokes `searchAndPrintResults` implementation of this requirement along with the output.

***Listing 6-10.*** Example of a less than filter

```
@Test
@DisplayName("Check that search operation using less than or equals
filter works")
public void should_works_lessThanOrEqualsFilter() {
    Filter filter = new LessThanOrEqualsFilter("postalCode", "57018");
    List<Patron> results = searchFilter.searchAndPrintResults(filter);
    assertAll(
            () -> assertNotNull(results),
            () -> assertEquals(56, results.size())
    );
}
```

```
Results found in search: 56

Full name: Aaccf Amar
Full name: Aaren Atp
Full name: Abbi Abbott
Full name: Abby Abdo
Full name: Abdallah Abdul-Nour
. . . . . . . . .
. . . . . . . . .
```

As mentioned, the search includes entries with postal code 57018. The LDAP specification does not provide a less than (<) operator. However, it is possible to combine `NotFilter` with `GreaterThanOrEqualsFilter` to obtain "less than" functionality. Here is an implementation of this idea:

```
NotFilter lessThanFilter = new NotFilter(new GreaterThanOrEqualsFilter
("postalCode", "557018"));
```

# AndFilter

The AndFilter is used to combine multiple search filter expressions to create complex search filters. The resulting filter will match entries that meet all the subfilter conditions. For example, the AndFilter is suitable for implementing an earlier requirement to get all the patrons that live in the Midvale area and have an email address. The following code shows this implementation:

```
AndFilter andFilter = new AndFilter();
andFilter.and(new EqualsFilter("postalCode", "95571"));
andFilter.and(new PresentFilter("mail"));
```

Invoking the encode method on this filter results in (&(postalCode=95571) (email=*)). Listing 6-11 shows the test case that creates the AndFilter and calls the searchAndPrintResults method.

***Listing 6-11.*** Example of an and filter

```
@Test
@DisplayName("Check that search operation using and filter works")
public void should_works_andFilter() {
AndFilter andFilter = new AndFilter();
andFilter.and(new EqualsFilter("postalCode", "95571"));
andFilter.and(new PresentFilter("mail"));
    List<Patron> results = searchFilter.searchAndPrintResults(filter);
    assertAll(
            () -> assertNotNull(results),
            () -> assertEquals(1, results.size())
    );
}
```

Results found in search: 1

Full name: Abbey Abbie

# OrFilter

Like the `AndFilter`, an `OrFilter` can combine multiple search filters. However, the resulting filter will match entries meeting any subfilter conditions. Here is one implementation of the `OrFilter`:

```
OrFilter orFilter = new OrFilter();
orFilter.add(new EqualsFilter("postalcode", "51911"));
orFilter.add(new EqualsFilter("postalcode", "48200"));
```

This `OrFilter` will retrieve all patrons that live in either the 51911 or the 48200 postal code. The encode method returns the expression ( | (postalcode =51911) (postalcode=48200) ). The test case for the `OrFilter` is shown in Listing 6-12.

***Listing 6-12.***  Example of an or filter

```
@Test
@DisplayName("Check that search operation using or filter works")
public void should_works_orFilter() {
    OrFilter orFilter = new OrFilter();
    orFilter.or(new EqualsFilter("postalCode", "51911"));
    orFilter.or(new EqualsFilter("postalCode", "48200"));
    List<Patron> results = searchFilter.searchAndPrintResults(orFilter);
    assertAll(
            () -> assertNotNull(results),
            () -> assertEquals(2, results.size())
    );
}
```

```
Results found in search: 2

Full name: Aggi Aguinsky
Full name: Aggie Aguirre
```

# HardcodedFilter

The HardcodedFilter is a convenience class that makes adding static filter text while building search filters easy. Let's say you are writing an admin application that allows the administrator to enter a search expression in a text box. If you want to use this expression along with other filters for a search, you can use HardcodedFilter, as shown:

```
String searchExpression = "(sn=Aguirre)";
AndFilter filter = new AndFilter();
filter.and(new HardcodedFilter(searchExpression));
filter.and(new EqualsFilter("givenName", "Aggie"));
```

In this code, the searchExpression variable contains the user-entered search expression. HardcodedFilter also comes in very handy when the static portion of a search filter comes from a properties file or a configuration file. It is important to remember that this filter does not encode the passed-in text. So please use it cautiously, especially when dealing with user input directly.

This HardcodedFilter will retrieve all patrons following both expressions. The encode method returns the expression (&(sn=Aguirre)(givenName=Aggie)). The test case for the HardcodedFilter is shown in Listing 6-13.

***Listing 6-13.*** Example of a hardcoded filter

```
@Test
@DisplayName("Check that search operation using hardcoded filter works")
public void should_works_HardcodedFilter() {
    String searchExpression;

    AndFilter filter = new AndFilter();
    filter.and(new HardcodedFilter("(sn=Aguirre)"));
    filter.and(new EqualsFilter("givenName", "Aggie"));
    List<Patron> results = searchFilter.searchAndPrintResults(filter);
    assertAll(
            () -> assertNotNull(results),
            () -> assertEquals(1, results.size())
```

```
    );
}
```

Results found in search: 1
Full name: Aggie Aguirre

# WhitespaceWildcardsFilter

The WhitespaceWildcardsFilter is another convenience class that makes creating substring search filters easier. Like its superclass EqualsFilter, this class takes an attribute name and a value. However, as the name suggests, it converts all whitespaces in the attribute value to wildcards. Consider the following example:

```
WhitespaceWildcardsFilter filter = new WhitespaceWildcardsFilter("cn", "John Will");
```

This filter results in the following expression: (cn=*John*Will*). This filter can be useful while developing search and lookup applications. Listing 6-14 shows the test case of this filter and the result.

***Listing 6-14.*** Example of a whitespace wildcard filter

```
@Test
@DisplayName("Check that search operation using whitespace wildcard
filter works")
void should_works_WhitespaceWildcardsFilter() {
    WhitespaceWildcardsFilter filter = new WhitespaceWildcardsFilter("cn",
    "Abbey Abbie");

    List<Patron> results = searchFilter.searchAndPrintResults(filter);
    assertAll(() -> assertNotNull(results), () -> assertEquals(1, results.
    size()));
}
```

Results found in search: 1
Full name: Abbey Abbie

# Handling Special Characters

There will be times when you need to construct search filters with characters such as ( or a * that have special meanings in LDAP. To execute these filters successfully, it is important to escape the special characters properly. Escaping is done using the format \ xx, where xx denotes the hexadecimal representation of the character. Table 6-3 lists the special characters and their escape values.

*Table 6-3.* *Special Characters and Escape Values*

| Special Character | Escape Value |
| --- | --- |
| ( | \28 |
| ) | \29 |
| * | \2a |
| \ | \5c |
| / | \2f |

In addition to the characters in Table 6-3, if any of the following characters are used in a DN, they also need to be properly escaped: comma (,), equals sign (=), plus sign (+), less than (<), greater than (>), pound sign (#), and semicolon (;).

# LDAP Query Builder Parameters

There is an alternative way to use the filters to execute queries to find information on LDAP; Spring LDAP offers a QueryBuilder, which more or less follows the structure of a SQL sentence which reduces the complexity of understanding what the query does. Also, it is simple to combine a lot of conditions in one sentence.

The following parameters are supported using the QueryBuilder:

- *base*: Defines the starting point in the LDAP tree from which the search initiates.

- *searchScope*: Determines the extent to which the LDAP tree is explored during the search.

- *attributes*: Dictates the desired attributes to retrieve from the search. The default setting retrieves all attributes.

- *countLimit*: Sets the upper limit on the number of entries retrieved from the search.

- *timeLimit*: Establishes the maximum allowable duration for the search operation.

- *search filter*: Specifies the criteria entries must meet for consideration in the search results.

Let's create a simple example that combines some conditions to find all the patrons by last name, postal code, and with a uid present. Listing 6-15 shows a class that has a method with filters.

***Listing 6-15.*** Example of QueryBuilder

```
package com.apress.book.ldap.builder;

import com.apress.book.ldap.domain.Patron;
import com.apress.book.ldap.mapper.PatronContextMapper;
import org.slf4j.Logger;
import org.slf4j.LoggerFactory;
import org.springframework.beans.factory.annotation.Autowired;
import org.springframework.beans.factory.annotation.Qualifier;
import org.springframework.ldap.core.LdapTemplate;
import org.springframework.ldap.query.LdapQuery;
import org.springframework.ldap.support.LdapUtils;
import org.springframework.stereotype.Component;

import java.util.List;

import static org.springframework.ldap.query.LdapQueryBuilder.query;

@Component("searchFilter")
public class SearchBuilder {
```

```
private static final Logger logger = LoggerFactory.getLogger(com.
apress.book.ldap.filter.SearchFilter.class);

private LdapTemplate ldapTemplate;

public SearchBuilder(@Autowired @Qualifier("ldapTemplate") LdapTemplate
ldapTemplate) {
    this.ldapTemplate = ldapTemplate;
}

public List<Patron> getPatronByLastNameAndPostalCode(String lastName,
String postalCode) {

    logger.info("finding patrons with lastname {} and postalcode {}",
    lastName, postalCode);

    LdapQuery query = query()
            .countLimit(10)
            .base(LdapUtils.emptyLdapName())
            .where("objectclass").is("person")
            .and("sn").is(lastName)
            .and("postalCode").is(postalCode)
            .and("uid").isPresent();

    return ldapTemplate.search(query, new PatronContextMapper());
    }
}
```

As you can see, the query is a combination of most of the previous filters you read in the previous sections but uses the ***countLimit*** to restrict the number of patrons that the methods could return. Listing 6-16 shows a test case that checks whether the method works fine.

***Listing 6-16.*** Tests to check how the QueryBuilder works

```
package com.apress.book.ldap.builder;

import com.apress.book.ldap.domain.Patron;
import org.junit.jupiter.api.Test;
import org.junit.jupiter.api.extension.ExtendWith;
```

```
import org.springframework.beans.factory.annotation.Autowired;
import org.springframework.test.context.ContextConfiguration;
import org.springframework.test.context.junit.jupiter.SpringExtension;
import org.junit.jupiter.api.DisplayName;

import java.util.List;

import static org.junit.jupiter.api.Assertions.*;
@ExtendWith(SpringExtension.class)
@ContextConfiguration("classpath:repositoryContext-test.xml")
@DisplayName("Search Builder test cases")
public class SearchBuilderTest {

    @Autowired
    private SearchBuilder searchBuilder;

    @Test
    @DisplayName("Check that search operation using lastname and postal
  code works")
    public void should_works_builder() {
        List<Patron> results = searchBuilder.getPatronByLastNameAndPostalCo
        de("Abbott", "07007");
        assertAll(
                ()-> assertNotNull(results),
                ()-> assertEquals(1, results.size()),
                ()-> assertEquals("Abbi Abbott", results.get(0).
                    getFullName())
        );
    }
}
```

Table 6-4 shows you all the possible methods you can use on the QueryBuilder and the function of each.

*Table 6-4.* *QueryBuilder Methods*

| Method | Description |
|---|---|
| query() | This method represents the init of the query you want to execute. |
| filter() | Sets the filter criteria for the LDAP query. You can use methods like and(), or(), not(), and various comparison methods to build complex filters. |
| build() | Constructs the final LDAP query based on the configured parameters. |
| base() | Specifies the base DN (distinguished name) from which the LDAP query should start. |
| countLimit() | Sets the maximum number of entries to be returned by the query. |
| timeLimit() | Sets the maximum time (in milliseconds) that the LDAP query can execute. |
| attributes() | Specifies the attributes to be retrieved in the query. You can pass attribute names as arguments. |
| and() | The and method allows you to combine multiple filters using the "and" operator. |
| or() | The or method allows you to combine multiple filters using the "or" operator. |
| not() | You can negate a filter using the not method. |
| is() | This method works as an equal filter that checks if the value of one attribute is equal to a certain value |
| isPresent() | This method checks if a particular attribute exists. |
| gte() | This method checks if the attribute is greater than a certain value. |
| lte() | This method checks if the attribute is less than a certain value. |
| like() | This method works in the same way as the LikeFilter. |

# Summary

In this chapter, you learned how to simplify LDAP searches using search filters. I started the chapter with an overview of LDAP search concepts. Then you looked at different search filters that you can use to retrieve data in various ways. Also, you learned how you can do the same using QueryBuilder, which is similar to writing a SQL sentence.

In the next chapter, you will look at sorting and paging the results obtained from an LDAP server.

# CHAPTER 7

# Sorting and Paging Results

## LDAP Controls

LDAP controls provide a standardized way to modify the behavior of LDAP operations. A control can be viewed simply as a message a client sends to an LDAP server (or vice versa). Controls sent as part of a client request can provide additional information to the server indicating how the operation should be interpreted and executed. For example, an LDAP delete operation can specify a delete subtree control. Upon receiving a delete request, the default behavior of an LDAP server is to just delete the entry. However, when a delete subtree control is appended to the delete request, the server automatically deletes the entry and all its subordinate entries. Such controls are referred to as request controls.

It is also possible for LDAP servers to send controls as part of their response message indicating how the operation was processed. For example, an LDAP server may return a password policy control during a bind operation, indicating that the client's password has expired or will expire soon. Such controls sent by the server are referred to as response controls. It is possible to send any number of request or response controls along with an operation.

LDAP controls, both request and response, comprise three components:

- *An object identifier (OID) that uniquely identifies the control*: These OIDs prevent conflicts between control names and are usually defined by the vendor that creates the control. This is a required component of control.

153

© Balaji Varanasi and Andres Sacco 2023
B. Varanasi and A. Sacco, *Practical Spring LDAP*, https://doi.org/10.1007/979-8-8688-0002-3_7

- *Indicate whether the control is critical or noncritical for the operation*: This is also a required component and can be either TRUE or FALSE.

- *Optional information specific to the control*: For example, the paged control used for paging search results needs the page size to determine the number of entries to return on a page.

The formal definition of an LDAP control, as specified in RFC 2251,[1] is shown in Figure 7-1. This LDAP specification, however, does not define any concrete controls. LDAP vendors usually provide control definitions, and their support varies vastly from one server to another.

```
Controls ::= SEQUENCE Of Control

Control  ::= SEQUENCE
    {
            controlType          LDAPOID,
            criticality          BOOLEAN DEFAULT FALSE,
            controlValue         OCTED STRING OPTIONAL
    }
```

**Figure 7-1.** *LDAP control specification*

When an LDAP server receives a control as part of an operation, its behavior depends on the control and its associated information. The flow chart in Figure 7-2 shows the server behavior upon receiving a request control.

---

[1] https://www.ietf.org/rfc/rfc2251.txt

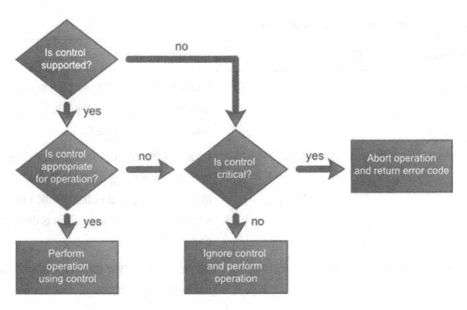

***Figure 7-2.*** *LDAP server control interaction*

Some commonly supported LDAP controls, along with their OID and description, are shown in Table 7-1.

***Table 7-1.*** *Commonly Used Controls*

| Control Name | OID | Description (RFC) |
| --- | --- | --- |
| Sort Control | 1.2.840.113556.1.4.473 | Requests the server to sort the search results before sending them to the client. This is part of RFC 2891. |
| Paged Search Control | 1.2.840.113556.1.4.319 | Requests the server to return search results in pages containing a specified number of entries. Only sequential iteration of the search results is allowed. This is defined as part of RFC 2696. |
| Subtree Delete Control | 1.2.840.113556.1.4.805 | Requests the server delete the entry and all its descendent entries. |
| Virtual List View Control | 2.16.840.1.113730.3.4.9 | This is similar to Page search results but allows the client to request arbitrary subsets of entries. This control is described in the Internet-Drafts file VLV 04. |
| Password Policy Control | 1.3.6.1.4.1.42.2.27.8.5.1 | Server-sent control that holds information about failed operation (e.g., authentication) due to password policy problems, such as a password needs to be reset, an account has been locked, or a password has expired or is expiring. |
| Manage DSA/IT Control | 2.16.840.1.113730.3.4.2 | Requests the server to treat "ref" attribute entries (referrals) as regular LDAP entries. |
| Persistent Search Control | 2.16.840.1.113730.3.4.3 | This control allows the client to receive notifications of changes in the LDAP server for entries that match search criteria. |

# Identifying Supported Controls

Before a particular control can be used, ensuring that the LDAP server you are using supports that control is important. The LDAP specification mandates every LDAP v3–compliant server publish all the supported controls in the `supportedControl` attribute of the Root *DSA-Specific Entry* (DSE). Thus, searching the Root DSE entry for the supportedControl attribute will list all the controls. Listing 7-1 shows the code that connects to the OpenDJ server running on port 11389 and prints the control list to the console.

***Listing 7-1.*** The class to detect the supported controls

```
package com.apress.book.ldap;

import org.slf4j.Logger;
import org.slf4j.LoggerFactory;

import java.util.Properties;
import javax.naming.NamingEnumeration;
import javax.naming.NamingException;
import javax.naming.directory.Attribute;
import javax.naming.directory.Attributes;
import javax.naming.directory.DirContext;
import javax.naming.directory.InitialDirContext;

public class SupportedControlApplication {

    private static final Logger logger = LoggerFactory.getLogger(Supported
    ControlApplication.class);
    public void displayControls() {

        String ldapUrl = "ldap://localhost:11389";
        try {

            Properties environment = new Properties();
            environment.setProperty(DirContext.INITIAL_CONTEXT_FACTORY,
            "com.sun.jndi.ldap.LdapCtxFactory");
            environment.setProperty(DirContext.PROVIDER_URL, ldapUrl);

            DirContext context = new InitialDirContext(environment);

            Attributes attributes = context.getAttributes("", new String[]
            { "supportedcontrol" });

            Attribute supportedControlAttribute = attributes.
            get("supportedcontrol");
```

```
            NamingEnumeration controlOIDList = supportedControlAttribute.
            getAll();
            while (controlOIDList != null && controlOIDList.hasMore()) {
                logger.info(controlOIDList.next().toString());
            }

            context.close();
        } catch (NamingException e) {
            logger.error(e.getClass() + ": " + e.getMessage());
        }
    }

    public static void main(String[] args) throws NamingException {
        SupportedControlApplication supportedControlApplication = new
        SupportedControlApplication();
        supportedControlApplication.displayControls();
    }
}
```

Listing 7-2 is the output after running the code from Listing 7-1.

***Listing 7-2.*** The result of the execution of the support control class

```
1.2.826.0.1.3344810.2.3
1.2.840.113556.1.4.1413
1.2.840.113556.1.4.319
1.2.840.113556.1.4.473
1.2.840.113556.1.4.805
1.3.6.1.1.12
1.3.6.1.1.13.1
1.3.6.1.1.13.2
1.3.6.1.4.1.26027.1.5.2
1.3.6.1.4.1.42.2.27.8.5.1
1.3.6.1.4.1.42.2.27.9.5.2
1.3.6.1.4.1.42.2.27.9.5.8
1.3.6.1.4.1.4203.1.10.1
1.3.6.1.4.1.4203.1.10.2
1.3.6.1.4.1.7628.5.101.1
```

```
2.16.840.1.113730.3.4.12
2.16.840.1.113730.3.4.16
2.16.840.1.113730.3.4.17
2.16.840.1.113730.3.4.18
2.16.840.1.113730.3.4.19
2.16.840.1.113730.3.4.2
2.16.840.1.113730.3.4.3
2.16.840.1.113730.3.4.4
2.16.840.1.113730.3.4.5
2.16.840.1.113730.3.4.9
```

The OpenDJ installation provides a command-line ldapsearch tool that can also be used for listing the supported controls; the same situation happens if you are using a Docker image with OpenDJ. Assuming that you are using OpenDJ, you need to access the root directory where the LDAP server is located and use the command to get a list of supported controls:

```
ldapsearch --baseDN "" --searchScope base --port 11389 "(objectclass=*)"
supportedControl
```

Figure 7-3 displays the results of running this command. Notice that you used the scope base to search the Root DSE and did not provide a base DN. Also, the supported control OIDs in the figure match the OIDs received after running the Java code in Listing 7-1.

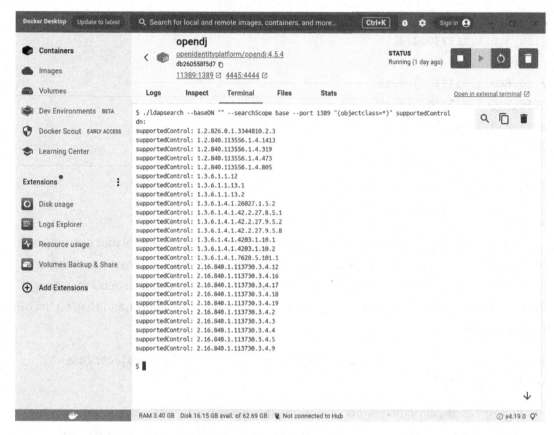

*Figure 7-3.*  *OpenDJ ldapsearch command*

# JNDI and Controls

The javax.naming.ldap package in the JNDI API supports LDAP V3–specific features such as controls and extended operations. While controls modify or augment the behavior of existing operations, extended operations allow additional operations to be defined. The UML diagram in Figure 7-4 highlights some of the important control classes in the javax.naming.ldap package.

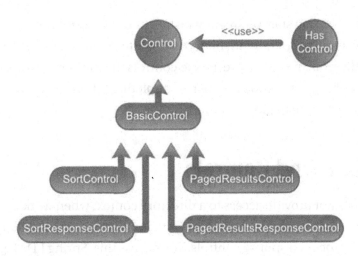

**Figure 7-4.** *Java LDAP control class hierarchy*

The javax.naming.ldap.Control interface provides an abstraction for both request and response controls. Several implementations of this interface, such as SortControl and PagedResultsControl, are provided as part of the JDK. Additional controls, such as Virtual-ListViewControl and PasswordExpiringResponseControl, are available as part of the LDAP booster pack.

A core component in the javax.naming.ldap package is the LdapContext interface. This interface extends the javax.naming.DirContext interface and provides additional methods for performing LDAP V3 operations. The InitialLdapContext class in the javax.naming.ldap package provides a concrete implementation of this interface.

Using controls with the JNDI API is very straightforward. The code in Listing 7-3 provides the algorithm for using controls.

**Listing 7-3.** Algorithm to use controls

```
LdapContext context = new InitialLdapContext();
Control[] requestControls = // Concrete control instance array
context.setRequestControls(requestControls);
/* Execute a search operation using the context*/
context.search(parameters);
Control[] responseControls = context.getResponseControls();
// Analyze the response controls
```

In this algorithm, you start by creating instances of the controls you would like to include in the request operation. Then, you operate and process the results of the operation. Finally, you analyze any response controls that the server has sent over. In the coming sections, you will look at concrete implementations of this algorithm in conjunction with sort and paging controls.

# Spring LDAP and Controls

Spring LDAP does not provide access to a directory context when working with LdapTemplate's search methods. As a result, you don't have a way to add request controls to the context or process response controls. To address this, Spring LDAP provides a directory context processor that automates adding and analyzing LDAP controls to a context. Listing 7-4 shows the DirContextProcessor API code.

*Listing 7-4.*  DirContextProcessor interface

```
package org.springframework.ldap.core;

import javax.naming.NamingException;
import javax.naming.directory.DirContext;

public interface DirContextProcessor {
    void preProcess(DirContext var1) throws NamingException;

    void postProcess(DirContext var1) throws NamingException;
}
```

Concrete implementations of the DirContextProcessor interface are passed to the LdapTemplate's search methods. The preProcess method gets called before a search is performed. Hence, the concrete implementations will have logic in the preProcess method to add request controls to the context. The postProcess method will be called after the search execution. So, the concrete implementations will have logic in the postProcess method to read and analyze any response controls that the LDAP server would have sent.

Figure 7-5 shows the UML representation of the DirContextProcessor and all its implementations.

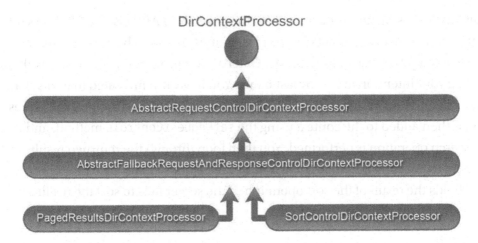

***Figure 7-5.*** *DirContextProcessor class hierarchy*

The AbstractRequestControlDirContextProcessor implements the preProcess
method of the DirContextProcessor and applies a single RequestControl on an
LdapContext. The AbstractRequestDirContextProcessor delegates the actual creation of
the request controls to the subclasses through the createRequestControl template method.

The AbstractFallbackRequestAndResponseControlDirContextProcessor class
extends the AbstractRequestControlDirContextProcessor and heavily uses reflection
to automate DirContext processing. It performs the tasks of loading control classes,
creating their instances, and applying them to the context. It also takes care of most
of the post-processing of the response control, delegating a template method to the
subclass that does the actual value retrieval.

The PagedResultsDirContextProcessor and SortControlDirContextProcessor
are used for managing paging and sorting controls. You will be looking at them in the
coming sections.

# Sort Control

The sort control provides a mechanism to request an LDAP server to sort the results of a
search operation before sending them over to the client. This control is specified in RFC
2891.[2] The sort request control accepts one or more LDAP attribute names and supplies
them to the server for sorting.

---

[2] https://www.ietf.org/rfc/rfc2891.txt

163

Let's look at using the sort control with the plain JNDI API. Listing 7-5 shows the code for sorting all search results by their last names. You start by creating a new instance of the `javax.naming.ldap.SortControl` and provide it with the `sn` attribute indicating your intention to sort by last name. You have also indicated that this is a critical control by providing the CRITICAL flag to the same constructor. This request control is then added to the context using the `setRequestControls` method, and the LDAP search operation is performed. You then loop through the returned results and print them to the console. Finally, you look at the response controls. The sort response control holds the result of the sort operation. If the server fails to sort the results, you indicate this by throwing an exception.

***Listing 7-5.***  A sorting example using JNDI

```
package com.apress.book.ldap.sorting;

import org.slf4j.Logger;
import org.slf4j.LoggerFactory;

import java.util.Properties;

import javax.naming.NamingEnumeration;
import javax.naming.NamingException;
import javax.naming.directory.DirContext;
import javax.naming.directory.SearchControls;
import javax.naming.directory.SearchResult;
import javax.naming.ldap.Control;
import javax.naming.ldap.InitialLdapContext;
import javax.naming.ldap.LdapContext;
import javax.naming.ldap.SortControl;
import javax.naming.ldap.SortResponseControl;

public class SortingJndi {

    private static final Logger logger = LoggerFactory.
    getLogger(SortingJndi.class);

    // We will be getting the LDAP context
    private LdapContext getContext() {
        Properties environment = new Properties();
```

```
environment.setProperty(DirContext.INITIAL_CONTEXT_FACTORY, "com.
sun.jndi.ldap.LdapCtxFactory");
environment.setProperty(DirContext.PROVIDER_URL, "ldap://
localhost:11389");
environment.setProperty(DirContext.SECURITY_PRINCIPAL,
"cn=Directory Manager");
environment.setProperty(DirContext.SECURITY_CREDENTIALS, "secret");

try {
    // The second argument is the list of controls that we
        need to send
    // as part of the connection request
    return new InitialLdapContext(environment, null);
} catch (NamingException e) {
    logger.error(e.getClass() + ": " + e.getMessage());
    return null;
}
}

public void sortByLastName() {
    try {
        LdapContext context = getContext();
        Control lastNameSort = new SortControl("sn", Control.CRITICAL);

        context.setRequestControls(new Control[] { lastNameSort });

        SearchControls searchControls = new SearchControls();
        searchControls.setSearchScope(SearchControls.SUBTREE_SCOPE);
        NamingEnumeration results = context.search("dc=inflinx,dc=com",
        "(objectClass=inetOrgPerson)",
                searchControls);

        // Iterate over search results and display patron entries
        while (results != null && results.hasMore()) {
            SearchResult entry = (SearchResult) results.next();
            logger.info(entry.getAttributes().get("sn") + " ( " +
            (entry.getName()) + " )");
        }
```

```java
            // Now that we have looped, we need to look at the response
            controls
            Control[] responseControls = context.getResponseControls();
            if (null != responseControls) {
                for (Control control : responseControls) {
                    if (control instanceof SortResponseControl) {
                        SortResponseControl sortResponseControl =
                        (SortResponseControl) control;
                        if (!sortResponseControl.isSorted()) {
                            // Sort did not happen. Indicate this with an
                            exception
                            throw sortResponseControl.getException();
                        }
                    }
                }
            }

            context.close();
        } catch (Exception e) {
            logger.error(e.getClass() + ": " + e.getMessage());
        }
    }

    public static void main(String[] args) {

        SortingJndi sortingJndi = new SortingJndi();
        sortingJndi.sortByLastName();
    }
}
```

The output should display the sorted patrons as follows:

```
sn: Aalders ( uid=patron4,ou=patrons )
sn: Aasen ( uid=patron5,ou=patrons )
sn: Abadines ( uid=patron6,ou=patrons )
sn: Abazari ( uid=patron7,ou=patrons )
sn: Abbatantuono ( uid=patron8,ou=patrons )
sn: Abbate ( uid=patron9,ou=patrons )
```

```
sn: Abbie ( uid=patron10,ou=patrons )
sn: Abbott ( uid=patron11,ou=patrons )
sn: Abdalla ( uid=patron12,ou=patrons )
```

.....................................

Now, let's look at implementing the same behavior using Spring LDAP. Listing 7-6 shows the associated code. In this implementation, you create a new org. springframework.ldap.control.SortControlDirContextProcessor instance. The SortControlDirContextProcessor constructor takes the LDAP attribute name that should be used as the sort key during control creation. The next step is to create the SearchControls and a filter to limit the search. Finally, you invoke the search method, passing in the created instances along with a mapper to map the data.

***Listing 7-6.*** A sorting example using Spring

```
package com.apress.book.ldap.sorting;

import java.util.List;

import javax.naming.directory.SearchControls;

import org.slf4j.Logger;
import org.slf4j.LoggerFactory;
import org.springframework.beans.factory.annotation.Autowired;
import org.springframework.beans.factory.annotation.Qualifier;
import org.springframework.ldap.control.SortControlDirContextProcessor;
import org.springframework.ldap.core.DirContextOperations;
import org.springframework.ldap.core.DirContextProcessor;
import org.springframework.ldap.core.LdapTemplate;
import org.springframework.ldap.core.support.AbstractContextMapper;
import org.springframework.ldap.filter.EqualsFilter;
import org.springframework.stereotype.Component;

@Component("sorting")
public class SpringSorting {

    private static final Logger logger = LoggerFactory.
    getLogger(SpringSorting.class);

    private LdapTemplate ldapTemplate;
```

```java
    public SpringSorting(@Autowired @Qualifier("ldapTemplate") LdapTemplate
    ldapTemplate) {
        this.ldapTemplate = ldapTemplate;
    }
    public List<String> sortByLastName() {

        DirContextProcessor scdcp = new SortControlDirContextProces
        sor("sn");

        SearchControls searchControls = new SearchControls();
        searchControls.setSearchScope(SearchControls.SUBTREE_SCOPE);

        EqualsFilter equalsFilter = new EqualsFilter("objectClass",
        "inetOrgPerson");

        @SuppressWarnings("unchecked")
        AbstractContextMapper<String> lastNameMapper = new
        AbstractContextMapper<String>() {
            @Override
            protected String doMapFromContext(DirContextOperations
            context) {
                return context.getStringAttribute("sn");
            }
        };

        List<String> lastNames = ldapTemplate.search("", equalsFilter.
        encode(), searchControls, lastNameMapper, scdcp);

        for (String ln : lastNames) {
            logger.info(ln);
        }
        return lastNames;
    }
}
```

Invoking this method will produce the same output as the previous implementation without Spring.

To check if everything works fine using a good practice, let's create a test like the one shown in Listing 7-7.

***Listing 7-7.*** Test case of the sorting

```
package com.apress.book.ldap.sorting;

import org.junit.jupiter.api.DisplayName;
import org.junit.jupiter.api.Test;
import org.junit.jupiter.api.extension.ExtendWith;
import org.springframework.beans.factory.annotation.Autowired;
import org.springframework.test.context.ContextConfiguration;
import org.springframework.test.context.junit.jupiter.SpringExtension;

import java.util.List;

import static org.junit.jupiter.api.Assertions.*;
@ExtendWith(SpringExtension.class)
@ContextConfiguration("classpath:repositoryContext-test.xml")
@DisplayName("Spring Sorting uses cases")
class SpringSortingTest {

    @Autowired
    private SpringSorting springSorting;

    @Test
    @DisplayName("Sorting by lastname")
    void should_sort_byLastName() {
        List<String> results = springSorting.sortByLastName();
        assertAll(() -> assertNotNull(results), () -> assertEquals(101,
        results.size()),
                () -> assertEquals("Aalders", results.get(0)));
    }
}
```

The complete application context configuration file is given in Listing 7-8 located in the **src/test/resources** folder.

***Listing 7-8.*** Application context configuration

```
<?xml version="1.0" encoding="UTF-8"?>
<beans xmlns="http://www.springframework.org/schema/beans"
       xmlns:xsi="http://www.w3.org/2001/XMLSchema-instance"
```

```
        xmlns:ldap="http://www.springframework.org/schema/ldap"
        xmlns:context="http://www.springframework.org/schema/context"
        xsi:schemaLocation="http://www.springframework.org/schema/beans
                      https://www.springframework.org/schema/beans/
                      spring-beans.xsd http://www.springframework.org/
                      schema/ldap https://www.springframework.org/
                      schema/ldap/spring-ldap.xsd
                  http://www.springframework.org/schema/context http://
                  www.springframework.org/schema/context/spring-
                  context.xsd">

<context:component-scan base-package="com.apress.book.ldap" />

<bean id="placeholderConfig" class="org.springframework.beans.factory.
config.PropertyPlaceholderConfigurer">
    <property name="location" value="classpath:ldap.properties" />
</bean>

<ldap:context-source id="contextSource"
                password="${ldap.password}"
                url="${ldap.url}"
                username="${ldap.userDn}"/>

<!-- Populates the LDAP server with initial data -->
<bean class="org.springframework.ldap.test.LdifPopulator" depends-
on="embeddedLdapServer">
    <property name="contextSource" ref="contextSource" />
    <property name="resource" value="classpath:patrons.ldif" />
    <property name="base" value="${ldap.base}" />
    <property name="clean" value="${ldap.clean}" />
    <property name="defaultBase" value="${ldap.base}" />
</bean>

<bean id="embeddedLdapServer" class="org.springframework.ldap.test.
unboundid.EmbeddedLdapServerFactoryBean">
    <property name="partitionName" value="inflinx"/>
    <property name="partitionSuffix" value="${ldap.base}" />
```

```
      <property name="port" value="${ldap.port}" />
    </bean>

    <bean id="ldapTemplate" class="org.springframework.ldap.core.
    LdapTemplate">
        <constructor-arg ref="contextSource" />
    </bean>
</beans>
```

If you run the test, everything will work fine.

# Implementing Custom DirContextProcessor

In Spring LDAP, `SortControlDirContextProcessor` can sort only on one LDAP attribute. The JNDI API, however, allows you to sort on multiple attributes. Since there will be cases where you would like to sort your search results on multiple attributes, let's implement a new `DirContextProcessor` that will allow you to do this in Spring LDAP.

As you have seen, the sort operation requires a request control and will send a response control. So, the easiest way to implement this functionality is to extend the `AbstractFallbackRequestAndResponseControlDirContextProcessor`. Listing 7-9 shows the initial code with empty abstract method implementation. As you will see, you are using three instance variables to hold the state of the control. The `sortKeys`, as the name suggests, will hold the attribute names you will be sorting on. The `sorted` and the `resultCode` variables will hold the information extracted from the response control.

***Listing 7-9.*** Basic implementation of multiple sorting

```
package com.apress.book.ldap.control;

import javax.naming.ldap.Control;

import org.springframework.ldap.control.
AbstractFallbackRequestAndResponseControlDirContextProcessor;

public class SortMultipleControlDirContextProcessor
```

171

```java
    extends AbstractFallbackRequestAndResponseControlDir
    ContextProcessor {

// The keys to sort on
private String[] sortKeys;

// Did the results get sorted?
private boolean sorted;

// The result code of the operation
private int resultCode;

@Override
public Control createRequestControl() {
    //implemented later
    return null;
}

@Override
protected void handleResponse(Object control) {
    //implemented later
}

public String[] getSortKeys() {
    return sortKeys;
}

public boolean isSorted() {
    return sorted;
}

public int getResultCode() {
    return resultCode;
}
}
```

The next step is to provide the necessary information to AbstractFallback RequestAndResponseControlDirContextProcessor for loading the controls. The AbstractFallbackRequestAndResponseControlDirContextProcessor expects two pieces of information from subclasses: the fully qualified class names of the request and response controls to be used and the fully qualified class names of the controls that should be used as a fallback. Listing 7-10 shows the constructor code that does this.

***Listing 7-10.*** Initialization of the context

```
public SortMultipleControlDirContextProcessor(String... sortKeys) {
    if (sortKeys.length == 0) {
        throw new IllegalArgumentException("You must provide lease one key
        to sort on");
    }
    this.sortKeys = sortKeys;
    this.sorted = false;
    this.resultCode = -1;

    this.defaultRequestControl = "javax.naming.ldap.SortControl";
    this.defaultResponseControl = "javax.naming.ldap.SortResponseControl";
    this.fallbackRequestControl = "com.sun.jndi.ldap.ctl.SortControl";
    this.fallbackResponseControl = "com.sun.jndi.ldap.ctl.
    SortResponseControl";

    loadControlClasses(); //This method exist on the super class
}
```

Notice that you have provided the control classes that come with the JDK as the default controls to be used and the controls that come with the LDAP booster pack as the fallback controls. On the last line of the constructor, you instruct the `AbstractFallbackRequestAndResponseControlDirContextProcessor` class to load the classes into JVM for usage.

The next step in the process is implementing the `createRequestControl` method. Since the superclass `AbstractFallbackRequestAndResponseControlDirContextProcessor` will take care of the actual creation of the control, all you need to do is provide the information necessary for creating the control. The following code shows this:

```
@Override
public Control createRequestControl() {
    return super.createRequestControl(new Class[] { String[].class,
    boolean.class },
            new Object[] { sortKeys, critical });
}
```

The final step in the implementation is to analyze the response control and retrieve the information regarding the completed operation. Listing 7-11 shows the code involved. Notice that you are using reflection to retrieve the sorted and result code information from the response control.

***Listing 7-11.*** Implementation of the handle response

```
@Override
protected void handleResponse(Object control) {
    this.sorted = (Boolean) invokeMethod("isSorted", responseControlClass,
    control);
    this.resultCode = (Integer) invokeMethod("getResultCode",
    responseControlClass, control);
}
```

Now that you have created a new DirContextProcessor instance that allows you to sort on multiple attributes, let's take it for a spin. Listing 7-12 shows a sortByLocation method which exists on the class SpringSorting that uses the SortMultipleControlDirContextProcessor. The method uses the attributes st and l for sorting the results.

***Listing 7-12.*** A concrete example

```
//Existing imports and packages

@Component("sorting")
public class SpringSorting {

    private static final Logger logger = LoggerFactory.
    getLogger(SpringSorting.class);

    private LdapTemplate ldapTemplate;
```

```java
public SpringSorting(@Autowired @Qualifier("ldapTemplate") LdapTemplate
ldapTemplate) {

    this.ldapTemplate = ldapTemplate;
}

public List<String> sortByLocation() {

    String[] locationAttributes = { "st", "l" };
    SortMultipleControlDirContextProcessor smcdcp = new SortMultiple
    ControlDirContextProcessor(locationAttributes);

    SearchControls searchControls = new SearchControls();
    searchControls.setSearchScope(SearchControls.SUBTREE_SCOPE);

    EqualsFilter equalsFilter = new EqualsFilter("objectClass",
    "inetOrgPerson");

    @SuppressWarnings("unchecked")
    AbstractContextMapper<String> locationMapper = new
    AbstractContextMapper<String>() {
        @Override
        protected String doMapFromContext(DirContextOperations
         context) {
            return context.getStringAttribute("st") + "," + context.
            getStringAttribute("l");
        }
    };

    List<String> results = ldapTemplate.search("", equalsFilter.
    encode(), searchControls, locationMapper, smcdcp);

    for (String r : results) {
        logger.info(r);
    }
    return results;
}

//Previous source code
}
```

Let's create a test that checks if the search method works fine or not. Listing 7-13 checks the content of the first element on the list.

***Listing 7-13.*** Test case to check if the search by location works

```java
package com.apress.book.ldap.sorting;

import org.junit.jupiter.api.DisplayName;
import org.junit.jupiter.api.Test;
import org.junit.jupiter.api.extension.ExtendWith;
import org.springframework.beans.factory.annotation.Autowired;
import org.springframework.test.context.ContextConfiguration;
import org.springframework.test.context.junit.jupiter.SpringExtension;

import java.util.List;

import static org.junit.jupiter.api.Assertions.*;

@ExtendWith(SpringExtension.class)
@ContextConfiguration("classpath:repositoryContext-test.xml")
@DisplayName("Spring Sorting uses cases")
class SpringSortingTest {

    @Autowired
    private SpringSorting springSorting;

    //Previous test
    @Test
    @DisplayName("Sorting by location")
    void should_sort_by_location() {
        List<String> results = springSorting.sortByLocation();
        assertAll(() -> assertNotNull(results), () -> assertEquals(101,
        results.size()),
                () -> assertEquals("AK,Abilene", results.get(0)));
    }
}
```

One last thing, in the case that you want to use ***LdapQueryBuilder*** to create the query, you will have problems using the sorting feature because it's not supported by default, and you need to do a lot of complex logic to obtain results; for that reason, this chapter only covers the basic approach to sorting the results.

## Paged Search Controls

The paged search control allows LDAP clients to control the rate at which the results of an LDAP search operation are returned. The LDAP clients create a page control with a specified page size and associate it with the search request. Upon receiving the request, the LDAP server will return the results in chunks, each containing the specified number of results. The paged search control is handy when dealing with large directories or building search applications with paging capabilities. This control is described in RFC 2696.[3]

Figure 7-6 describes the LDAP client and server interaction using a page control.

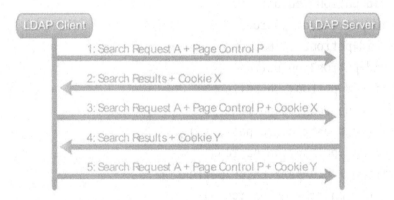

***Figure 7-6.*** *Page control interaction*

---

**Note**    LDAP servers often use the sizeLimit directive to restrict the number of results returned for a search operation. If a search produces more results than the specified sizeLimit, a size limit exceeds exception javax.naming. SizeLimitExceededException is thrown. The paging method does not let you pass through this limit.

---

[3] https://www.ietf.org/rfc/rfc2696.txt

The LDAP client sends the search request along with the page control. Upon receiving the request, the LDAP server executes the search operation and returns the first page of results. Additionally, it sends a cookie that needs to be used to request the next paged results set. This cookie enables the LDAP server to maintain the search state. The client must not make any assumptions about the internal structure of the cookie. When the client requests the next batch of results, it sends the same search request page control and the cookie. The server responds with the new result set and a new cookie. When no more search results are returned, the server sends an empty cookie.

Paging using the paged search control is unidirectional and sequential. The client can't jump between pages or go back. Now that you know the basics of the paging control, Listing 7-14 shows its implementation using the plain JNDI API.

Upon invoking the method, the paginated patrons will be displayed on the console as shown in Listing 7-14.

***Listing 7-14.*** An example of paging using JNDI

```
sn: Amar ( uid=patron0,ou=patrons )
sn: Atp ( uid=patron1,ou=patrons )
sn: Atpco ( uid=patron2,ou=patrons )
sn: Atrc ( uid=patron3,ou=patrons )
sn: Aalders ( uid=patron4,ou=patrons )
sn: Aasen ( uid=patron5,ou=patrons )
sn: Abadines ( uid=patron6,ou=patrons )
sn: Abazari ( uid=patron7,ou=patrons )
sn: Abbatantuono ( uid=patron8,ou=patrons )
sn: Abbate ( uid=patron9,ou=patrons )
sn: Abbie ( uid=patron10,ou=patrons )
sn: Abbott ( uid=patron11,ou=patrons )
sn: Abdalla ( uid=patron12,ou=patrons )
sn: Abdo ( uid=patron13,ou=patrons )
sn: Abdollahi ( uid=patron14,ou=patrons )
sn: Abdou ( uid=patron15,ou=patrons )
sn: Abdul-Nour ( uid=patron16,ou=patrons )
sn: Abdulla ( uid=patron17,ou=patrons )
sn: Abdullah ( uid=patron18,ou=patrons )
sn: Abe ( uid=patron19,ou=patrons )
```

```
---End page ---
sn: Abedi ( uid=patron20,ou=patrons )
sn: Abel ( uid=patron21,ou=patrons )
sn: Abell ( uid=patron22,ou=patrons )
..............
```

In Listing 7-14, you start implementing by obtaining a context on the LDAP server. Then, you create the PagedResultsControl and specify the page size as its constructor parameter. You add the control to the context and perform the search operation. Then, you loop through the search results and display the information on the console. As the next step, you examine the response controls to identify the server sent PagedResultsResponseControl. From that control, you extract the cookie and an estimated total number of results for this search. The resulting count is optional information, and the server can simply return zero, indicating an unknown count. Finally, you create a new PagedResultsControl with the page size and the cookie as its constructor parameter. This process is repeated until the server sends an empty (null) cookie, indicating no more results to be processed.

Spring LDAP abstracts most of the code in Listing 7-14, making it easy to deal with page controls using the PagedResultsDirContextProcessor.

In this implementation, you create the PagedResultsDirContextProcessor with the page size and a cookie. Note that you are using the org.springframework.ldap. control.PagedResultsCookie class for abstracting the cookie sent by the server. The cookie value initially starts with a null. Then, you perform the search and loop through the results. The cookie the server sends is extracted from the DirContextProcessor and is used to check for future search requests. You also use a LastNameMapper class to extract the last name from the results context. Listing 7-15 gives the implementation of the LastNameMapper class.

***Listing 7-15.*** Implementation mapper

```java
private class LastNameMapper extends AbstractContextMapper<String> {
    @Override
    protected String doMapFromContext(DirContextOperations context) {
        return context.getStringAttribute("sn");
    }
}
```

Consider that you can create a mapper in the same way as you see in the previous chapter, where there is a public class with all the mapping, but in this chapter, for simplicity, it's a private class with just one attribute.

Now let's create a test which validates Listing 7-15 like shown in Listing 7-16.

***Listing 7-16.*** Test case related with the pagination

```
package com.apress.book.ldap.paging;

import org.junit.jupiter.api.DisplayName;
import org.junit.jupiter.api.Test;
import org.junit.jupiter.api.extension.ExtendWith;
import org.springframework.beans.factory.annotation.Autowired;
import org.springframework.test.context.ContextConfiguration;
import org.springframework.test.context.junit.jupiter.SpringExtension;
import static org.junit.jupiter.api.Assertions.*;
import static org.junit.jupiter.api.Assertions.assertEquals;

@ExtendWith(SpringExtension.class)
@ContextConfiguration("classpath:repositoryContext-test.xml")
@DisplayName("Spring Paging uses cases")
class SpringPagingTest {

    @Autowired
    private SpringPaging springPaging;

    @Test
    @DisplayName("Check if all the results are paginated")
    void should_paginate_all_results() {
        springPaging.pagedResults();
    }
}
```

Upon invoking the test, the paginated patrons will be displayed on the console as shown:

```
Starting Page: 1
Amar
Atp
```

```
Abbie
Ahad
Abbott
Abdalla
Abdo
Abdollahi
Abdou
Abdul-Nour
Abdulla
Abdullah
Abe
Atpco
Abedi
Abel
Abell
Abella
Abello
Abelow
Starting Page: 2
Abernathy
Abernethy
```

Another way to implement this pagination mechanism to return just one page is by introducing modifications in Listing 7-15 to something like Listing 7-17.

***Listing 7-17.*** An example of paging using Spring

```
package com.apress.book.ldap.paging;

import java.util.List;

import javax.naming.directory.SearchControls;

import com.apress.book.ldap.domain.Page;
import com.apress.book.ldap.domain.Pagination;
import org.slf4j.Logger;
import org.slf4j.LoggerFactory;
import org.springframework.beans.factory.annotation.Autowired;
```

```java
import org.springframework.beans.factory.annotation.Qualifier;
import org.springframework.ldap.control.PagedResultsCookie;
import org.springframework.ldap.control.PagedResultsDirContextProcessor;
import org.springframework.ldap.core.DirContextOperations;
import org.springframework.ldap.core.LdapTemplate;
import org.springframework.ldap.core.support.AbstractContextMapper;
import org.springframework.ldap.filter.EqualsFilter;
import org.springframework.stereotype.Component;

@Component("springPaging")
public class SpringPaging {

    private static final Logger logger = LoggerFactory.
    getLogger(SpringPaging.class);

    private LdapTemplate ldapTemplate;

    public SpringPaging(@Autowired @Qualifier("ldapTemplate") LdapTemplate
    ldapTemplate) {
        this.ldapTemplate = ldapTemplate;
    }

    //previous code

    public Pagination pagedResults(Page page) {
        int pageNumber = 0;
        PagedResultsCookie cookie = null;

        SearchControls searchControls = new SearchControls();
        searchControls.setSearchScope(SearchControls.SUBTREE_SCOPE);

        if (page.getCookie() != null) {
            pageNumber = page.getActualPage();
            cookie = page.getCookie();
        }

        logger.info("Page: " + page);
        PagedResultsDirContextProcessor processor = new
        PagedResultsDirContextProcessor(20, cookie);
```

```
    EqualsFilter equalsFilter = new EqualsFilter("objectClass",
    "inetOrgPerson");

    List<String> lastNames = ldapTemplate.search("", equalsFilter.
    encode(), searchControls, new LastNameMapper(),
            processor);

    for (String l : lastNames) {
        logger.info(l);
    }

    return new Pagination(lastNames,
            new Page(processor.getPageSize(), processor.
            getResultSize(), pageNumber + 1, processor.getCookie()));
    }

    //previous code

}
```

The definition of the class Page is simple. It contains just the information about the actual page and the limit like Listing 7-18.

***Listing 7-18.*** An example of a page class

```
import org.springframework.ldap.control.PagedResultsCookie;

public class Page {

    int pageSize;
    int numberElements;

    int actualPage;

    PagedResultsCookie cookie;

    public Page() {

    }
    public Page(int pageSize, int numberElements, int actualPage,
                    PagedResultsCookie cookie) {
        this.pageSize = pageSize;
```

```
        this.numberElements = numberElements;
        this.actualPage = actualPage;
        this.cookie = cookie;
    }
    //setters and getters
}
```

The class Pagination includes all the elements of the actual page and the information to paginate the results like Listing 7-19.

***Listing 7-19.*** An example of a pagination class

```
import java.util.List;

public class Pagination {
    List<String> result;

    Page page;

    public Pagination(List<String> result, Page page) {
        this.result = result;
        this.page = page;
    }
    //setters and getters
}
```

After that, let's modify our previous test class to include a test which validates if the method works fine or not. Listing 7-20 shows how it looks like.

***Listing 7-20.*** An example of a pagination class

```
package com.apress.book.ldap.paging;

import com.apress.book.ldap.domain.Page;
import com.apress.book.ldap.domain.Pagination;
import org.junit.jupiter.api.DisplayName;
import org.junit.jupiter.api.Test;
import org.junit.jupiter.api.extension.ExtendWith;
import org.springframework.beans.factory.annotation.Autowired;
import org.springframework.test.context.ContextConfiguration;
```

```java
import org.springframework.test.context.junit.jupiter.SpringExtension;

import static org.junit.jupiter.api.Assertions.*;
import static org.junit.jupiter.api.Assertions.assertEquals;

@ExtendWith(SpringExtension.class)
@ContextConfiguration("classpath:repositoryContext-test.xml")
@DisplayName("Spring Paging uses cases")
class SpringPagingTest {

    @Autowired
    private SpringPaging springPaging;

    //previous test
    @Test
    @DisplayName("Check the results of the first page")
    void should_paginate_first_pade() {
        Pagination result = springPaging.pagedResults(new Page());

        assertAll(() -> assertNotNull(result), () -> assertEquals(1,
        result.getPage().getActualPage()),
                () -> assertEquals(20, result.getPage().getPageSize()),
                () -> assertEquals(101, result.getPage().
                    getNumberElements()),
                () -> assertEquals("Amar", result.getResult().get(0)));
    }
}
```

Upon invoking the test, the paginated patrons will be displayed on the console as shown:

```
Starting Page: 1
Amar
Atp
Abbie
Ahad
Abbott
Abdalla
Abdo
```

```
Abdollahi
Abdou
Abdul-Nour
Abdulla
Abdullah
Abe
Atpco
Abedi
Abel
Abell
Abella
Abello
Abelow
```

This is a possible implementation to paginate the results, but you can create your way to do it.

# Summary

In this chapter, you learned the basic concepts associated with LDAP controls. You then looked at the sort control, which can be used to perform server-side sorting of the results. You saw how Spring LDAP simplifies the sort control usage significantly. The paging control can be used to page LDAP results, which is useful under heavy traffic conditions.

In the next chapter, you will look at using Spring LDAP ODM technology for implementing the data access layer.

# CHAPTER 8

# Object-Directory Mapping

Enterprise Java developers employ object-oriented (OO) techniques to create modular, complex applications. In the OO paradigm, objects are central to the system and represent entities in the real world. Each object has an identity, state, and behavior. Objects can be related to other objects through inheritance or composition. On the other hand, LDAP directories represent data and relationships in a hierarchical tree structure. This difference leads to an object-directory paradigm mismatch and can cause problems in communication between OO and directory environments.

Spring LDAP provides an Object-Directory Mapping (ODM) framework that bridges the gap between the object and directory models. The ODM framework allows us to map concepts between the two models and orchestrates the process of automatically transforming LDAP directory entries into Java objects. ODM is similar to the Object-Relational Mapping (ORM) methodology that bridges the gap between object and relational database worlds. Frameworks such as Hibernate[1] and TopLink[2] have made ORM popular and an essential part of the developer's toolset. Also, other frameworks like Spring Data[3] use behind-the-scenes Hibernate and offer the same support to access a database.

Though Spring LDAP ODM shares the same concepts as ORM, it has the following differences:

- Caching LDAP entries is not possible by default, but you can use libraries like Caffeine, Guava, or EhCache to encapsulate the logic that accesses the LDAP.

- ODM metadata is expressed through class-level annotations.

- No XML configuration is available.

---

[1] https://hibernate.org/

[2] https://projects.eclipse.org/projects/ee4j.eclipselink

[3] https://spring.io/projects/spring-data/

B. Varanasi and A. Sacco, *Practical Spring LDAP*, https://doi.org/10.1007/979-8-8688-0002-3_8

- Lazy loading of entries is not possible.

- A query language, such as HQL, does not exist. Loading of objects is done via DN lookups and standard LDAP search queries, or you can use the methods provided by Spring LDAP to write the query using methods.

# Spring ODM Basics

The Spring LDAP ODM is distributed as a separate module from the core LDAP project. To include the Spring LDAP ODM[4] in the project, the following dependency needs to be added to the project's pom.xml file:

```
<dependency>
    <groupId>org.springframework.ldap</groupId>
    <artifactId>spring-ldap-odm</artifactId>
    <version>${org.springframework.ldap.version}</version>
    <exclusions>
        <exclusion>
            <artifactId>commons-logging</artifactId>
            <groupId>commons-logging</groupId>
        </exclusion>
    </exclusions>
</dependency>
```

The Spring LDAP ODM is available under the org.springframework.ldap.odm package and its subpackages.

The previous dependency is necessary to execute any kind of operation and use the advantages of ODM, but during the different versions of Spring LDAP, the ways to execute different operations were changed from using the class OdmManager to LdapTemplate.

---

[4]https://github.com/spring-projects/spring-ldap/tree/main/odm

**Note**    Before version 2.0.0, the way to execute operations was by using the
class OdmManager and some annotations to indicate which property represents
an attribute on LDAP. Figure 8-1 represents the structure of the classes that were
used on the versions prior to Spring LDAP 2.0.0.

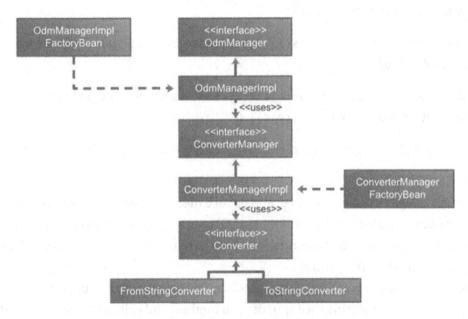

***Figure 8-1.*** *Previous Spring LDAP ODM core classes*

Central to the LDAP ODM is the OdmManager, which provides generic search and
CRUD operations. It acts as a mediator and transforms data between LDAP entries and
Java objects. The Java objects are annotated to provide the transformation metadata.
On Listing 8-1, you will see the source code of the OdmManager with all the methods.

***Listing 8-1.*** OdmManager API

```
package org.springframework.ldap.odm.core;

import java.util.List;

import javax.naming.Name;
import javax.naming.directory.SearchControls;

import org.springframework.ldap.query.LdapQuery;
```

```
public interface OdmManager {

    <T> T read(Class<T> clazz, Name dn);

    void create(Object entry);

    void update(Object entry);

    void delete(Object entry);

    <T> List<T> findAll(Class<T> clazz, Name base, SearchControls
    searchControls);

    <T> List<T> search(Class<T> clazz, Name base, String filter,
    SearchControls searchControls);

    <T> List<T> search(Class<T> clazz, LdapQuery query);
}
```

The OdmManager's create, update, and delete methods take a Java object and use its information to perform corresponding LDAP operations. The read method takes two parameters: a Java class that determines the type to return and a fully qualified DN that is used to look up the LDAP entry.

The unique implementation of this interface, OdmManagerImpl, is deprecated and behind the scenes transforms the input of each method and calls to the same operations of LdapTemplate.

The class LdapTemplate implements the interface LdapOperations which provides a standard way to access LDAP and execute the different operations. Listing 8-2 shows the most relevant methods that you can use to execute different operations.

***Listing 8-2.*** Declaration of the interface LdapOperations

```
package org.springframework.ldap.core;

import java.util.List;
import java.util.stream.Stream;
import javax.naming.Name;
import javax.naming.directory.Attributes;
import javax.naming.directory.ModificationItem;
import javax.naming.directory.SearchControls;
import org.springframework.ldap.NamingException;
```

```
import org.springframework.ldap.filter.Filter;
import org.springframework.ldap.odm.core.ObjectDirectoryMapper;
import org.springframework.ldap.query.LdapQuery;
public interface LdapOperations {

    <T> T findByDn(Name dn, Class<T> clazz);

    <T> T findOne(LdapQuery query, Class<T> clazz);

    <T> List<T> find(LdapQuery query, Class<T> clazz);

    <T> List<T> findAll(Class<T> clazz);

    <T> List<T> findAll(Name base, SearchControls searchControls,
    Class<T> clazz);

    <T> List<T> findAll(Name base, Filter filter, SearchControls
    searchControls, Class<T> clazz);

    void create(Object entry);

    void update(Object entry);

    void delete(Object entry);
}
```

As you can see in Listing 8-2, some methods receive an object; the object represents our domain object like Patron or Employee but with certain annotations that provide the necessary metadata to Spring to execute the different operations.

# ODM Metadata

The org.springframework.ldap.odm.annotations package contains annotations that can be used to turn simple Java POJOs into ODM manageable entities. Listing 8-3 shows the Patron Java class you will convert into an ODM entity.

*Listing 8-3.* Patron entity without setters and getters

```
package com.apress.book.ldap.domain;

import java.util.List;
```

```
import javax.naming.Name;

public class Patron {

    private Name dn;

    private String lastName;

    private String firstName;

    private String telephoneNumber;

    private String fullName;

    private String mail;

    private List<String> objectClasses;

    private int employeeNumber;

     //Setters and getters

     @Override
     public String toString() {
         return "Dn: " + dn + ", firstName: " + firstName + ", fullName: "
         + fullName + ", Telephone Number: " + telephoneNumber;
     }
}
```

You will start the conversion by annotating the class with @Entry. This marker annotation tells the ODM that the class is an entity. It also provides the objectClass definitions in LDAP that the entity maps to. Listing 8-4 shows the annotated Patron class.

*Listing 8-4.* Patron entity with the declaration of the type of entity

```
package com.apress.book.ldap.domain;

import java.util.List;

import javax.naming.Name;
import org.springframework.ldap.odm.annotations.Entry;
```

```
@Entry(objectClasses = { "inetorgperson", "organizationalperson", "person",
"top" })
public class Patron {
  // Fields and getters and setters
}
```

The next annotation you need to add is the @org.springframework.ldap.odm.
annotations.Id. This annotation specifies the entry's DN and can only be placed on a
field derivative of the javax.naming.Name class. You will create a new field called dn in
the Patron class to address this. Listing 8-5 shows the modified Patron class.

***Listing 8-5.*** Patron entity with the declaration of the type of entity and the id

```
package com.apress.book.ldap.domain;
import java.util.List;

import javax.naming.Name;

import org.springframework.ldap.odm.annotations.Entry;
import org.springframework.ldap.odm.annotations.Id;

@Entry(objectClasses = { "inetorgperson", "organizationalperson", "person",
"top" })
public class Patron {
  @Id
  private Name dn;
  // Fields and getters and setters
}
```

The @Id annotation in the Java Persistence API specifies the identifier property of
the entity bean. Additionally, its placement determines the default access strategy the
JPA provider will use for mapping. If the @Id is placed over a field, field access is used.
The property access will be used if placed over a getter method. However, Spring LDAP
ODM only allows field access.

The @Entry and @Id are the only annotations required to make the Patron class
an ODM entity. By default, all the fields in the Patron entity class will automatically
become persistable. The default strategy is to use the name of the entity field as the
LDAP attribute name while persisting or reading. In the Patron class, this would work
for attributes such as telephoneNumber or mail because the field name and the LDAP

attribute name are the same. However, this would cause problems with fields such as firstName and fullName, as their names differ from the LDAP attribute names. To address this, ODM provides the @Attribute annotation that maps the entity fields to object class fields. This annotation allows you to specify the name of the LDAP attribute, an optional syntax OID, and an optional type declaration. Listing 8-6 shows the completely annotated Patron entity class.

***Listing 8-6.*** Patron entity with the attributes and their annotations

```
package com.apress.book.ldap.domain;
import java.util.List;

import javax.naming.Name;

import org.springframework.ldap.odm.annotations.Attribute;
import org.springframework.ldap.odm.annotations.Entry;
import org.springframework.ldap.odm.annotations.Id;

@Entry(objectClasses = { "inetorgperson", "organizationalperson", "person",
"top" })
public class Patron {

    @Id
    private Name dn;

    @Attribute(name = "sn")
    private String lastName;

    @Attribute(name = "givenName")
    private String firstName;

    private String telephoneNumber;

    @Attribute(name = "cn")
    private String fullName;

    private String mail;

    @Attribute(name = "objectClass")
    private List<String> objectClasses;
```

```
@Attribute(name = "employeeNumber", syntax = "2.16.840.1.113730.3.1.3")
private int employeeNumber;

// Fields and getters and setters

@Override
public String toString() {
    return "Dn: " + dn + ", firstName: " + firstName + ", fullName: " +
    fullName + ", Telephone Number: " + telephoneNumber;
}
}
```

Sometimes, you wouldn't want to persist certain fields of an entity class. Typically, these involve fields that are computed. Such fields can be annotated with @Transient annotation, indicating that ODM should ignore the field.

# ODM Service Class

Spring-based enterprise applications typically have a service layer that holds the application's business logic. Classes in the service layer delegate persistent specifics to a DAO or repository layer. In Chapter 5, you implemented a DAO using LdapTemplate. Listing 8-7 shows the interface of the service class you will be implementing.

*Listing 8-7.* Patron service interface

```
package com.apress.book.ldap.service;

import com.apress.book.ldap.domain.Patron;

public interface PatronService {

    void create(Patron patron);

    void delete(String id);

    void update(Patron patron);

    Patron find(String id);
}
```

The service class implementation is in Listing 8-8. In the implementation, you inject an instance of LdapTemplate. The create and update method implementations simply delegate the calls to the LdapTemplate. The find method converts the passed-in id parameter to the fully qualified DN and delegates the retrieval to LdapTemplate's findByDn method. Finally, the delete method uses the find method to read the patron and uses the LdapTemplate's delete method to delete it.

***Listing 8-8.*** Patron service implementation

```
package com.apress.book.ldap.service;

import org.springframework.beans.factory.annotation.Autowired;
import org.springframework.beans.factory.annotation.Qualifier;
import org.springframework.ldap.core.DistinguishedName;
import org.springframework.ldap.core.LdapTemplate;
import org.springframework.stereotype.Service;
import com.apress.book.ldap.domain.Patron;

@Service("patronService")
public class PatronServiceImpl implements PatronService {

    private static final String PATRON_BASE  = "ou=patrons,dc=inflinx,
    dc=com";

    private LdapTemplate ldapTemplate;

    public PatronServiceImpl(@Autowired @Qualifier("ldapTemplate")
    LdapTemplate ldapTemplate) {
        this.ldapTemplate = ldapTemplate;
    }

    @Override
    public void create(Patron patron) {
        ldapTemplate.create(patron);
    }

    @Override
    public void update(Patron patron) {
        ldapTemplate.update(patron);
    }
```

```
    @Override
    public Patron find(String id) {
        DistinguishedName dn = new DistinguishedName(PATRON_BASE);
        dn.add("uid", id);
        return ldapTemplate.findByDn(dn, Patron.class);
    }

    @Override
    public void delete(String id) {
        ldapTemplate.delete(find(id));
    }
}
```

The JUnit test to verify the `PatronService` implementation is shown in Listing 8-9.

***Listing 8-9.*** JUnit test of the service

```
package com.apress.book.ldap.service;

import org.junit.jupiter.api.DisplayName;
import org.junit.jupiter.api.Test;
import org.junit.jupiter.api.extension.ExtendWith;
import org.springframework.beans.factory.annotation.Autowired;
import org.springframework.ldap.NameNotFoundException;
import org.springframework.ldap.core.DistinguishedName;
import org.springframework.test.context.ContextConfiguration;

import com.apress.book.ldap.domain.Patron;
import org.springframework.test.context.junit.jupiter.SpringExtension;

import static org.junit.jupiter.api.Assertions.*;

@ExtendWith(SpringExtension.class)
@ContextConfiguration("classpath:repositoryContext-test.xml")
class PatronServiceImplTest {

    @Autowired
    private PatronService patronService;

    @Test
```

```java
@DisplayName("Check that operation add create a new entry on
the LDAP")
void should_create_a_patron() {
    Patron patron = new Patron();
    patron.setDn(new DistinguishedName("uid=patron10001,ou=patrons,
    dc=inflinx,dc=com"));

    patron.setFirstName("Patron");

    patron.setLastName("Test 1");
    patron.setFullName("Patron Test 1");
    patron.setMail("balaji@inflinx.com");
    patron.setEmployeeNumber(1234);
    patron.setTelephoneNumber("8018640759");
    patronService.create(patron);
    // Lets read the patron
    Patron result = patronService.find("patron10001");
    assertAll(
            () -> assertNotNull(result),
            () -> assertEquals(patron.getDn().toString(), result.
                getDn().toString())
    );
}

@Test
void should_find_a_patron() {
    Patron result = patronService.find("patron100");
    assertAll(
            () -> assertNotNull(result),
            () -> assertEquals("uid=patron100,ou=patrons,dc=inflinx,
            dc=com", result.getDn().toString())
    );
}

@Test
@DisplayName("Check that operation search return a patron")
void should_delete_a_patron() {
```

```
        patronService.delete("patron92");

        assertThrows(NameNotFoundException.class, ()-> patronService.
        find("patron92"));
    }

    @Test
    @DisplayName("Check that operation update an entry on the LDAP")
    void should_update_a_patron() {
        Patron patron = patronService.find("patron1");
        assertNotNull(patron);

        patron.setTelephoneNumber("8018640850");
        patronService.update(patron);

        patron = patronService.find("patron1");
        assertEquals(patron.getTelephoneNumber(), "8018640850");
    }

    @Test
    @DisplayName("Check that operation remove works")
    void should_delete_a_patron() {
        patronService.delete("patron92");

        assertThrows(NameNotFoundException.class, () -> patronService.
        find("patron92"));
    }
}
```

The `repositoryContext-test.xml` file, located in the folder **src/test/resources**, contains snippets of the configuration you have seen. Listing 8-10 gives the complete content of the XML file.

***Listing 8-10.*** Configuration of the test

```
<?xml version="1.0" encoding="UTF-8"?>
<beans xmlns="http://www.springframework.org/schema/beans"
     xmlns:xsi="http://www.w3.org/2001/XMLSchema-instance"
     xmlns:ldap="http://www.springframework.org/schema/ldap"
     xmlns:context="http://www.springframework.org/schema/context"
```

```
          xsi:schemaLocation="http://www.springframework.org/schema/beans
                      https://www.springframework.org/schema/beans/
                      spring-beans.xsd http://www.springframework.org/
                      schema/ldap https://www.springframework.org/
                      schema/ldap/spring-ldap.xsd
                  http://www.springframework.org/schema/context http://
                  www.springframework.org/schema/context/spring-
                  context.xsd">

<context:component-scan base-package="com.apress.book.ldap" />

<bean id="placeholderConfig" class="org.springframework.beans.factory.
config.PropertyPlaceholderConfigurer">
    <property name="location" value="classpath:ldap.properties" />
</bean>
<ldap:context-source id="contextSource"
                  password="${ldap.password}"
                  url="${ldap.url}"
                  username="${ldap.userDn}"/>

<!-- Populates the LDAP server with initial data -->
<bean class="org.springframework.ldap.test.LdifPopulator" depends-
on="embeddedLdapServer">
    <property name="contextSource" ref="contextSource" />
    <property name="resource" value="classpath:patrons.ldif" />
    <property name="base" value="${ldap.base}" />
    <property name="clean" value="${ldap.clean}" />
    <property name="defaultBase" value="${ldap.base}" />
</bean>

<bean id="embeddedLdapServer" class="org.springframework.ldap.test.
unboundid.EmbeddedLdapServerFactoryBean">
    <property name="partitionName" value="inflinx"/>
    <property name="partitionSuffix" value="${ldap.base}" />
    <property name="port" value="${ldap.port}" />
</bean>
```

```
<bean id="ldapTemplate" class="org.springframework.ldap.core.
LdapTemplate">
    <constructor-arg ref="contextSource" />
</bean>
</beans>
```

# Creating Custom Converter

Consider the scenario where your Patron class uses a custom PhoneNumber class for storing a patron's phone number. Now, when a Patron class needs to be persisted, you need to convert the PhoneNumber class to String type. Similarly, when you read a Patron class from LDAP, the data in the telephone attribute needs to be converted into a PhoneNumber class. The default ToStringConverter and FromStringConverter will not be useful for such conversion. Listing 8-11 shows the new class PhoneNumber with the attributes that represent the phone in a different format.

***Listing 8-11.*** PhoneNumber class with all the attributes

```
package com.apress.book.ldap.custom;

public class PhoneNumber {
    private int areaCode;
    private int exchange;
    private int extension;

    public PhoneNumber(int areaCode, int exchange, int extension) {
        this.areaCode = areaCode;
        this.exchange = exchange;
        this.extension = extension;
    }

    //Setters and getters

    public boolean equals(Object obj) {
        if(obj == null || obj.getClass() != this.getClass()) { return
        false; }
        PhoneNumber p = (PhoneNumber) obj;
```

```
            return (this.areaCode ==  p.areaCode) && (this.exchange ==
            p.exchange) && (this.extension == p.extension);
    }

    public String toString() {
            return String.format("+1 %03d %03d %04d", areaCode, exchange,
            extension);
    }

    // satisfies the hashCode contract
    public int hashCode() {
            int result = 17;
            result = 37 * result + areaCode;
            result = 37 * result + exchange;
            result = 37 * result + extension;

            return result;
    }
}
```

Now, let's modify the Patron class as you can see in Listing 8-12.

***Listing 8-12.*** Patron entity with the modifications of the phone number

```
package com.apress.book.ldap.custom;

import java.util.List;

import javax.naming.Name;

import org.springframework.ldap.odm.annotations.Attribute;
import org.springframework.ldap.odm.annotations.Entry;
import org.springframework.ldap.odm.annotations.Id;

@Entry(objectClasses = { "inetorgperson", "organizationalperson", "person",
"top" })
public class Patron {

    @Id
    private Name dn;
```

```java
@Attribute(name = "sn")
private String lastName;

@Attribute(name = "givenName")
private String firstName;

@Attribute(name = "telephoneNumber")
private PhoneNumber phoneNumber;

@Attribute(name = "cn")
private String fullName;

private String mail;

@Attribute(name = "objectClass")
private List<String> objectClasses;

@Attribute(name = "employeeNumber", syntax = "2.16.840.1.113730.3.1.3")
private int employeeNumber;

// Fields and getters and setters

@Override
public String toString() {
    return "Dn: " + dn + ", firstName: " + firstName + ", fullName: " +
    fullName + ", Telephone Number: " + phoneNumber;
}
}
```

To convert PhoneNumber to String, you create a new FromPhoneNumberConverter converter. Listing 8-13 shows the implementation. The implementation simply involves calling the toString method to perform the conversion.

***Listing 8-13.*** Converter from an object PhoneNumber to String

```java
package com.apress.book.ldap.converter;

import com.apress.book.ldap.custom.PhoneNumber;
import org.springframework.ldap.odm.typeconversion.impl.Converter;

public class FromPhoneNumberConverter implements Converter  {
```

```
    @Override
    public <T> T convert(Object source, Class<T> toClass) throws
    Exception {
        T result = null;
        if(PhoneNumber.class.isAssignableFrom(source.getClass()) &&
        toClass.equals(String.class)) {
            result = toClass.cast(source.toString());
        }
        return result;
    }
}
```

Next, you need an implementation to convert the LDAP string attribute to Java
PhoneNumber type. To do this, you create the ToPhoneNumberConverter on the same
package, as shown in Listing 8-14.

***Listing 8-14.*** Converter from a String to PhoneNumber

```
package com.apress.book.ldap.converter;

import com.apress.book.ldap.custom.PhoneNumber;
import org.springframework.ldap.odm.typeconversion.impl.Converter;

public class ToPhoneNumberConverter implements Converter {

    @Override
    public <T> T convert(Object source, Class<T> toClass) throws
    Exception {
        T result = null;

        if (String.class.isAssignableFrom(source.getClass()) && toClass
        == PhoneNumber.class) {
            // Simple implementation
            String[] tokens = ((String)source).split(" ");
            int i = 0;
            if(tokens.length == 4) {
                i = 1;
            }
```

```
            result = toClass.cast(new PhoneNumber(Integer.
            parseInt(tokens[i]), Integer.parseInt(tokens[i+1]), Integer.
            parseInt(tokens[i+2])));
        }

        return result;
    }
}
```

Since that LDAPTemplate replaced OdmManager, many things have changed,
so to use the converters, one alternative is to create a new implementation of
ConverterManager to simplify the configuration process. Listing 8-15 shows the
DefaultConverterManagerImpl class. As you can see, it uses the ConverterManagerImpl
class internal to its implementation.

***Listing 8-15.*** New converter manager

```
package com.apress.book.ldap.converter;

import com.apress.book.ldap.custom.PhoneNumber;
import org.springframework.ldap.odm.typeconversion.ConverterManager;
import org.springframework.ldap.odm.typeconversion.impl.Converter;
import org.springframework.ldap.odm.typeconversion.impl.
ConverterManagerImpl;
import org.springframework.ldap.odm.typeconversion.impl.converters.
FromStringConverter;
import org.springframework.ldap.odm.typeconversion.impl.converters.
ToStringConverter;

public class DefaultConverterManagerImpl implements ConverterManager {
    private static final Class[] classSet = {
            java.lang.Byte.class,
            java.lang.Integer.class,
            java.lang.Long.class,
            java.lang.Double.class,
            java.lang.Boolean.class};
    private ConverterManagerImpl converterManager;
    public DefaultConverterManagerImpl() {
```

```java
        converterManager = new ConverterManagerImpl();
        Converter fromStringConverter = new FromStringConverter();
        Converter toStringConverter = new ToStringConverter();
        for(Class clazz : classSet) {
            converterManager.addConverter(String.class, null, clazz,
            fromStringConverter);
            converterManager.addConverter(clazz, null, String.class,
            toStringConverter);
        }

        Converter toPhoneNumberConverter = new ToPhoneNumberConverter();
        converterManager.addConverter(String.class, null, PhoneNumber.
        class, toPhoneNumberConverter);

        Converter fromPhoneNumberConverter = new FromPhoneNumber
        Converter();
        converterManager.addConverter(PhoneNumber.class, null, String.
        class, fromPhoneNumberConverter);
    }
    @Override
    public boolean canConvert(Class<?> fromClass, String syntax, Class<?>
    toClass) {
        return converterManager.canConvert(fromClass, syntax, toClass);
    }
    @Override
    public <T> T convert(Object source, String syntax, Class<T> toClass) {
        return converterManager.convert(source,syntax,toClass);
    }
}
```

Finally, you tie up everything in the configuration, creating a new file named
repositoryContext-test-converter.xml on the **src/test/resources**, as shown in
Listing 8-16.

***Listing 8-16.*** Converter manager configuration

```xml
<?xml version="1.0" encoding="UTF-8"?>
<beans xmlns="http://www.springframework.org/schema/beans"
       xmlns:xsi="http://www.w3.org/2001/XMLSchema-instance"
       xmlns:ldap="http://www.springframework.org/schema/ldap"
       xmlns:context="http://www.springframework.org/schema/context"
       xsi:schemaLocation="http://www.springframework.org/schema/beans
                           https://www.springframework.org/schema/beans/
                           spring-beans.xsd http://www.springframework.org/
                           schema/ldap https://www.springframework.org/
                           schema/ldap/spring-ldap.xsd
                   http://www.springframework.org/schema/context http://
                   www.springframework.org/schema/context/spring-
                   context.xsd">

    <context:component-scan base-package="com.apress.book.ldap" />

    <bean id="placeholderConfig" class="org.springframework.beans.factory.
    config.PropertyPlaceholderConfigurer">
        <property name="location" value="classpath:ldap.properties" />
    </bean>
    <ldap:context-source id="contextSource"
                    password="${ldap.password}"
                    url="${ldap.url}"
                    username="${ldap.userDn}"/>

    <!-- Populates the LDAP server with initial data -->
    <bean class="org.springframework.ldap.test.LdifPopulator" depends-
    on="embedded
    LdapServer">
        <property name="contextSource" ref="contextSource" />
        <property name="resource" value="classpath:patrons.ldif" />
        <property name="base" value="${ldap.base}" />
        <property name="clean" value="${ldap.clean}" />
        <property name="defaultBase" value="${ldap.base}" />
    </bean>
```

```
<bean id="embeddedLdapServer" class="org.springframework.ldap.test.
unboundid.EmbeddedLdapServerFactoryBean">
    <property name="partitionName" value="inflinx"/>
    <property name="partitionSuffix" value="${ldap.base}" />
    <property name="port" value="${ldap.port}" />
</bean>

<bean id="ldapTemplate" class="org.springframework.ldap.core.
LdapTemplate">
    <constructor-arg ref="contextSource" />
    <property name="objectDirectoryMapper" ref="defaultObjectDirectory
    Mapper"/>
</bean>

<bean id="defaultObjectDirectoryMapper" class="org.springframework.
ldap.odm.core.impl.DefaultObjectDirectoryMapper">
    <property name="converterManager" ref="converterManager"/>
</bean>

<bean id="converterManager" class="com.apress.book.ldap.converter.
DefaultConverter
ManagerImpl" />
</beans>
```

As you can see in Listing 8-16, you use the new converter manager as a replacement of the original and add on the configuration of the LdapTemplate.

The modified test case for testing the newly added converters is shown in Listing 8-17.

***Listing 8-17.*** Test cases to check the converters

```
package com.apress.book.ldap.custom;

import org.junit.jupiter.api.Test;
import org.junit.jupiter.api.extension.ExtendWith;
import org.springframework.beans.factory.annotation.Autowired;
import org.springframework.ldap.core.DistinguishedName;
import org.springframework.test.context.ContextConfiguration;
import org.springframework.test.context.junit.jupiter.SpringExtension;
```

```java
import org.junit.jupiter.api.DisplayName;

import static org.junit.jupiter.api.Assertions.*;
@ExtendWith(SpringExtension.class)
@ContextConfiguration("classpath:repositoryContext-test-converter.xml")
@DisplayName("Patron Service Custom test cases")
class PatronServiceImplCustomTest {

    @Autowired
    private PatronService patronService;

    @Test
    @DisplayName("Check that operation add create a new entry on
    the LDAP")
    void should_create_a_patron() {
        Patron patron = new Patron();
        patron.setDn(new DistinguishedName("uid=patron10001,ou=patrons,dc
        =inflinx,dc=com"));

        patron.setFirstName("Patron");

        patron.setLastName("Test 1");
        patron.setFullName("Patron Test 1");
        patron.setMail("balaji@inflinx.com");
        patron.setEmployeeNumber(1234);
        patron.setPhoneNumber(new PhoneNumber(801, 864, 8050));
        patronService.create(patron);
        // Lets read the patron
        Patron result = patronService.find("patron10001");
        assertAll(
                    () -> assertNotNull(result),
                    () -> assertEquals(patron.getDn().toString(), result.
                        getDn().toString()),
                    () -> assertEquals(801, patron.getPhoneNumber().
                        getAreaCode()),
                    () -> assertEquals(864, patron.getPhoneNumber().
                        getExchange()),
```

```
                () -> assertEquals(8050, patron.getPhoneNumber().
                    getExtension())
        );
    }

    @Test
    @DisplayName("Check that operation search return a patron")
    void should_find_a_patron() {
        Patron result = patronService.find("patron100");
        assertAll(
                () -> assertNotNull(result),
                () -> assertEquals("uid=patron100,ou=patrons,dc=inflinx
                    ,dc=com", result.getDn().toString()),
                () -> assertEquals(232, result.getPhoneNumber().
                    getAreaCode()),
                () -> assertEquals(25, result.getPhoneNumber().
                    getExchange()),
                () -> assertEquals(4008, result.getPhoneNumber().
                    getExtension())
        );
    }

    @Test
    @DisplayName("Check that operation update an entry on the LDAP")
    void should_update_a_patron() {
        Patron patron = patronService.find("patron1");
        assertNotNull(patron);

        patron.setPhoneNumber(new PhoneNumber(1, 2, 3));
        patronService.update(patron);
        Patron result = patronService.find("patron1");
        assertAll(
                () -> assertNotNull(result),
                () -> assertEquals("uid=patron1,ou=patrons,dc=inflinx,
                    dc=com", result.getDn().toString()),
                () -> assertEquals(1, result.getPhoneNumber().
                    getAreaCode()),
```

```
                () -> assertEquals(2, result.getPhoneNumber().
                    getExchange()),
                () -> assertEquals(3, result.getPhoneNumber().
                    getExtension())
        );
    }
}
```

With these little modifications, you can use complex objects that represent a simple attribute on your LDAP.

# Summary

Spring LDAP's Object-Directory Mapping (ODM) bridges the gap between object and directory models. In this chapter, you learned the basics of ODM and looked at annotations for defining ODM mappings. You then took a deep dive into the ODM framework and built a Patron service and custom converters.

Up to this point in the book, you have created several variations of service and DAO implementations. In the next chapter, you will explore Spring LDAP's transaction support.

# CHAPTER 9

# LDAP Transactions

In this chapter, you will learn

- The basics of transactions

- Spring transaction abstraction

- Spring LDAP support for transactions

## Transaction Basics

Transactions are an integral part of enterprise applications. Put simply, a transaction is a series of operations that are performed together. All its operations must succeed for a transaction to be completed or committed. If, for any reason, one operation fails, the entire transaction fails and is rolled back. In that scenario, all the previous operations that have succeeded must be undone. This ensures that the end state matches the state in place before the transaction starts.

In your day-to-day world, you run into transactions all the time. Consider an online banking scenario where you wish to transfer $300 from your savings account to your checking account. This operation involves debiting the savings account by $300 and crediting the checking account by $300. If the debiting part of the operation were to succeed and the crediting part failed, you would end up with $300 less in your combined accounts. (Ideally, we all would like the debit operation to fail and the credit operation to succeed, but the bank might knock on our door the next day.) Banks ensure that accounts never end up in such inconsistent states by using transactions.

© Balaji Varanasi and Andres Sacco 2023
B. Varanasi and A. Sacco, *Practical Spring LDAP*, https://doi.org/10.1007/979-8-8688-0002-3_9

Transactions are usually associated with the following four well-known characteristics, often called ACID properties:

- *Atomicity*: This property ensures that a transaction executes completely or not at all. So, in our preceding example, we either successfully transfer the money or our transfer fails. This all-or-nothing property is also called a single or logical unit of work.

- *Consistency*: This property ensures that a transaction leaves the system in a consistent state after its completion. For example, all the integrity constraints, such as a primary key or referential integrity, are satisfied with a database system.

- *Isolation*: This property ensures that a transaction executes independently of other parallel transactions. Changes or side effects of a transaction that has not yet been completed will never be seen in other transactions. In the money transfer scenario, another account owner will only see the balances before or after the transfer. They will only be able to see the intermediate balances if the transaction takes longer to complete. Many database systems relax this property and provide several levels of isolation. Table 9-1 lists the primary transaction levels and descriptions. As the isolation level increases, transaction concurrency decreases, and transaction consistency increases.

- *Durability*: This property ensures that the results of a committed transaction never get lost due to a failure. Revisiting the bank transfer scenario, when you receive a confirmation that the transfer has succeeded, the durability property ensures that this change becomes permanent.

***Table 9-1.*** *Isolation Levels*

| Isolation Level | Description |
| --- | --- |
| Read Uncommitted | This isolation level allows a query in a running transaction to see changes made by other uncommitted transactions. Changes made by this transaction become visible to other transactions even before it is completed. This is the lowest level of isolation and can more appropriately be considered as lack of isolation. Since it violates one of the ACID properties, most database vendors do not support it. |
| Read Committed | This isolation level allows a query in a running transaction to see only data committed before the query began. However, all uncommitted changes or changes committed by concurrent transactions during query execution will not be seen. This is the default isolation level for most databases, including Oracle, MySQL, and PostgreSQL. |
| Repeatable Read | This isolation level allows a query in a running transaction to read the same data every time it is executed. To achieve this, the transaction acquires locks on all the rows examined (not just fetched) until completion. |
| Serializable | This is the strictest and most expensive of all the isolation levels. Interleaving transactions are stacked up so that transactions are executed one after another rather than concurrently. With this isolation level, queries will only see the data that has been committed before the start of the transaction and will never see uncommitted changes or commits by concurrent transactions. |

# Local vs. Global Transactions

Transactions are often categorized into local or global transactions depending on the number of resources participating. Examples of these resources include a database system or a JMS queue. Resource managers, such as a JDBC driver, are typically used to manage resources.

Local transactions are transactions that involve a single resource. The most common example is a transaction associated with a single database. These transactions are usually managed via objects used to access the resource. In the case of a JDBC database transaction, implementations of the `java.sql.Connection` interfaces are used to access the database. These implementations also provide `commit` and `rollback` methods for managing transactions. In the case of a JMS queue, the `javax.jms.Session` instance provides methods for controlling transactions.

Global transactions, on the other hand, deal with multiple resources. For example, a global transaction can read a message from a JMS queue and write a record to the database all in one transaction.

Global transactions are managed using a transaction manager external to the resources. It is responsible for communicating with resource managers and making the final commit or rollback decision on distributed transactions. In Java/JEE, global transactions are implemented using the Java Transaction API (JTA). JTA provides standard interfaces for transaction managers and transaction participating components.

Transaction managers employ a "two-phase commit" protocol to coordinate global transactions. As the name suggests, the two-phase commit protocol has two phases:

- *Prepare phase*: In this phase, all participating resource managers are asked if they are ready to commit their work. Upon receiving the request, the resource managers attempt to record their state. If successful, the resource manager responds positively. If it cannot be committed, the resource manager responds negatively and reverses the local changes.

- *Commit phase*: If the transaction manager receives all positive responses, it commits the transaction and notifies all the commit participants. If it receives one or more negative responses, it rolls back the entire transaction and notifies all the participants.

The two-phase commit protocol is shown in Figure 9-1.

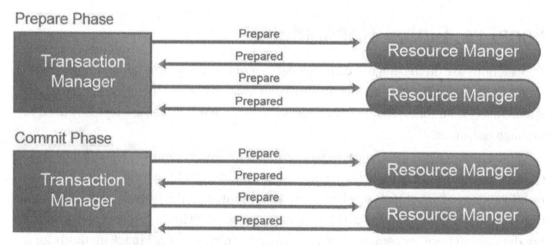

*Figure 9-1.*  *Two-phase commit protocol*

# Programmatic vs. Declarative Transactions

Developers have two choices when adding transaction capabilities to their application.

# Programmatically

In this scenario, the transaction management code for starting, committing, or rolling back transactions surrounds the business code. This can provide extreme flexibility but can also make maintenance difficult. The following code gives an example of the programmatic transaction using JTA and EJB 3.0:

```
@Stateless
@TransactionManagement(TransactionManagementType.BEAN)
public class OrderManager {

    @Resource
    private UserTransaction transaction;

    public void create(Order order) {
        try {
            transaction.begin();
            // business logic for processing order
            verifyAddress(order);
            processOrder(order);
            sendConfirmation(order);
            transaction.commit();
        } catch(Exception ex) {
            transaction.rollback();
        }
    }
}
```

# Declaratively

In this scenario, the container is responsible for starting, committing, or rolling back transactions. The developer usually specifies the transaction behavior via annotations or XML. This model cleanly separates the transaction management code from business logic. The following code gives an example of declarative transactions using JTA and EJB 3.0. When an exception happens during order processing, the setRollbackOnly method on the session context is called; this marks that the transaction must be rolled back.

```
@Stateless
@TransactionManagement(TransactionManagementType.CONTAINER)
public class OrderManager {

    @Resource
    private SessionContext context;

    @TransactionAttribute(TransactionAttributeType.REQUIRED)
    public void create(Order order) {
        try {
            // business logic for processing order
            verifyAddress(order);
            processOrder(order);
            sendConfirmation(order);
        } catch(Exception ex) {
            context.setRollbackOnly();
        }
    }
}
```

# Spring Transaction Abstraction

The Spring Framework provides a consistent programming model for handling both global and local transactions. The transaction abstraction hides the inner workings of different transaction APIs, such as JTA, JDBC, JMS, and JPA. It allows developers to write transaction-enabled code in an environment-neutral way. Behind the scenes, Spring simply delegates the transaction management to the underlying transaction providers.

Both programmatic and declarative transaction management models are supported without requiring any EJBs. The declarative approach is usually recommended, which we will use in this book.

Central to Spring's transaction management is the `PlatformTransactionManager` abstraction. It exposes key aspects of transaction management in a technology-independent manner. It is responsible for creating and managing transactions and is required for declarative and programmatic transactions. Several implementations of this interface, such as `JtaTransactionManager`,[1] `DataSourceTransactionManager`,[2] `JdbcTransactionManager`,[3] and `JmsTransactionManager`,[4] are available out of the box. The `PlatformTransactionManager`[5] API is shown in Listing 9-1.

***Listing 9-1.*** Source code of the PlatformTransactionManager

```
public interface PlatformTransactionManager extends TransactionManager {
    TransactionStatus getTransaction(@Nullable TransactionDefinition
    definition) throws TransactionException;

    void commit(TransactionStatus status) throws TransactionException;

    void rollback(TransactionStatus status) throws TransactionException;
}
```

The getTransaction method in the `PlatformTransactionManager` is used to retrieve an existing transaction. If no active transaction is found, this method might create a new transaction based on the transactional properties specified in the `TransactionDefinition` instance. The following is the list of properties that `TransactionDefinition` interface abstracts:

---

[1] https://docs.spring.io/spring-framework/docs/current/javadoc-api/org/springframework/transaction/jta/JtaTransactionManager.html

[2] https://docs.spring.io/spring-framework/docs/current/javadoc-api/org/springframework/jdbc/datasource/DataSourceTransactionManager.html

[3] https://docs.spring.io/spring-framework/docs/current/javadoc-api/org/springframework/jdbc/support/JdbcTransactionManager.html

[4] https://docs.spring.io/spring-framework/docs/current/javadoc-api/org/springframework/jms/connection/JmsTransactionManager.html

[5] https://docs.spring.io/spring-framework/docs/current/javadoc-api/org/springframework/transaction/PlatformTransactionManager.html

- *Read-only*: This property indicates whether this transaction is read-only.

- *Timeout*: This property mandates the time the transaction must complete. If the transaction fails to complete in the specified time, it will be rolled back automatically.

- *Isolation*: This property controls the degree of isolation among transactions. The possible isolation levels are discussed in Table 9-1.

- *Propagation*: Consider the scenario where an active transaction exists, and Spring encounters code that needs to be executed in a transaction. One option in that scenario is to execute the code in the existing transaction. Another option is to suspend the existing transaction and start a new transaction to execute the code. The propagation property can be used to define such transaction behavior. Possible values that include it on the `Propagation`[6] enum are `PROPAGATION_REQUIRED`, `PROPAGATION_REQUIRES_NEW`, `PROPAGATION_SUPPORTS`, etc.

The `getTransaction` method returns an instance of `TransactionStatus` representing the status of the current transaction. Application code can use this interface to check whether this is a new transaction or has been completed. The interface can also be used to request a transaction rollback programmatically. The other two methods in the `PlatformTransactionManager` are `commit` and `rollback`, which, as their names suggest, can be used to commit or roll back the transaction.

# Declarative Transactions Using Spring

Spring provides two ways to declaratively add transaction behavior to applications: pure XML and annotations. The annotation approach is very popular and greatly simplifies the configuration. To demonstrate declarative transactions, consider the simple scenario of inserting a new record in a `Person` table in a database. Listing 9-2 gives the `PersonRepositoryImpl` class with a `create` method implementing this scenario.

---

[6] https://docs.spring.io/spring-framework/docs/current/javadoc-api/org/springframework/transaction/annotation/Propagation.html

***Listing 9-2.*** Source code of an example to insert a row

```java
import org.springframework.jdbc.core.JdbcTemplate;
import org.springframework.stereotype.Repository;

@Repositorypublic class PersonRepositoryImpl implements PersonRepository{
   private JdbcTemplate jdbcTemplate;

   @Override
   public void create(String firstName, String lastName) {
      String sql = "INSERT INTO PERSON (FIRST_NAME, " + "LAST_NAME) VALUES
      (?, ?)";
      jdbcTemplate.update(sql, new Object[]{firstName, lastName});
   }
}
```

Listing 9-3 shows the `PersonRepository` interface that the preceding class implements.

***Listing 9-3.*** Example of a repository

```java
public interface PersonRepository {
   void create(String firstName, String lastName);
}
```

The next step is to make the `create` method transactional. This is done by annotating the method with `@Transactional`, as shown in Listing 9-4. (Note that I annotated the method in the implementation, not the interface method.)

***Listing 9-4.*** Example of a transaction

```java
import org.springframework.transaction.annotation.Transactional;
import org.springframework.stereotype.Repository;

@Repository
public class PersonRepositoryImpl implements PersonRepository {
   ...........
```

```
@Transactional
public void create(String firstName, String lastName) {
...........
}
}
```

The @Transactional annotation has several properties that can be used to specify additional information, such as propagation and isolation. Listing 9-5 shows the method with default isolation and REQUIRES_NEW propagation.

***Listing 9-5.*** Example of a method with the default propagation

```
@Transactional(propagation=Propagation.REQUIRES_NEW, isolation=Isolation.
DEFAULT)
public void create(String  firstName, String lastName) {
  //Logic of the method
}
```

The next step is to specify a transaction manager for Spring to use. Since you are going after a single database, the org.springframework.jdbc.datasource. DataSourceTransactionManager shown in Listing 9-6 is ideal for your case. From Listing 9-6, you can see that the DataSourceTransactionManager needs a data source to obtain and manage connections to the database.

***Listing 9-6.*** Example configuration of the transaction data source

```
<bean id="transactionManager" class="org.springframework.jdbc.datasource.
DataSourceTransactionManager">
    <property name="dataSource" ref="dataSource"/>
</bean>
```

The complete application context configuration file for declarative transaction management is given in Listing 9-7.

***Listing 9-7.*** Example of all the configuration

```
<?xml version="1.0" encoding="UTF-8"?>
<beans xmlns="http://www.springframework.org/schema/beans"
xmlns:xsi="http://www.w3.org/2001/XMLSchema-instance"
```

```
xmlns:context="http://www.springframework.org/schema/context"
xmlns:tx="http://www.springframework.org/schema/tx"
xmlns:aop="http://www.springframework.org/schema/aop"
xsi:schemaLocation="http://www.springframework.org/schema/beans
http://www.springframework.org/schema/beans/spring-beans.xsd
http://www.springframework.org/schema/context
http://www.springframework.org/schema/context/spring-context.xsd
http://www.springframework.org/schema/tx
http://www.springframework.org/schema/tx/spring-tx.xsd
http://www.springframework.org/schema/aop
http://www.springframework.org/schema/tx/spring-aop.xsd">

    <context:component-scan base-package="com.apress.book.ldap" />
    <bean id="transactionManager" class="org.springframework.jdbc.
    datasource.DataSourceTransactionManager">
        <property name="dataSource" ref="dataSource"/>
    </bean>
    <tx:annotation-driven transaction-manager="transactionManager"/>
    <aop:aspectj-autoproxy />
</beans>
```

The <tx:annotation-driven/> tag indicates that you are using annotation-based transaction management. This tag, along with <aop:aspectj-autoproxy />, instructs Spring to use Aspect-Oriented Programming (AOP) and create proxies that manage transactions on behalf of the annotated class. So, when a call is made to a transactional method, the proxy intercepts the call and uses the transaction manager to obtain a transaction (new or existing). The called method is then invoked, and if the method completes successfully, the proxy using the transaction manager will commit the transaction. If the method fails, throwing an exception, the transaction will be rolled back. This AOP-based transaction processing is shown in Figure 9-2.

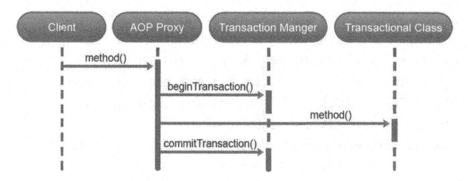

**Figure 9-2.** *AOP-based Spring transaction*

---

**Note**    The explanation about transactions has the goal that the reader understand the main idea and which things imply a transaction.

---

# LDAP Transaction Support

The LDAP protocol requires that all LDAP operations (modify or delete) follow ACID properties. This transactional behavior ensures consistency of the information stored in the LDAP server. However, LDAP does not define transactions across multiple operations. Consider the scenario where you want to add two LDAP entries as one atomic operation. Completing the operation means that both entries get added to the LDAP server. If there is a failure and one of the entries can't be added, the server will automatically undo the addition of the other entry. Such transactional behavior is not part of the LDAP specification and does not exist in the world of LDAP. Also, the lack of transactional semantics, such as commit and rollback, makes it impossible to assure data consistency across multiple LDAP servers.

Though transactions are not part of the LDAP specification, servers such as IBM Tivoli Directory Server and ApacheDS provide transaction support. The Begin transaction (OID 1.3.18.0.2.12.5) and End transaction (OID 1.3.18.0.2.12.6) extended controls supported by the IBM Tivoli Directory Server can restrict a set of operations inside a transaction. The RFC 5805[7] attempts to standardize transactions in LDAP and is currently in an experimental state.

---

**Note**    OIDs or object identifiers are used on LDAP in common elements on a schema, controls, and extended operations.

---

# Spring LDAP Transaction Support

The lack of transactions in LDAP might initially seem surprising. More importantly, it can hinder enterprises' widespread adoption of directory servers. To address this, Spring LDAP offers non-LDAP/JNDI-specific compensating transaction support. This transaction support integrates tightly with the Spring transaction management infrastructure you saw in the earlier section. Figure 9-3 shows the components responsible for Spring LDAP transaction support.

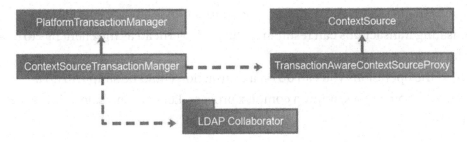

***Figure 9-3.***  *Spring LDAP transaction support*

The ContextSourceTransactionManager class implements PlatformTransaction Manager and manages LDAP-based transactions. This class and its collaborators keep track of the LDAP operations performed inside the transaction and record the state before each operation. If the transaction were to roll back, the transaction manager would take steps to restore the original state. The transaction manager uses a TransactionAwareContextSourceProxy to achieve this behavior instead of working

---

[7]https://datatracker.ietf.org/doc/html/rfc5805

directly with `LdapContextSource`. This proxy class also ensures that a single `javax.naming.directory.DirContext` instance is used throughout the transaction and will not be closed until the transaction is finished.

# Compensating Transactions

A compensating transaction undoes the effects of a previously committed transaction and restores the system to a previous consistent state. Consider a transaction that involves booking an airline ticket. A compensating transaction in that scenario is an operation that cancels the reservation. In the case of LDAP, if an operation adds a new LDAP entry, the corresponding compensating transaction simply involves removing that entry.

Compensating transactions are useful for resources such as LDAP and web services without standard transactional support. However, it is important to remember that compensating transactions provide an illusion and can never replace real transactions. So, if a server crashes or the connection to the LDAP server is lost before the compensating transaction completes, you will have inconsistent data. Also, concurrent transactions might see invalid data since the transaction is already committed. Compensating transactions can result in additional overhead as the client has to deal with extra undo operations.

Most of the operations you can do on a transaction could be simple to do a rollback but, in some cases, imply a complex process. Let's see in Table 9-2 what each operation is.

***Table 9-2.*** *Operations and Rollback Process*

| Operation | Description | Rollback |
|---|---|---|
| bind | This operation implies creating a record using a DN. | Unbind the entry recorded using the DN. |
| rename | This operation implies changing the name of an entry. | Revert the name to the previous status. |
| unbind | This operation implies making a record from a DN and creating a temporary DN. | Use the entry on a temporary location to rename and go back to the previous status. |
| rebind | Create a record from a DN and add new attributes; this implies calculating a new DN. | Use the entry on a temporary location to rename and return to the previous status. |
| modifyAttributes | This operation will modify certain attributes of a record. | Check which attribute changes to revert the operation. |

As you can read in the previous table, most of the operations imply creating a temporary record with the previous information, so in the case that something bad happens, LDAP will rename the record with the previous name. You will feel that everything works as a database transaction.

You need to consider the renaming strategies, which imply how Spring LDAP will define the name of the previous record to move to a temporal location. Until this book's version, there are only two different strategies:

- *DefaultTempEntryRenamingStrategy*: This is the simplest strategy because it implies adding a suffix on the DN of each record. You can specify a particular *temporal-suffix* of every value you want. On the following block, you will see what the configuration of the ***transaction-manager*** looks like:

```
<ldap:transaction-manager context-source-ref="contextSourceTarget"
id="transactionManager">

        <ldap:default-renaming-strategy temp-suffix="temporal-suffix"/>

</ldap:transaction-manager>
```

- *DifferentSubtreeTempEntryRenamingStrategy*: On this strategy, the temporal record will append a part on the DN. For example, if you have a record *cn=Doe, ou=Patrons*, the temporal information will exist on *cn=Doe, ou=tempEntries*. On the following block, you will see what the configuration of the ***transaction-manager*** looks like:

```
<ldap:transaction-manager context-source-ref="contextSourceTarget"
id="transactionManager">

        <ldap:different-subtree-renaming-strategy subtree-node="ou=patrons,
        dc=inflinx,dc=com"/>

</ldap:transaction-manager>
```

To understand Spring LDAP transactions better, let's create a Patron service with transactional behavior. Listing 9-8 shows the `PatronService` interface with just a create method.

***Listing 9-8.*** The interface of the service to create a Patron

```
package com.apress.book.ldap.transactions;

import java.util.List;

import com.apress.book.ldap.domain.Patron;

public interface PatronService {

    void create(Patron patron);
}
```

Listing 9-9 shows the implementation of this service interface. The `create` method implementation simply delegates the call to the DAO layer.

***Listing 9-9.*** Implementing the service to create a Patron

```
package com.apress.book.ldap.transactions;

import java.util.List;

import com.apress.book.ldap.domain.Patron;
import com.apress.book.ldap.repository.PatronDao;
import org.slf4j.Logger;
import org.slf4j.LoggerFactory;
import org.springframework.beans.factory.annotation.Autowired;
```

```
import org.springframework.beans.factory.annotation.Qualifier;
import org.springframework.stereotype.Service;
import org.springframework.transaction.annotation.Transactional;
@Service("patronService")
@Transactional

public class PatronServiceImpl implements PatronService {

    private static final Logger logger = LoggerFactory.
    getLogger(PatronServiceImpl.class);

    private PatronDao patronDao;
    public PatronServiceImpl(@Autowired @Qualifier("patronDao") PatronDao
    patronDao) {
        this.patronDao = patronDao;
    }

    @Override
    public void create(Patron patron) {
        logger.info("Begining the transaction");
        patronDao.create(patron);
        logger.info("Ending the patron creation");
    }
}
```

Notice the use of @Transactional annotation at the top of the class declaration. Listing 9-10 shows the PatronDao interface of the Dao.

***Listing 9-10.*** The Dao interface to create a Patron

```
package com.apress.book.ldap.repository;

import java.util.List;

import com.apress.book.ldap.domain.Patron;

public interface PatronDao {

    void create(Patron patron);
}
```

Listing 9-11 shows the implementation of PatronDao.

***Listing 9-11.***  The Dao implementation to create a Patron

```
package com.apress.book.ldap.repository;

import com.apress.book.ldap.domain.Patron;
import com.apress.book.ldap.mapper.PatronContextMapper;
import org.slf4j.Logger;
import org.slf4j.LoggerFactory;
import org.springframework.beans.factory.annotation.Autowired;
import org.springframework.beans.factory.annotation.Qualifier;
import org.springframework.ldap.core.DirContextAdapter;
import org.springframework.ldap.core.DirContextOperations;
import org.springframework.ldap.core.DistinguishedName;
import org.springframework.ldap.core.LdapTemplate;
import org.springframework.ldap.filter.EqualsFilter;
import org.springframework.stereotype.Repository;
import org.springframework.transaction.annotation.Transactional;

@Repository("patronDao")
@Transactional
public class PatronDaoImpl implements PatronDao {

    private static final Logger logger = LoggerFactory.
    getLogger(PatronDaoImpl.class);

    private static final String PATRON_BASE = "ou=patrons,dc=inflinx,
    dc=com";

    private LdapTemplate ldapTemplate;

    public PatronDaoImpl(@Autowired @Qualifier("ldapTemplate") LdapTemplate
    ldapTemplate) {
        this.ldapTemplate = ldapTemplate;
    }

    @Override
    public void create(Patron patron) {
        logger.info("Inside the create method ...");
```

```
    DistinguishedName dn = new DistinguishedName(PATRON_BASE);
    dn.add("uid", patron.getUid());

    DirContextAdapter context = new DirContextAdapter(dn);
    context.setAttributeValues("objectClass",
            new String[] { "top", "uidObject", "person",
            "organizationalPerson", "inetOrgPerson" });
    context.setAttributeValue("sn", patron.getLastName());
    context.setAttributeValue("cn", patron.getFullName());
    ldapTemplate.bind(context);
    }
}
```

As you can see from these two listings, you create a Patron DAO and its implementation following the concepts discussed in Chapter 5. The next step is to create a Spring configuration file that will autowire the components and include the transaction semantics. Listing 9-12 gives the contents of the configuration file which is located in the **src/test/resources** with the name repositoryContext-test.xml. Here, you are using the locally installed OpenDJ LDAP server.

***Listing 9-12.*** All the configurations to applications to use transactions

```
<?xml version="1.0" encoding="UTF-8"?>
<beans xmlns="http://www.springframework.org/schema/beans"
        xmlns:xsi="http://www.w3.org/2001/XMLSchema-instance"
        xmlns:ldap="http://www.springframework.org/schema/ldap"
        xmlns:context="http://www.springframework.org/schema/context"
        xmlns:tx="http://www.springframework.org/schema/tx"
        xsi:schemaLocation="http://www.springframework.org/schema/beans
        https://www.springframework.org/schema/beans/spring-beans.xsd
                        http://www.springframework.org/schema/ldap
                        https://www.springframework.org/schema/ldap/
                        spring-ldap.xsd
                http://www.springframework.org/schema/tx http://www.
                springframework.org/schema/tx/spring-tx.xsd
```

```
                        http://www.springframework.org/schema/context
                        http://www.springframework.org/schema/context/
                        spring-context.xsd">

  <context:component-scan base-package="com.apress.book.ldap" />

  <ldap:context-source id="contextSourceTarget"
                                  password="secret"
                                  url="ldap://127.0.0.1:18880"
                                  username="uid=admin,ou=system"/>

  <!-- Populates the LDAP server with initial data -->
  <bean class="org.springframework.ldap.test.LdifPopulator" depends-
  on="embeddedLdapServer">
        <property name="contextSource" ref="contextSource" />
        <property name="resource" value="classpath:patrons.ldif" />
        <property name="base" value="dc=inflinx,dc=com" />
        <property name="clean" value="true" />
        <property name="defaultBase" value="dc=inflinx,dc=com" />
  </bean>

  <bean id="embeddedLdapServer" class="org.springframework.ldap.test.
  unboundid.EmbeddedLdapServerFactoryBean">
        <property name="partitionName" value="inflinx"/>
        <property name="partitionSuffix" value="dc=inflinx,dc=com" />
        <property name="port" value="18880" />
  </bean>

  <bean id="ldapTemplate" class="org.springframework.ldap.core.
  LdapTemplate">
        <constructor-arg ref="contextSource" />
  </bean>

  <bean id="contextSource" class="org.springframework.ldap.transaction.
  compensating.manager.TransactionAwareContextSourceProxy">
        <constructor-arg ref="contextSourceTarget" />
  </bean>
```

```
<ldap:transaction-manager context-source-ref="contextSourceTarget"
id="transactionManager">
        <ldap:default-renaming-strategy temp-suffix="temporal-
        suffix"/>
</ldap:transaction-manager>
<tx:annotation-driven transaction-manager="transactionManager" />
</beans>
```

In this configuration, you start by defining a new LdapContextSource and providing it with your LDAP information. Up to this point, you referred to this bean with the id contextSource and injected it for use by LdapTemplate. However, in this new configuration, you are calling it contextSourceTarget. You then configure an instance of TransactionAwareContextSourceProxy and inject the contextSource bean into it. This newly configured TransactionAwareContextSourceProxy bean has the id contextSource and is used by LdapTemplate. Finally, you configure the transaction manager using the ContextSourceTransactionManager class. As discussed earlier, this configuration allows a single DirContext instance to be used during a single transaction, enabling transaction commit/rollback.

With this information in place, let's verify if your create method and configuration behave correctly during a transaction rollback. To simulate a transaction rollback, let's modify the create method in the PatronServiceImpl class to throw a RuntimeException, as shown:

```
@Override
public void create(Patron patron) {
    logger.info("Begining the transaction");
    patronDao.create(patron);
    logger.info("Ending the patron creation");
    throw new RuntimeException(); // Will roll back the transaction
}
```

The next step in verifying the expected behavior is to write a test case that calls PatronServiceImpl's create method to create a new Patron. The test case is shown in Listing 9-13. The repositoryContext-test.xml file contains the XML configuration defined in Listing 9-12.

*Listing 9-13.*  A test case that validates if the create method works or not

```
package com.apress.book.ldap.transactions;

import com.apress.book.ldap.domain.Patron;
import org.junit.jupiter.api.DisplayName;
import org.junit.jupiter.api.Test;
import org.junit.jupiter.api.extension.ExtendWith;
import org.springframework.beans.factory.annotation.Autowired;

import org.springframework.transaction.IllegalTransactionStateException;

import org.springframework.test.context.ContextConfiguration;
import org.springframework.test.context.junit.jupiter.SpringExtension;

import static org.junit.jupiter.api.Assertions.*;

@ExtendWith(SpringExtension.class)
@ContextConfiguration("classpath:repositoryContext-test.xml")
@DisplayName("Patron service with transactions use cases")
class PatronServiceImplTest {

    @Autowired
    private PatronService patronService;

    @Test
    @DisplayName("Transaction will be abort during the process")
    void should_not_create_a_patron() {
        Patron patron = new Patron();

        patron.setUid("patron10001");
        patron.setLastName("Patron10001");
        patron.setFullName("Test Patron10001");

        assertThrows(RuntimeException.class, () -> {
            patronService.create(patron);
        });

        assertThrows( IllegalTransactionStateException.class, () -> {
```

```
    patronService.find("patron10001");
  });
}
```

}

When you run the test, Spring LDAP should create a new patron; rolling back the transaction would remove the newly created patron. The inner workings of Spring LDAP's compensating transactions can be seen in the OpenDJ log file. The log file is named *access* and is located in the OPENDJ_INSTALL\logs folder, but consider that you will see it only if you use a real LDAP instead of an embedded one, which only shows the application logs on the console.

Listing 9-14 shows a portion of the log file for this create operation. You will notice that when the create method on the PatronDaoImpl gets invoked, an "ADD REQ" command is sent to the OpenDJ server to add the new Patron entry. When Spring LDAP rolls back the transaction, a new "DELETE REQ" command is sent to remove the entry.

***Listing 9-14.*** Logs of the OpenDJ with the transactions

```
[14/Sep/2023:15:03:09 -0300] CONNECT conn=52 from=127.0.0.1:54792
to=127.0.0.1:11389 protocol=LDAP
[14/Sep/2023:15:03:09 -0300] BIND REQ conn=52 op=0 msgID=1 type=SIMPLE
dn="cn=Directory Manager"
[14/Sep/2023:15:03:09 -0300] BIND RES conn=52 op=0 msgID=1 result=0
authDN="cn=Directory Manager,cn=Root DNs,cn=config" etime=0
[14/Sep/2023:15:03:09 -0300]                    ADD REQ                conn=52 op=1
msgID=2 dn="uid=patron10001,ou=patrons,dc=inflinx,dc=com"
[14/Sep/2023:15:03:09 -0300] ADD RES conn=52 op=1 msgID=2 result=0 etime=2
[14/Sep/2023:15:03:09 -0300]                    DELETE REQ              conn=52 op=2
msgID=3 dn="uid=patron10001,ou=patrons,dc=inflinx,dc=com"
[14/Sep/2023:15:03:09 -0300] DELETE RES conn=52 op=2 msgID=3
result=0 etime=4
[14/Sep/2023:15:03:09 -0300] UNBIND REQ conn=52 op=3 msgID=4
[14/Sep/2023:15:03:09 -0300] DISCONNECT conn=52 reason="Client Unbind""
```

Remember that you will only see all these logs if you change the configuration to a real LDAP. If you use an Embedded LDAP like Unboundid, you will see more or less the information to understand what happened, but in another format like Listing 9-15.

***Listing 9-15.*** Logs of the application with the result of the operations

```
15:10:30.570 [main] DEBUG o.s.l.t.c.m.ContextSourceTransactionManager -
Creating new transaction with name [com.apress.book.ldap.transactions.
PatronServiceImpl.create]: PROPAGATION_REQUIRED,ISOLATION_DEFAULT
15:10:30.571 [main] DEBUG o.s.l.c.s.AbstractContextSource - Got Ldap
context on server 'ldap://127.0.0.1:18880'
15:10:30.571 [main] INFO  c.a.b.l.t.PatronServiceImpl - Begining the
transaction
15:10:30.571 [main] INFO  c.a.b.ldap.repository.PatronDaoImpl - Inside the
create method ...
15:10:30.572 [main] DEBUG o.s.l.t.c.LdapCompensatingTransactionOperation
Factory - Bind operation recorded
15:10:30.572 [main] DEBUG o.s.l.t.c.BindOperationExecutor - Performing bind
operation
15:10:30.573 [main] DEBUG o.s.l.t.c.m.TransactionAwareDirContextInvocation
Handler - Closing context
15:10:30.573 [main] DEBUG o.s.l.t.c.m.TransactionAwareDirContextInvocation
Handler - Leaving transactional context open
15:10:30.574 [main] INFO  c.a.b.l.t.PatronServiceImpl - Ending the patron
creation
15:10:30.574 [main] DEBUG o.s.l.t.c.m.ContextSourceTransactionManager -
Initiating transaction rollback
15:10:30.574 [main] DEBUG o.s.t.c.s.DefaultCompensatingTransactionOperation
Manager - Performing rollback
15:10:30.574 [main] DEBUG o.s.t.c.s.AbstractCompensatingTransactionManager
Delegate - Cleaning stored transaction synchronization
15:10:30.574 [main] DEBUG o.s.l.t.c.m.ContextSourceTransactionManager
Delegate - Closing target context
```

This test verified that Spring LDAP's compensating transaction infrastructure would automatically remove the newly added entry if the transaction were to roll back for any reason.

Let's continue implementing the `PatronServiceImpl` methods and verify their transactional behaviors. Listings 9-16 and 9-17 show the `delete` method added to the `PatronService` interface and `PatronServiceImpl` class, respectively. Again, the actual delete method implementation is straightforward and simply involves calling the `PatronDaoImpl`'s delete method.

***Listing 9-16.*** The interface of the service to create and delete a Patron

```
package com.apress.book.ldap.transactions;

import java.util.List;

import com.apress.book.ldap.domain.Patron;

public interface PatronService {

    void create(Patron patron);

    void delete(String id);
}
```

Listing 9-17 shows the implementation of the service.

***Listing 9-17.*** The implementation of the service to delete a Patron

```
// Import and annotations removed for brevity
public class PatronServiceImpl implements PatronService {
    // Create method removed for brevity
    @Override
    public void delete(String id) {
       patronDao.delete(id);
    }
}
```

Now let's define the method on the PatronDao that appears in Listing 9-18.

**_Listing 9-18._** The Dao interface to make a Patron

```
package com.apress.book.ldap.repository;
import java.util.List;

import com.apress.book.ldap.domain.Patron;

public interface PatronDao {

    void create(Patron patron);
    void delete(String id);
}
```

Listing 9-19 shows the `PatronDaoImpl`'s `delete` method implementation.

**_Listing 9-19._** The Dao implementation to create a Patron

```
package com.apress.book.ldap.repository;
import java.util.List;

import com.apress.book.ldap.domain.Patron;

// Annotation and imports removed for brevity
public class PatronDaoImpl implements PatronDao {
    // Removed other methods for brevity
    @Override
    public void delete(String id) {
        DistinguishedName dn = new DistinguishedName(PATRON_BASE);
        dn.add("uid", id);
        ldapTemplate.unbind(dn);
    }
}
```

With this code in hand, let's write a test case that invokes your `delete` method in a transaction. Listing 9-20 shows the test case. The "uid=patron98" is an existing entry in your OpenDJ server and was created during the LDIF import in Chapter 3.

***Listing 9-20.*** Test to check if the delete works fine

```
// Annotation and imports removed for brevity
class PatronServiceImplTest {
    //Removed other methods for brevity
    @Test
    @DisplayName("Transaction will works")
    public void should_delete_a_patron() {
        patronService.delete("patron98");
    }
}
```

When you run this test case and invoke the `PatronServiceImpl`'s `delete` method in a transaction, Spring LDAP's transaction infrastructure simply renames the entry under a newly calculated temporary DN. With a rename, Spring LDAP is moving your entry to a different location on the LDAP server. Upon a successful commit, the temporary entry is removed. On a rollback, the entry is renamed and thus will be moved from the temporary location to its original location.

Now, run the method and watch the *access* log under OpenDJ. Listing 9-21 shows the log file portion for the delete operation. Notice that the delete operation results in a "MODIFYDN REQ" command that renames the entry to be deleted. Upon a successful commit, the renamed entry is removed via the "DELETE REQ" command.

***Listing 9-21.*** Logs of the OpenDJ with the transactions

```
[14/Sep/2023:16:21:56 -0300] CONNECT conn=54 from=127.0.0.1:54824
to=127.0.0.1:11389 protocol=LDAP
[14/Sep/2023:16:21:56 -0300] BIND REQ conn=54 op=0 msgID=1 type=SIMPLE
dn="cn=Directory Manager"
[14/Sep/2023:16:21:56 -0300] BIND RES conn=54 op=0 msgID=1 result=0
authDN="cn=Directory Manager,cn=Root DNs,cn=config" etime=1
[14/Sep/2023:16:21:56 -0300]              MODIFYDN REQ              conn=54
op=1 msgID=2 dn="uid=patron97,ou=patrons,dc=inflinx,dc=com"
newRDN="uid=patron97_temp" deleteOldRDN=true newSuperior="ou=patrons,
dc=inflinx,dc=com
[14/Sep/2023:16:21:56 -0300] MODIFYDN RES conn=54 op=1 msgID=2
result=0 etime=4
```

```
[14/Sep/2013:16:21:56 -0300]            DELETE REQ            conn=54 op=2
msgID=3 dn="uid=patron97_temp,ou=patrons,dc=inflinx,dc=com"
[14/Sep/2023:16:21:56 -0300] DELETE RES conn=54 op=2 msgID=3
result=0 etime=2
[14/Sep/2023:16:21:56 -0300] UNBIND REQ conn=54 op=3 msgID=4
[14/Sep/2023:16:21:56 -0300] DISCONNECT conn=54 reason="Client Unbind"
```

Listing 9-22 shows you the logs on the application console.

***Listing 9-22.*** Logs of the application with the result of the operations

```
17:07:25.338 [main] DEBUG o.s.l.t.c.m.ContextSourceTransactionManager -
Creating new transaction with name [com.apress.book.ldap.transactions.
PatronServiceImpl.delete]: PROPAGATION_REQUIRED,ISOLATION_DEFAULT
17:07:25.339 [main] DEBUG o.s.l.c.s.AbstractContextSource - Got Ldap
context on server 'ldap://127.0.0.1:18880'
17:07:25.341 [main] DEBUG o.s.l.t.c.UnbindOperationExecutor - Performing
operation for unbind - renaming to temporary entry.
17:07:25.343 [main] DEBUG o.s.l.t.c.m.TransactionAwareDirContextInvocation
Handler - Closing context
17:07:25.343 [main] DEBUG o.s.l.t.c.m.TransactionAwareDirContextInvocation
Handler - Leaving transactional context open
17:07:25.343 [main] DEBUG o.s.l.t.c.m.ContextSourceTransactionManager -
Initiating transaction commit
17:07:25.343 [main] DEBUG o.s.t.c.s.DefaultCompensatingTransactionOperation
Manager - Performing commit
17:07:25.343 [main] DEBUG o.s.l.t.c.UnbindOperationExecutor - Committing
unbind operation - unbinding temporary entry
17:07:25.343 [main] DEBUG o.s.t.c.s.AbstractCompensatingTransactionManager
Delegate - Cleaning stored transaction synchronization
17:07:25.343 [main] DEBUG o.s.l.t.c.m.ContextSourceTransactionManager
Delegate - Closing target context
```

Let's simulate a rollback for the delete method in the PatronServiceImpl class, as shown in Listing 9-23.

***Listing 9-23.*** The implementation of the service to delete a Patron

```
// Import and annotations removed for brevity
public class PatronServiceImpl implements PatronService {
    // Create method removed for brevity
    @Override
    public void delete(String id) {
        patronDao.delete(id);
        throw new RuntimeException(); // Need this to simulate a rollback
    }
}
```

Let's update the test case with a new `Patron` ID that you know still exists in the OpenDJ server, as shown in Listing 9-24.

***Listing 9-24.*** Test to check if the delete works fine

```
// Annotation and imports removed for brevity
class PatronServiceImplTest {
    //Removed other methods for brevity
    @Test
    void should_delete_a_patron() {
        assertThrows(RuntimeException.class, () -> {
            patronService.delete("patron96");
        });
    }
}
```

When this code is run, the expected behavior is that Spring LDAP will rename the patron96 entry by changing its DN and then, upon rollback, will rename it again to the right DN. Listing 9-25 shows the OpenDJ's *access* log for the preceding operation. Note that the delete operation first results in the renaming of the entry by sending the first MODIFYDN REQ. Upon a rollback, a second "MODIFYDN REQ" is sent to rename the entry back to the original location.

241

***Listing 9-25.*** Logs of the OpenDJ with the transactions

```
[14/Sep/2023:16:33:43 -0300] CONNECT conn=55 from=127.0.0.1:54829
to=127.0.0.1:11389 protocol=LDAP
[14/Sep/2023:16:33:43 -0300] BIND REQ conn=55 op=0 msgID=1 type=SIMPLE
dn="cn=Directory Manager"
[14/Sep/2023:16:33:43 -0300] BIND RES conn=55 op=0 msgID=1 result=0
authDN="cn=Directory Manager,cn=Root DNs,cn=config" etime=0
[14/Sep/2023:16:33:43 -0300]              MODIFYDN REQ              conn=55
op=1 msgID=2 dn="uid=patron96,ou=patrons,dc=inflinx,dc=com"
newRDN="uid=patron96_temp" deleteOldRDN=true newSuperior="ou=patrons,
dc=inflinx,dc=com
[14/Sep/2023:16:33:43 -0300] MODIFYDN RES conn=55 op=1 msgID=2
result=0 etime=1
[14/Sep/2023:16:33:43 -0300]              MODIFYDN REQ              conn=55
op=2 msgID=3 dn="uid=patron96_temp,ou=patrons,dc=inflinx,dc=com"
newRDN="uid=patron96" deleteOldRDN=true newSuperior="ou=patrons,dc=infl
inx,dc=com
[14/Sep/2023:16:33:43 -0300] MODIFYDN RES conn=55 op=2 msgID=3
result=0 etime=0
[14/Sep/2023:16:33:43 -0300] UNBIND REQ conn=55 op=3 msgID=4
[14/Sep/2023:16:33:43 -0300] DISCONNECT conn=55 reason="Client Unbind"
```

Listing 9-26 shows you the logs on the application console.

***Listing 9-26.*** Logs of the application with the result of the operations

```
17:19:17.284 [main] DEBUG o.s.l.t.c.m.ContextSourceTransactionManager -
Creating new transaction with name [com.apress.book.ldap.transactions.
PatronServiceImpl.delete]: PROPAGATION_REQUIRED,ISOLATION_DEFAULT
17:19:17.285 [main] DEBUG o.s.l.c.s.AbstractContextSource - Got Ldap
context on server 'ldap://127.0.0.1:18880'
17:19:17.286 [main] DEBUG o.s.l.t.c.UnbindOperationExecutor - Performing
operation for unbind - renaming to temporary entry.
17:19:17.288 [main] DEBUG o.s.l.t.c.m.TransactionAwareDirContextInvocation
Handler - Closing context
```

```
17:19:17.288 [main] DEBUG o.s.l.t.c.m.TransactionAwareDirContextInvocation
Handler - Leaving transactional context open
17:19:17.288 [main] DEBUG o.s.l.t.c.m.ContextSourceTransactionManager -
Initiating transaction rollback
17:19:17.288 [main] DEBUG o.s.t.c.s.DefaultCompensatingTransactionOperation
Manager - Performing rollback
17:19:17.289 [main] DEBUG o.s.t.c.s.AbstractCompensatingTransactionManager
Delegate - Cleaning stored transaction synchronization
17:19:17.289 [main] DEBUG o.s.l.t.c.m.ContextSourceTransactionManager
Delegate - Closing target context
```

For an update operation, as you can guess by now, the Spring LDAP infrastructure calculates the compensating ModificationItem list for the modifications made on the entry. On a commit, nothing needs to be done. But upon a rollback, the computed compensating ModificationItem list will be written back.

# Summary

In this chapter, you explored the basics of transactions and looked at Spring LDAP's transaction support. Spring LDAP records the state in the LDAP tree before operating. If a rollback were to happen, Spring LDAP would perform compensating operations to restore the previous state. Remember that this compensating transaction support gives an illusion of atomicity but doesn't guarantee it.

In the next chapter, you will explore other Spring LDAP features, such as connection pooling and LDIF parsing.

# CHAPTER 10

# Odds and Ends

In this chapter, you will learn

- How to perform authentication using Spring LDAP

- How to parse LDIF files

- LDAP connection pooling

## Authentication Using Spring LDAP

Authentication is a common operation performed against LDAP servers. This usually involves verifying a username and password against the information stored in the directory server.

One approach for implementing authentication using Spring LDAP is via the getContext method of the `ContextSource` class. Here is the getContext method API:

```
DirContext getContext(String principal, String credentials) throws
NamingException
```

The `principal` parameter is the fully qualified DN of the user, and the `credentials` parameter is the user's password. The method uses the passed-in information to authenticate against LDAP. Upon successful authentication, the method returns a `DirContext` instance representing the user's entry. Authentication failures are communicated to the caller via an exception. Listing 10-1 defines the interface with the method to validate whether someone could be authenticated.

© Balaji Varanasi and Andres Sacco 2023
B. Varanasi and A. Sacco, *Practical Spring LDAP*, https://doi.org/10.1007/979-8-8688-0002-3_10

***Listing 10-1.*** DAO interface with the authenticate method

```
package com.apress.book.ldap.repository;

public interface AuthenticationDao {
    boolean authenticate(String userid, String password);
}
```

Listing 10-2 gives a DAO implementation for authenticating patrons in your Library application using the getContext technique.

***Listing 10-2.*** Basic implementation of the authentication method

```
package com.apress.book.ldap.repository;

import javax.naming.directory.DirContext;

import org.slf4j.Logger;
import org.slf4j.LoggerFactory;
import org.springframework.beans.factory.annotation.Autowired;
import org.springframework.beans.factory.annotation.Qualifier;
import org.springframework.ldap.NamingException;
import org.springframework.ldap.core.ContextSource;
import org.springframework.ldap.core.DistinguishedName;
import org.springframework.ldap.support.LdapUtils;
import org.springframework.stereotype.Repository;

@Repository("authenticationDao")
public class AuthenticationDaoImpl implements AuthenticationDao {

    private static final Logger logger = LoggerFactory.
    getLogger(AuthenticationDaoImpl.class);
    public static final String BASE_DN = "ou=patrons,dc=inflinx,dc=com";

    private ContextSource contextSource;
    public AuthenticationDaoImpl(@Autowired @Qualifier("contextSource")
    ContextSource contextSource) {
        this.contextSource = contextSource;
    }
```

```
@Override
public boolean authenticate(String userid, String password) {

    DistinguishedName dn = new DistinguishedName(BASE_DN);
    dn.add("uid", userid);

    DirContext authenticatedContext = null;
    try {
        authenticatedContext = contextSource.getContext(dn.toString(),
        password);
        return Boolean.TRUE;
    } catch (NamingException ex) {
        logger.error("{}: {}", ex.getClass(), ex.getMessage());
        return Boolean.FALSE;
    } finally {
        LdapUtils.closeContext(authenticatedContext);
    }
}
}
```

The getContext method requires a fully qualified DN of the user entry. Hence, the authentication method starts by creating a DistinguishedName instance with the supplied "ou=patrons,dc=inflinx,dc=com" base. Then, you append the provided userid to the DN to create the patron's fully qualified DN. The authentication method then invokes the getContext method, passing in the string representation of the patron's DN and password. A successful authentication simply exits the method with a return value of true. Notice that in the finally block, you are closing the obtained context.

Listing 10-3 shows a JUnit test to verify the proper working of this authenticate method.

***Listing 10-3.*** Test to check if the authentication method works

```
package com.apress.book.ldap.repository;

import org.junit.jupiter.api.DisplayName;
import com.apress.book.ldap.repository.AuthenticationDao;
import org.junit.jupiter.api.Test;
import org.junit.jupiter.api.extension.ExtendWith;
```

```java
import org.springframework.beans.factory.annotation.Autowired;
import org.springframework.beans.factory.annotation.Qualifier;
import org.springframework.test.context.ContextConfiguration;
import org.springframework.test.context.junit.jupiter.SpringExtension;

import static org.junit.jupiter.api.Assertions.assertFalse;
import static org.junit.jupiter.api.Assertions.assertTrue;

@ExtendWith(SpringExtension.class)
@ContextConfiguration("classpath:repositoryContext-test.xml")
@DisplayName("Authentication Dao test cases")
class AuthenticationDaoTest {
    @Autowired
    @Qualifier("authenticationDao")
    private AuthenticationDao authenticationDao;

    @Test
    @DisplayName("Check is the authentication mechanism works fine")
    void should_authentication_works() {
        boolean authResult = authenticationDao.authenticate("patron0",
        "password");

        assertTrue(authResult);
        authResult = authenticationDao.authenticate("patron0",
        "invalidPassword");
        assertFalse(authResult);
    }
}
```

The repositoryContext-test.xml, located in the folder **src/test/resources**, associated with Listing 10-3 is shown in Listing 10-4. In this scenario, you are working with your installed OpenDJ LDAP server.

***Listing 10-4.*** Structure of the configuration

```xml
<?xml version="1.0" encoding="UTF-8"?>
<beans xmlns="http://www.springframework.org/schema/beans"
       xmlns:xsi="http://www.w3.org/2001/XMLSchema-instance"
       xmlns:context="http://www.springframework.org/schema/context"
```

```
    xsi:schemaLocation="http://www.springframework.org/schema/beans
    http://www.springframework.org/schema/beans/spring-beans.xsd
     http://www.springframework.org/schema/context http://www.
    springframework.org/schema/context/spring-context.xsd">

<context:component-scan base-package="com.apress.book.ldap" />

<bean id="contextSource" class="org.springframework.ldap.core.support.
LdapContextSource">
    <property name="url" value="ldap://localhost:11389" />
    <property name="userDn" value="cn=Directory Manager" />
    <property name="password" value="secret" />
    <property name="base" value="ou=employees,dc=inflinx,dc=com"/>
</bean>

<bean id="ldapTemplate" class="org.springframework.ldap.core.
LdapTemplate">
    <constructor-arg ref="contextSource"  />
</bean>

</beans>
```

The only drawback with the implementation shown in Listing 10-4 is that the getContext method requires the fully qualified DN of the patron entry. There could be scenarios where the client's code might not know the fully qualified DN of the user. In Listing 10-2, you append a hard-coded value to create the fully qualified DN. This approach will fail if you want to use the Listing 10-2 code to authenticate your library's employees. To address such situations, Spring LDAP added several variations of the following authenticate method to the LdapTemplate class:

```
boolean authenticate(String base, String filter,  String password)
```

This authenticate method uses the supplied base DN and filter parameters to perform a search for the user's LDAP entry. If an entry is found, the fully qualified DN of the user is extracted. Then, this DN and the password are passed to the ContextSource's getContext method to perform authentication. This is a two-step process, but it alleviates the need for fully qualified DN up front. Listing 10-5 contains the modified authentication implementation. Notice that the authenticate method signature in the DAO implementation has not changed. It still accepts the username and password as its parameters. However, the implementation has become much simpler thanks to the authentication method abstraction. The implementation passes an empty base DN since you want the search to be performed relative to the base DN used during ContextSource creation.

***Listing 10-5.*** A second possible implementation of the authentication

```
package com.apress.book.ldap.repository;

import org.springframework.beans.factory.annotation.Autowired;
import org.springframework.beans.factory.annotation.Qualifier;
import org.springframework.ldap.core.LdapTemplate;
import org.springframework.stereotype.Repository;

@Repository("authenticationDao2")
public class AuthenticationDaoImpl2 implements AuthenticationDao {

    public static final String BASE_DN = "ou=patrons,dc=inflinx,dc=com";

    private LdapTemplate ldapTemplate;

    public AuthenticationDaoImpl2(@Autowired @Qualifier("ldapTemplate")
    LdapTemplate ldapTemplate) {
        this.ldapTemplate = ldapTemplate;
    }

    @Override
    public boolean authenticate(String userid, String password) {
        return ldapTemplate.authenticate(BASE_DN, "(uid=" + userid + ")",
        password);
    }
}
```

Listing 10-6 shows the JUnit test case to verify the preceding authenticate method implementation.

*Listing 10-6.* Test to check if the authentication method works

```
package com.apress.book.ldap.repository;

import org.junit.jupiter.api.DisplayName;
import org.junit.jupiter.api.Test;
import org.junit.jupiter.api.extension.ExtendWith;
import org.springframework.beans.factory.annotation.Autowired;
import org.springframework.beans.factory.annotation.Qualifier;
import org.springframework.test.context.ContextConfiguration;
import org.springframework.test.context.junit.jupiter.SpringExtension;

import static org.junit.jupiter.api.Assertions.assertFalse;
import static org.junit.jupiter.api.Assertions.assertTrue;

@ExtendWith(SpringExtension.class)
@ContextConfiguration("classpath:repositoryContext-test.xml")
@DisplayName("Authentication Dao 2 test cases")
class AuthenticationDao2Test {

    @Autowired
    @Qualifier("authenticationDao2")
    private AuthenticationDao authenticationDao;

    @Test
    @DisplayName("Check is the authentication mechanism works fine")
    void should_authentication_works() {
        boolean authResult = authenticationDao.authenticate("patron0",
        "password");
        assertTrue(authResult);

        authResult = authenticationDao.authenticate("patron0",
        "invalidPassword");
        assertFalse(authResult);
    }
}
```

# Handling Authentication Exceptions

The previous authenticate methods in LdapTemplate simply tell you whether authentication succeeded or failed. There will be cases where you are interested in the actual exception that caused the failure. For those scenarios, LdapTemplate provides overloaded versions of the authenticate method. The API for one of the overloaded authenticate methods is as follows:

```
boolean authenticate(String base, String filter,  String  password,
AuthenticationErrorCallback errorCallback);
```

Any exceptions that occur during the execution of the preceding authenticate method will be passed on to an AuthenticationErrorCallback instance provided as the method parameter. This collected exception can be logged or used for post-authentication processes. Listings 10-7 and 10-8 show the AuthenticationErrorCallback API and its simple implementation. The execute method in the callback can decide what to do with the raised exception. In your simple implementation, you just store it and make it available to the LdapTemplate's search caller.

***Listing 10-7.***  The interface with the default method executes

```
package org.springframework.ldap.core;
public interface AuthenticationErrorCallback {
    void execute(Exception ex);
}
```

***Listing 10-8.***  A possible definition of a callback

```
package com.apress.book.ldap.exception;

import org.springframework.ldap.core.AuthenticationErrorCallback;

public class EmployeeAuthenticationErrorCallback implements
AuthenticationErrorCallback {

    private Exception authenticationException;

    @Override
```

```
    public void execute(Exception    ex) {
        this.authenticationException = ex;
    }

    public Exception getAuthenticationException() {
        return authenticationException;
    }
}
```

Listing 10-9 shows the modified AuthenticationDao implementation and the error callback; here, you simply log the failed exception to the console.

***Listing 10-9.*** A third possible implementation of the authentication

```
package com.apress.book.ldap.repository;

import com.apress.book.ldap.exception.EmployeeAuthenticationErrorCallback;
import org.slf4j.Logger;
import org.slf4j.LoggerFactory;
import org.springframework.beans.factory.annotation.Autowired;
import org.springframework.beans.factory.annotation.Qualifier;
import org.springframework.ldap.core.LdapTemplate;
import org.springframework.stereotype.Repository;

@Repository("authenticationDao3")
public class AuthenticationDaoImpl3 implements AuthenticationDao {

    private static final Logger logger = LoggerFactory.getLogger
    (AuthenticationDaoImpl3.class);

    public static final String BASE_DN = "ou=patrons,dc=inflinx,dc=com";

    private LdapTemplate ldapTemplate;

    public AuthenticationDaoImpl3(@Autowired @Qualifier("ldapTemplate")
    LdapTemplate ldapTemplate) {
        this.ldapTemplate = ldapTemplate;
    }

    @Override
    public boolean authenticate(String userid, String password) {
```

```
        EmployeeAuthenticationErrorCallback errorCallback = new
        EmployeeAuthentication
        ErrorCallback();
        boolean isAuthenticated = ldapTemplate.authenticate( BASE_DN,
        "(uid=" + userid + ")", password, errorCallback);
        if (!isAuthenticated) {
            logger.info(errorCallback.getAuthenticationException().
            getMessage());
        }
        return isAuthenticated;
    }
}
```

Listing 10-10 shows the JUnit test to check how this method of authentication works.

***Listing 10-10.*** Test to check if the authentication method works

```
package com.apress.book.ldap.repository;

import org.junit.jupiter.api.DisplayName;
import org.junit.jupiter.api.Test;
import org.junit.jupiter.api.extension.ExtendWith;
import org.springframework.beans.factory.annotation.Autowired;
import org.springframework.beans.factory.annotation.Qualifier;
import org.springframework.test.context.ContextConfiguration;
import org.springframework.test.context.junit.jupiter.SpringExtension;

import static org.junit.jupiter.api.Assertions.assertFalse;

@ExtendWith(SpringExtension.class)
@ContextConfiguration("classpath:repositoryContext-test.xml")
@DisplayName("Authentication Dao 3 test cases")
class AuthenticationDao3Test {
    @Autowired
    @Qualifier("authenticationDao3")
    private AuthenticationDao authenticationDao;
```

```
@Test
@DisplayName("Check is the authentication mechanism works fine")
void should_authentication_works() {
    boolean authResult = authenticationDao.authenticate("patron0",
    "invalidPassword");
    assertFalse(authResult);
}
}
```

Upon running the JUnit test in Listing 10-10, you should see the following error message in the console:

```
10:29:36.008 [main] INFO  c.a.b.l.r.AuthenticationDaoImpl3 - [LDAP: error
code 49 - Unable to bind as user 'uid=patron0,ou=patrons,dc=inflinx,dc=com'
because the provided password was incorrect.]
```

The test returns success because check what happens if you put a wrong password, in the case that you want to check the opposite change the password and use the method **assertTrue**.

There are other alternative methods, but these options give you the basic mechanism to authenticate a user. Another possibility to do the same is Spring Security,[1] which has a mechanism to combine with LDAP, similar to the examples you read in this chapter. Unfortunately, Spring Security is a complex topic to explain in just a few words, so it's out of the scope of this book.

# Parsing LDIF Data

The LDAP Data Interchange Format is a standards-based data interchange format for representing LDAP directory data in a flat-file format. LDIF is discussed in detail in Chapter 1. As an LDAP developer or administrator, you may sometimes need to parse LDIF files and perform operations such as a bulk directory load. For such scenarios, Spring LDAP introduced a set of classes in the `org.springframework.ldap.ldif` package and its subpackages that make it easy to read and parse LDIF files.

---

[1]https://spring.io/projects/spring-security

CHAPTER 10 ODDS AND ENDS

Central to the org.springframework.ldap.ldif.parser package is the Parser interface, and its default implementation LdifParser. The LdifParser is responsible for reading individual lines from an LDIF file and converting them into Java objects. This object representation is possible through two newly added classes, namely, LdapAttribute and LdapAttributes.

The code in Listing 10-11 uses LdifParser to read and print the total number of records in an LDIF file. You start the implementation by creating an instance of LdifParser and passing in the file you want to parse. Before the parser can be used, you need to open it. Then, you use the parser's iterator-style interface for reading and counting individual records.

***Listing 10-11.*** Example of an LDIF parser

```
package com.apress.book.ldap.parser;

import java.io.File;
import java.io.IOException;

import org.slf4j.Logger;
import org.slf4j.LoggerFactory;
import org.springframework.core.io.ClassPathResource;
import org.springframework.ldap.core.LdapAttributes;
import org.springframework.ldap.ldif.parser.LdifParser;

public class SimpleLdifParser {
    private static final Logger logger = LoggerFactory.
    getLogger(SimpleLdifParser.class);
    public void parse(File file) throws IOException {
        LdifParser parser = new LdifParser(file);
        parser.open();
        int count = 0;
        while (parser.hasMoreRecords()) {
            LdapAttributes attributes = parser.getRecord();
            count++;
        }
        parser.close();
        logger.info(String.valueOf(count));
    }
```

```
public static void main(String[] args) throws IOException {
    SimpleLdifParser parser = new SimpleLdifParser();
    parser.parse(new ClassPathResource("patrons.ldif").getFile());
}
}
```

Before running the preceding class, ensure you have the patrons.ldif file in the folder **src/java/resources**. Upon running the class with the patrons.ldif file included with the Chapter 1 code, you should see the count 103 printed to the console like the following output:

```
14:37:04.933 [main] DEBUG o.s.ldap.ldif.parser.LdifParser - record parsed:
dn: ou=patrons,dc=inflinx,dc=com
ou: patrons
objectClass: top
objectClass: organizationalunit

14:37:04.935 [main] DEBUG o.s.ldap.ldif.parser.LdifParser - record parsed:
dn: uid=patron0,ou=patrons,dc=inflinx,dc=com
mobile: +1 189 955 5012
initials: ARA
givenName: Aaccf
street: 08904 Sixth Street
telephoneNumber: +1 688 926 3146
sn: Amar
userPassword: password
l: Fairbanks
mail: patron0@inflinx.com
objectClass: top
objectClass: person
objectClass: organizationalperson
objectClass: inetorgperson
uid: patron0
postalAddress: Aaccf Amar$08904 Sixth Street$Fairbanks, IA  10928
homePhone: +1 092 210 9726
postalCode: 10928
cn: Aaccf Amar
```

```
st: IA
.....................
.....................
.....................
```

The parsing implementation of `LdifParser` relies on three supporting policy definitions: separator policy, attribute validation policy, and record specification policy.

- The separator policy provides the separation rules for LDIF records in a file and is defined in RFC 2849.[2] It is implemented via the `org.springframework.ldap.ldif.support.SeparatorPolicy` class.

- The attribute validation policy, as the name suggests, ensures that all the attributes are structured properly in the LDIF file before parsing. It is implemented via the `AttributeValidationPolicy` interface and the `DefaultAttributeValidationPolicy` class. These two are located in the `org.springframework.ldap.ldif.support` package. The `DefaultAttributeValidationPolicy` uses regular expressions to validate attribute format according to RFC 2849.

- The record specification policy validates rules that each LDIF record must confirm. Spring LDAP provides the `Specification` interface and two implementations for this policy: `org.springframework.ldap.schema.DefaultSchemaSpecification` and `org.springframework.ldap.schema.BasicSchemaSpecification`. The `DefaultSchemaSpecification` has an empty implementation and does not validate the records. The `BasicSchemaSpecification` can perform basic checks, such as that an `objectClass` must exist for each LAP entry. For most cases, the `BasicSchemaSpecification` will suffice.

The modified `parse` method implementation and the three policy definitions are given in Listing 10-12.

---

[2]`https://datatracker.ietf.org/doc/html/rfc2849`

**Listing 10-12.**  Example of LDIF parser using the validators

```
package com.apress.book.ldap.parser;

import java.io.File;
import java.io.IOException;

import org.slf4j.Logger;
import org.slf4j.LoggerFactory;
import org.springframework.core.io.ClassPathResource;
import org.springframework.ldap.core.LdapAttributes;
import org.springframework.ldap.ldif.parser.LdifParser;
import org.springframework.ldap.ldif.support.
DefaultAttributeValidationPolicy;
import org.springframework.ldap.schema.BasicSchemaSpecification;

public class SimpleLdifParser2 {
    private static final Logger logger = LoggerFactory.
    getLogger(SimpleLdifParser2.class);
    public void parse(File file) throws IOException {
        LdifParser parser = new LdifParser(file);
        parser.setAttributeValidationPolicy(new
        DefaultAttributeValidationPolicy());
        parser.setRecordSpecification(new BasicSchemaSpecification());
        parser.open();
        int count = 0;
        while (parser.hasMoreRecords()) {
            LdapAttributes attributes = parser.getRecord();
            count++;
        }
        parser.close();
        logger.info(String.valueOf(count));
    }

    public static void main(String[] args) throws IOException {
        SimpleLdifParser2 parser = new SimpleLdifParser2();
```

```
        parser.parse(new ClassPathResource("patrons.ldif").getFile());
    }
}
```

Upon running the method in Listing 10-12, you should see the count 103 printed to the console like the following output:

```
14:37:04.933 [main] DEBUG o.s.ldap.ldif.parser.LdifParser - record parsed:
dn: ou=patrons,dc=inflinx,dc=com
ou: patrons
objectClass: top
objectClass: organizationalunit

14:37:04.935 [main] DEBUG o.s.ldap.ldif.parser.LdifParser - record parsed:
dn: uid=patron0,ou=patrons,dc=inflinx,dc=com
mobile: +1 189 955 5012
initials: ARA
givenName: Aaccf
street: 08904 Sixth Street
telephoneNumber: +1 688 926 3146
sn: Amar
userPassword: password
l: Fairbanks
mail: patron0@inflinx.com
objectClass: top
objectClass: person
objectClass: organizationalperson
objectClass: inetorgperson
uid: patron0
postalAddress: Aaccf Amar$08904 Sixth Street$Fairbanks, IA  10928
homePhone: +1 092 210 9726
postalCode: 10928
cn: Aaccf Amar
st: IA

.....................
.....................
.....................
```

# LDAP Connection Pooling

LDAP connection pooling is a technique where connections to the LDAP directory are reused rather than being created each time a connection is requested. Without connection pooling, each request to the LDAP directory causes a new connection to be created and then released when the connection is no longer required. Creating a new connection is resource-intensive, and this overhead can adversely affect performance. With connection pooling, connections are stored in the pool after they are created and are recycled for subsequent client requests.

Connections in a pool at any point can be in one of these three states:

- *In use*: The connection is open and currently in use.

- *Idle*: The connection is open and available for reuse.

- *Closed*: The connection is no longer available for use.

Figure 10-1 illustrates the possible actions on a connection at any given time.

***Figure 10-1.*** *Connection pool states*

# Built-In Connection Pooling

JNDI provides basic support for connection pooling via the "com.sun.jndi.ldap. connect.pool" environment property. Applications creating a directory context can set this property to true and indicate that connection pooling needs to be turned on. Listing 10-13 shows the plain JNDI code that utilizes pooling support.

***Listing 10-13.*** JNDI plain code with pooling

```
// Set up environment for creating initial context
Hashtable env = new Hashtable();
env.put(Context.INITIAL_CONTEXT_FACTORY, "com.sun.jndi.ldap.
LdapCtxFactory");
env.put(Context.PROVIDER_URL, "ldap://localhost:11389");
```

261

```
// Enable connection pooling
env.put("com.sun.jndi.ldap.connect.pool", "true");
// Create one initial context
(Get connection from pool) DirContext ctx = new InitialDirContext(env);
// do something useful with ctx
// Close the context when we're done
ctx.close(); // Return connection to pool
```

By default, the Spring LDAP contexts have the "com.sun.jndi.ldap.connect.
pool" property set to false. The native connection pooling can be turned on by setting
the pooled property of the LdapContextSource to true in the configuration file. The
following code shows the configuration change:

```
<bean id="contextSource" class="org.springframework.ldap.core.support.
LdapContextSource">
    <property name="url" value="ldap://localhost:11389" />
    <property name="base" value="dc=inflix,dc=com" />
    <property name="userDn" value="cn=Director Manager" />
    <property name="password" value="secret" />
    <property name="pooled" value="true"/>
</bean>
```

Though the native LDAP connection pooling is simple, it does suffer from certain
drawbacks. The pool of connections is maintained per the Java Runtime Environment. It
is not possible to maintain multiple connection pools per JVM. Also, there is no control
over the properties of the connection pool, such as the number of connections to be
maintained at any time or idle connection time. Providing any custom connection
validation to ensure that pooled connections are still valid is also impossible.

# Spring LDAP Connection Pooling

To address shortcomings with native JNDI pooling, Spring LDAP provides a custom
pooling library for LDAP connections. The Spring LDAP pooling library maintains its
own set of LDAP connections specific to each application.

> **Note**    Spring LDAP utilizes the Jakarta Commons Pool[3] library for its underlying pooling implementation.

To start, you need to add the dependency on the pom.xml file related with the pool which is not included by default on Spring LDAP:

```
<dependency>
    <groupId>commons-pool</groupId>
    <artifactId>commons-pool</artifactId>
    <version>1.6</version>
</dependency>
```

Central to Spring LDAP pooling is the org.springframework.ldap.pool.factory. PoolingContextSource, which is a specialized ContextSource implementation and is responsible for pooling DirContext instances. To utilize connection pooling, you start by configuring a Spring LDAP context source:

```
<bean id="contextSourceTarget" class="org.springframework.ldap.core.
support.LdapContextSource">
    <property name="url" value="ldap://localhost:11389" />
    <property name="base" value="dc=inflix,dc=com" />
    <property name="userDn" value="cn=Directory Manager" />
    <property name="password" value="secret" />
    <property name="pooled" value="false"/>
</bean>
```

Note that you have the pooled property of the context source set to false. This will allow the LdapContextSource to create brand-new connections when the need arises. Also, the id of the ContextSource is now set to contextSourceTarget instead of contextSource, which is what you usually use. The next step is to create a PoolingContextSource, as shown:

---

[3] https://commons.apache.org/proper/commons-pool/

```
<bean id="contextSource" class="org.springframework.ldap.pool.factory.
PoolingContextSource">
    <property name="contextSource" ref="contextSourceTarget" />
</bean>
```

The PoolingContextSource wraps the contextSourceTarget you configured earlier. This is required since the PoolingContextSource delegates the creation of DirContexts to the contextSourceTarget. Also, note that you have used the id contextSource for this bean instance. This allows you to keep the configuration changes to a minimum while using a PoolingContextSource instance in an LdapTemplate, as shown:

```
<bean id="ldapTemplate" class="org.springframework.ldap.core.LdapTemplate">
    <constructor-arg ref="contextSource" />
</bean>
```

The PoolingContextSource provides a variety of options that can be used to fine-tune connection pooling. Table 10-1 lists some of the important configuration properties.

*Table 10-1.* *PoolingContextSource Configuration Properties*

| Property | Description | Default |
|----------|-------------|---------|
| testOnBorrow | When set to true, the DirContext is validated before it is borrowed from the pool. If the DirContext fails validation, it is removed from the pool and a new attempt is made to borrow another DirContext. This testing might add a small delay in serving the borrow request. | False |
| testOnReturn | When set to true, this property indicates that DirContext will be validated before returning to the pool. | False |
| testWhileIdle | When set to true, this property indicates that idle DirContext instances in the pool should be validated at a specified frequency. Objects failing the validation will be dropped from the pool. | False |
| timeBetween EvictionRuns Millis | This property indicates the time in milliseconds to sleep between running idle context tests. A negative number indicates that idle test will never be run. | -1 |
| whenExhausted Action | Specifies the action to be taken when the pool is exhausted. The possible options are WHEN_EXHAUSTED_FAIL (0), WHEN_EXHAUSTED_BLOCK (1), and WHEN_EXHAUSTED_ GROW (2). | 1 |
| maxTotal | The maximum number of active connections that this pool can contain. A nonpositive integer indicates no limit. | -1 |
| maxIdle | The maximum number of idle connections of each type (read, read-write) that can be idle in the pool. | 8 |
| maxWait | The maximum number of milliseconds that a pool will wait for a connection to be returned to the pool before throwing an exception. A negative number indicates an indefinite wait. | -1 |

After all the basic configurations, let's create another file called repositoryContext-test-1.xml in the folder **src/test/resources** with the content of Listing 10-14.

***Listing 10-14.*** The declaration of pool

```xml
<?xml version="1.0" encoding="UTF-8"?>
<beans xmlns="http://www.springframework.org/schema/beans"
       xmlns:xsi="http://www.w3.org/2001/XMLSchema-instance"
       xmlns:ldap="http://www.springframework.org/schema/ldap"
       xmlns:context="http://www.springframework.org/schema/context"
       xsi:schemaLocation="http://www.springframework.org/schema/beans
                       https://www.springframework.org/schema/beans/
                       spring-beans.xsd http://www.springframework.org/
                       schema/ldap https://www.springframework.org/
                       schema/ldap/spring-ldap.xsd
                   http://www.springframework.org/schema/context http://
                   www.springframework.org/schema/context/spring-
                   context.xsd">

    <context:component-scan base-package="com.apress.book.ldap" />

    <bean id="placeholderConfig" class="org.springframework.beans.factory.
    config.PropertyPlaceholderConfigurer">
        <property name="location" value="classpath:ldap.properties" />
    </bean>
    <ldap:context-source id="contextSource"
                    password="${ldap.password}"
                    url="${ldap.url}"
                    username="${ldap.userDn}">
        <ldap:pooling/>
    </ldap:context-source>

    <!-- Populates the LDAP server with initial data -->
    <bean class="org.springframework.ldap.test.LdifPopulator" depends-
    on="embeddedLdapServer">
        <property name="contextSource" ref="contextSource" />
        <property name="resource" value="classpath:patrons.ldif" />
        <property name="base" value="${ldap.base}" />
        <property name="clean" value="${ldap.clean}" />
        <property name="defaultBase" value="${ldap.base}" />
```

```
    </bean>

    <bean id="embeddedLdapServer" class="org.springframework.ldap.test.
    unboundid.EmbeddedLdapServerFactoryBean">
        <property name="partitionName" value="inflinx"/>
        <property name="partitionSuffix" value="${ldap.base}" />
        <property name="port" value="${ldap.port}" />
    </bean>

    <bean id="ldapTemplate" class="org.springframework.ldap.core.
    LdapTemplate">
        <constructor-arg ref="contextSource" />
    </bean>

</beans>
```

Check in Listing 10-14 that the configuration of the pool is a little different from the previous listings because you can do it using different ways, but the result is the same.

Consider the file could not be used for authentication purposes because the user on the ContextSource performs a bind, which is accomplished by creating a new connection with the specified distinguished name and password.

# Pool Validation

Spring LDAP makes it easy to validate pooled connections. This validation ensures that the DirContext instances are properly configured and connected to the LDAP server before they are borrowed from the pool. The same validation is done before the contexts are returned to the pool or on the contexts sitting idle.

The PoolingContextSource delegates the validation to concrete instances of the org.springframework.ldap.pool.validation.DirContextValidator interface. In Listing 10-15, you can see that the DirContextValidator has only one method: validateDirContext. The first parameter, contextType, indicates if the context to be validated is a read-only or a read-write context. The second parameter is the actual context that needs to be validated.

*Listing 10-15.*  The declaration of the context validator

```
package org.springframework.ldap.pool.validation;
import javax.naming.directory.DirContext;
import org.springframework.ldap.core.ContextSource;
import org.springframework.ldap.pool.DirContextType;

public interface DirContextValidator {
    boolean validateDirContext(DirContextType contextType, DirContext
    dirContext);
}
```

Out of the box, Spring LDAP provides an aptly named default implementation of the DirContextValidator called org.springframework.ldap.pool.validation. DefaultDirContextValidator. This implementation simply searches using the context and verifies the returned javax.naming.NamingEnumeration. If the NamingEnumeration does not contain any results or an exception is thrown, the context fails the validation and will be removed from the pool. Applications requiring more sophisticated validation can create new implementations of the DirContextValidator interface.

Configuring pooling validation is shown in Listing 10-14. You start by creating a dirContextValidator bean of type DefaultDirContextValidator. Then, you modify the contextSource bean declaration to include the dirContextValidator bean. In Listing 10-16, you added the testOnBorrow and testWhileIdle properties.

*Listing 10-16.*  Modifications on the context validator

```
<bean id="dirContextValidator" class="org.springframework.ldap.pool.
validation.DefaultDirContextValidator" />
<bean id="contextSource" class="org.springframework.ldap.pool.factory.
PoolingContextSource">
    <property name="contextSource" ref="contextSourceTarget" />
    <property name="dirContextValidator" ref="dirContextValidator"/>
    <property name="testOnBorrow" value="true" />
    <property name="testWhileIdle" value="true" />
</bean>
```

An alternative way to do it is shown in Listing 10-14, but with a little modification on the **<ldap:pooling>** tag like Listing 10-16.

```
<ldap:context-source id="contextSource"
                password="${ldap.password}"
                url="${ldap.url}"
                username="${ldap.userDn}">
    <ldap:pooling test-on-borrow="true" test-while-idle="true"/>
</ldap:context-source>
```

# Summary

This brings us to the end of our journey. Throughout the book, you have learned the key features of Spring LDAP. With this knowledge, you should be ready to start developing Spring LDAP–based applications.

Finally, writing this book and sharing my insights with you have been a pleasure. I wish you all the best. Happy coding!

# APPENDIX A

# Setting Up Environment Tools

You will use some required tools to run all the examples in this book. In this appendix, I will show you how to install the most relevant of them, excluding the tools related to LDAP.

## Install Java

The first thing you need to install before starting to try something is the Java JDK. You need to consider that different alternatives of the JDK exist, but in all cases, you need to install version 21:

- OracleJDK :[1] This version was free until Java 11; after this version, you can use it for development/test environments, but you need to pay a license to use it on production. This version of the JDK offers you the most recent patches of bugs and new features because Oracle owns the language.

- OpenJDK :[2] When Oracle bought Sun Microsystems, it created this as an open source alternative that all developers can use in any environment without restrictions. The main problem with this version is the patches of the bugs take time to appear in a case that is not critical.

---

[1] https://www.oracle.com/java/technologies/
[2] https://openjdk.org/

© Balaji Varanasi and Andres Sacco 2023
B. Varanasi and A. Sacco, *Practical Spring LDAP*, https://doi.org/10.1007/979-8-8688-0002-3

- *Others*: There are many other alternatives to JDK, for example, AWS (Amazon Web Services) has Amazon Corretto,[3] which extends from OpenJDK and optimizes the applications' performance in this cloud provider's environments. Another alternative is Eclipse Temurin[4] which is very popular.

We use OpenJDK throughout all the chapters of this book, but you can choose any other alternative you want. Depending on the operating system, there are many ways to install the JDK:

- For Mac OS/Linux, you can use brew,[5] a tool to install/update different things:

  ➔  ~ brew install openjdk

  Another possibility is to use SDKMAN[6,] which is similar to brew and has multiple versions and implementations of the JDK:

  ➔  ~ sdk install java 21-ms

- For Windows platforms, you have two possibilities:

  - The first option is to install SDKMAN and run the same command as Mac OS/Linux.

  - The second option is to install Eclipse Temurin,[7] which allows you to download the OpenJDK for different platforms. In the case of Windows, you can download a file MSI, which makes the installation so easy.

---

[3] https://aws.amazon.com/corretto

[4] https://adoptium.net/es/temurin/releases/

[5] https://brew.sh/

[6] https://sdkman.io/

[7] https://adoptium.net/

After installing the JDK, you will check if the version of Java is available in your system. To do this, you will type the following:

➔   ~ java -version
openjdk 21 2023-09-19
OpenJDK Runtime Environment (build 21+35-2513)
OpenJDK 64-Bit Server VM (build 21+35-2513, mixed mode, sharing)

Consider that for executing all the examples, there are no limitations between which versions of Java you need to have installed on your machine. Still, all the examples are written using JDK 21, the version required for Spring Boot 3.0. Still, not many developers use that version on production because, according to Snyk,[8] more or less 61% of developers use version 11 in the production environments.

# Install Maven

The second thing you need to have on your machine to run all the examples or follow the examples is Maven. This tool provides a good way to manage and solve the conflict between different versions of the dependencies in your projects.

Depending on the operating system, there are many ways to install Maven. Some involve doing it manually, so you must download it from the official website[9] and configure the environment variables to recognize the *mvn* command. For simplicity, in this book, I will show you how to install using package manager tools:

- For Mac OS/Linux, you can use brew,[10] a tool to install/update different things:

  ➔   ~ brew install maven

  Also, you can install it using SDKMAN,[11] which follows the same approach as brew, which provides a simple way to install different libraries or tools:

  ➔   ~ sdk install maven

---

[8] https://snyk.io/jvm-ecosystem-report-2021/
[9] https://maven.apache.org/download.cgi
[10] https://brew.sh/
[11] https://sdkman.io/

Lastly, there is another way to do it, which is only available on some specific Linux distributions:

- Ubuntu

  → ~ sudo apt install maven

  - Fedora

    → ~ sudo dnf install maven

- For Windows platforms, you have two possibilities:

  - The first option is installing SDKMAN and running the same Mac OS/Linux command.

  - The second option involves downloading manually, unzipping all the content in one directory, and creating an environment variable named "M2_HOME" with the root directory's location inside the Maven folder you created.

After finishing the installation of Maven, you will check if the version is available in your system. To do this, you will type the following:

→ ~ mvn --version
Apache Maven 3.9.1
Maven home: /usr/share/maven

# Install Git

This tool is a version control system for tracking all the modifications different people can introduce. In particular, this tool is not required for using the source code of this book because GitHub provides a button to download all the repositories. Still, I included it in case you want to fork and introduce modifications to the repository.

As I mentioned in the previous section, to install this tool, you can use different package manager tools like

- Brew

  → ~ brew install git

- SDKMAN

  → `~ sdk install git`

Or, if you want to use another option, you can check on the official website of Git.[12] On that link, you will find that you can download an executable that installs everything in the case of Windows.

After you install this tool, the only thing that you need to do is check which version is on your system. To do this, you will type the following:

```
→  ~ git --version
git version 2.42.0
```

As a suggestion to not need to write on every commit some information like your username and email, you can configure globally using these commands:

```
→  ~ git config --global user.name "John Doe"
→  ~ git config --global user.email "johndoe@example.com"
```

# Install IntelliJ

You can see the instructions to install the IDE on the official page,[13] which mentions the minimum resources and operating system to use it. Consider that there are two versions of the IDE, as you can see in Figure A-1; one is the Community edition, which is entirely free, and you can use and install several plug-ins. The other version is the Ultimate, which is paid and offers some extra unnecessary features for this book.

---

[12] https://git-scm.com/downloads
[13] www.jetbrains.com/idea/download/?section=linux#section=linux

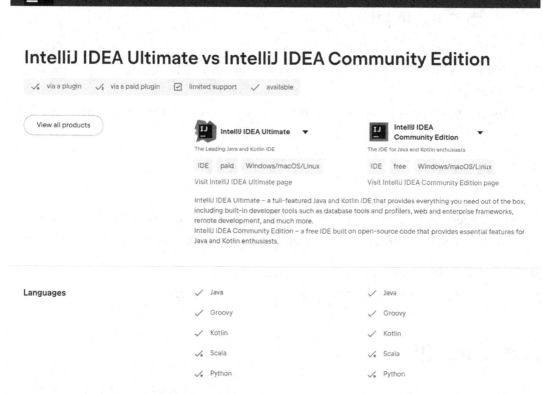

**Figure A-1.** *Official site to download the IDE*

Here are some helpful plug-ins that you can install on this IDE:

- Maven Helper[14]

- GitToolBox[15]

- Docker[16]

- Spring[17]

To install any of these plugins, go to Preferences ➤ Plugins, find by name, and install it as shown in Figure A-2.

---

[14] https://plugins.jetbrains.com/plugin/7179-maven-helper
[15] https://plugins.jetbrains.com/plugin/7499-gittoolbox
[16] https://plugins.jetbrains.com/plugin/7724-docker
[17] https://plugins.jetbrains.com/plugin/20221-spring/versions

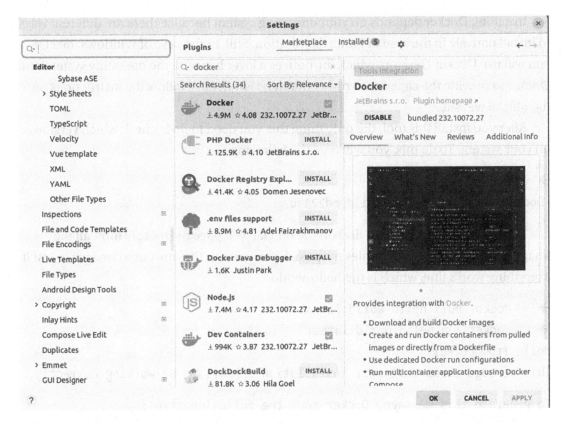

*Figure A-2.* *IntelliJ plug-in installation*

# Install Docker

Docker is one of the most popular options to run a container engine based on Linux. In the case of this book, you can use it to reduce the complexity of installing different LDAP vendors on your system, so using Docker, you can run it easily and remove it just to stop the container.

---

**Note** The idea of this book is to explain only some of the pros and cons of using Docker because many books, articles, and videos explain all the concepts related to technology in a lot of detail.

---

Installing Docker depends on your operating system because there are different ways to install natively in the case of Linux distribution. Still, in the case of Windows/macOS, you will use Docker Desktop, which introduces a layer between the operating system and Docker to provide the capacity to run containers. For details, follow the instructions on the official website.[18]

After you install this tool, the only thing that you need to do is check which version is on your system. To do this, you will type the following:

```
➜  ~ docker --version
Docker version 24.0.6, build ed223bc
```

To run a container, you can find on the official web page of Docker Hub[19] all the images that exist; for the examples proposed, you can run the most used images to test if everything works fine, which is the hello-world:

```
➜  ~ docker pull hello-world:latest
➜  ~ docker run hello-world:latest
Hello from Docker!
This message shows that your installation appears to be working correctly.

To generate this message, Docker took the following steps:
1. The Docker client contacted the Docker daemon.
2. The Docker daemon pulled the "hello-world" image from the Docker Hub.
   (amd64)
3. The Docker daemon created a new container from that image which runs the
   executable that produces the output you are currently reading.
4. The Docker daemon streamed that output to the Docker client, which sent
   it to your terminal.
```

---

[18] https://docs.docker.com/get-docker/
[19] https://hub.docker.com/

To try something more ambitious, you can run an Ubuntu container with:
$ docker run -it ubuntu bash

Share images, automate workflows, and more with a free Docker ID:
https://hub.docker.com/

For more examples and ideas, visit:
https://docs.docker.com/get-started/

You can check this blog,[20] which explains the most relevant commands and components.

---

[20] https://docs.docker.com/get-started/docker_cheatsheet.pdf

# APPENDIX B

# Recommended and Alternative Tools

This appendix will mention the first alternative of tools you will use in the different chapters and other options.

## IDEs

- *IntelliJ*:[1] IntelliJ is the most widely used IDE for Java development. IntelliJ IDEA Community Edition provides everything you need to start with Java and Spring. Also, you have the Ultimate version, which contains some extra features and other plug-ins. In Figure B-1, you can see how it looks like a project imported on the IDE.

---

[1] https://www.jetbrains.com/idea/

© Balaji Varanasi and Andres Sacco 2023
B. Varanasi and A. Sacco, *Practical Spring LDAP*, https://doi.org/10.1007/979-8-8688-0002-3

*Figure B-1.  IntelliJ with an imported project*

- *Eclipse:*[2] Eclipse is another IDE option for Java development that most old developers know. Most plug-ins are free and have a vast community of developers who frequently update them and many of Spring's plug-ins. Still, the most relevant ones appear on the Spring website,[3] so if you choose this tool, please follow the instructions to install the plug-ins. In Figure B-2, you can see how it looks like a project imported on Eclipse.

---

[2] https://www.eclipse.org/downloads/
[3] https://spring.io/tools

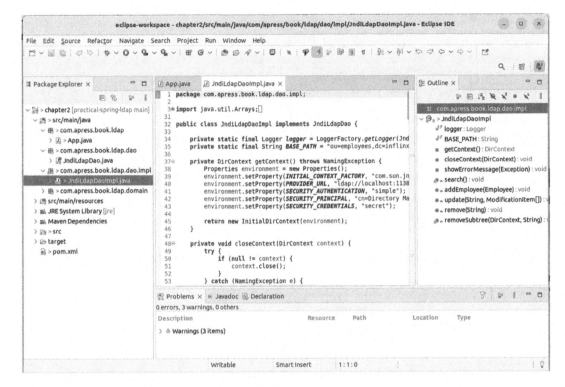

*Figure B-2.* *Eclipse with an imported project*

- *NetBeans:*[4] It's another alternative to develop applications using different programming languages. Nowadays, there is not a big community of users because the other alternatives have the best user interface and plug-ins that cover most developers' requirements. It's used by some developers when they start to learn their first language. In Figure B-3, you can see how it looks like a project imported on NetBeans.

---

[4] https://netbeans.apache.org/

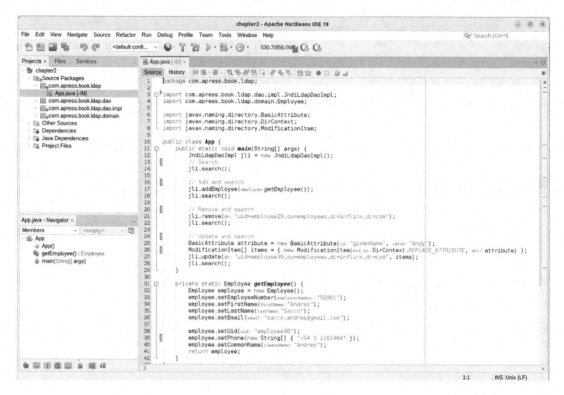

**Figure B-3.** *NetBeans with an imported project*

- *Visual Studio:*[5] This IDE is the newest alternative to creating and running applications using Java and many other languages. There are tons of plug-ins to provide support on different frameworks or technologies related to Java, like Spring Tools.[6] In Figure B-4, you can see how it looks like a project imported on VisualStudio.

---

[5] https://code.visualstudio.com/
[6] https://spring.io/tools

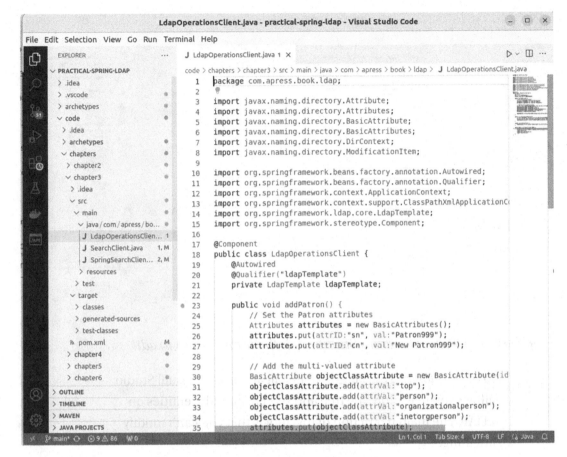

*Figure B-4.  Visual Studio with an imported project*

# LDAP UI

- *Apache Directory Studio:*[7] It's a tool that interacts with LDAP and
  executes different operations, offering support for multiple operating
  systems like Windows, macOS, and Linux. You can use it on any
  vendor of LDAP. Still, it's especially recommended for ApacheDS. In
  this book, you will use version 2.0.0-M17. In Figure B-5, you can see
  how it looks like the tool with the information imported on the LDAP.

---

[7] https://directory.apache.org/

**Figure B-5.** *Apache Directory Studio with the information to edit*

- *LDAP Explorer:*[8] This plug-in to install and use on Visual Studio allows you to explore the tree and search/filter the entities on LDAP. The main restriction of this tool is that you can't modify anything.

- *LDAP User Manager:*[9] This tool, which you can run using Docker, offers the possibility to execute many operations using a web page. You can configure many things, like a regex, to validate the user's name or email the information that a new user was created. This tool has new versions with a specific frequency, but the main problem is that it is not a group of developers or a company that provides support.

There are many other alternatives, but most are too old or need support for multiple operating systems, so they are not highly recommended.

---

[8] https://marketplace.visualstudio.com/items?itemName=fengtan.ldap-explorer
[9] https://hub.docker.com/r/wheelybird/ldap-user-manager

# APPENDIX C

# Set Up LDAP Server

Throughout the different chapters, you've learned about many tools necessary to run the examples in the book. In this appendix, you will learn different ways to install and configure the LDAP server and the UI to access and load the information.

## LDAP Server Setup

This section will look at installing an LDAP server to test your LDAP code. OpenDJ[1] is easy to install and configure among the available open source LDAP servers.

---

**Note**   Even if you already have a test LDAP server available, I recommend performing the following steps and installing the OpenDJ LDAP server. You will heavily use this instance to test the code in this book.

---

Download the OpenDJ distribution file OpenDJ-4.5.9.zip from the official website.[2] Unzip the distribution to a folder on your local system and then follow these steps to complete the installation:

1. Start the installation process by clicking the `setup.bat` file for Windows, or if you use macOS/Linux, you can do it by running the `setup.sh`. This will launch the install screen like Figure C-1.

---

[1] https://www.openidentityplatform.org/opendj
[2] https://github.com/OpenIdentityPlatform/OpenDJ/releases

287

© Balaji Varanasi and Andres Sacco 2023
B. Varanasi and A. Sacco, *Practical Spring LDAP*, https://doi.org/10.1007/979-8-8688-0002-3

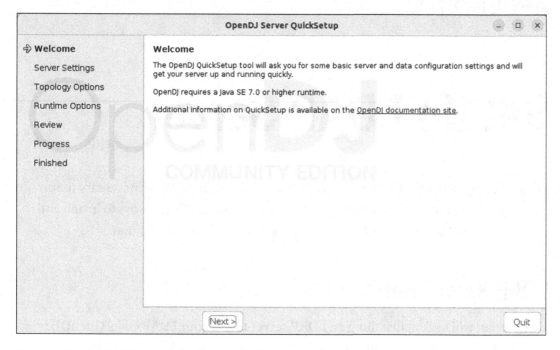

**Figure C-1.** *LDAP server welcome page*

---

**Note**    Run the installer as an administrator when installing under Windows 10 or up. Otherwise, you will run into an error when enabling the server as a Windows service.

For Linux or macOS, check if the file has permission to do the setup; if not, run the **chmod** command to assign the correct permission to the file.

---

2.   Enter the following values on the Server settings screen and click the Next button. I changed the Listener Port from 1389 to 11389 and the Administration Connector Port from 4444 to 4445; the main reason for doing that is to prevent any possible conflict if you are using those ports for another thing. Also, set the password as ***secret*** or any value you want, but remember to put the same value on the different examples before running it. Please use these settings for running code examples in this book (see Figure C-2).

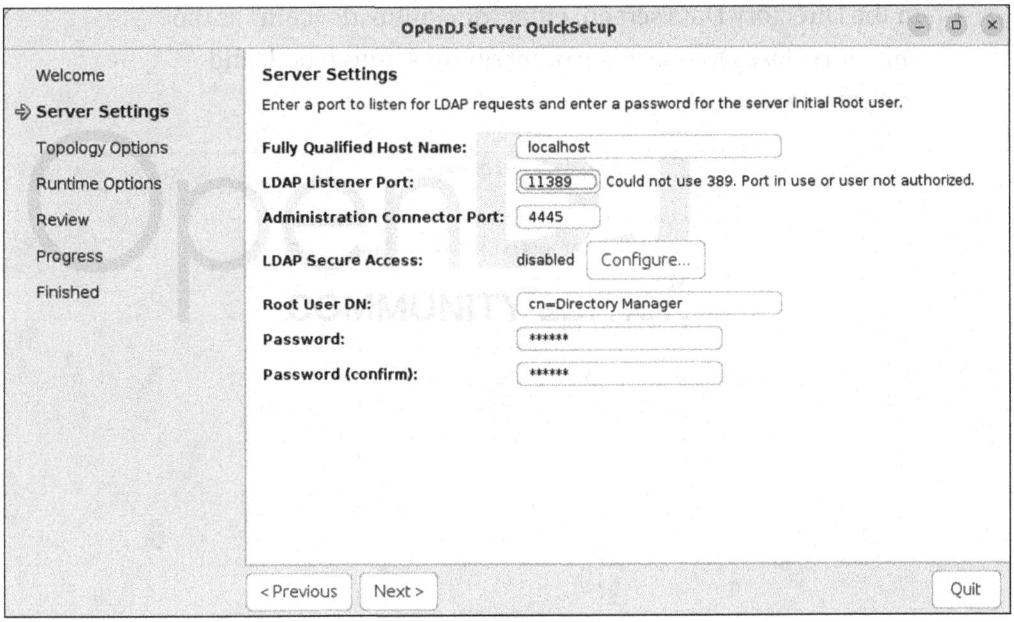

**Figure C-2.** *LDAP server settings*

3. In the Topology Options screen, leave the "This will be a standalone server" option and click Next (see Figure C-3).

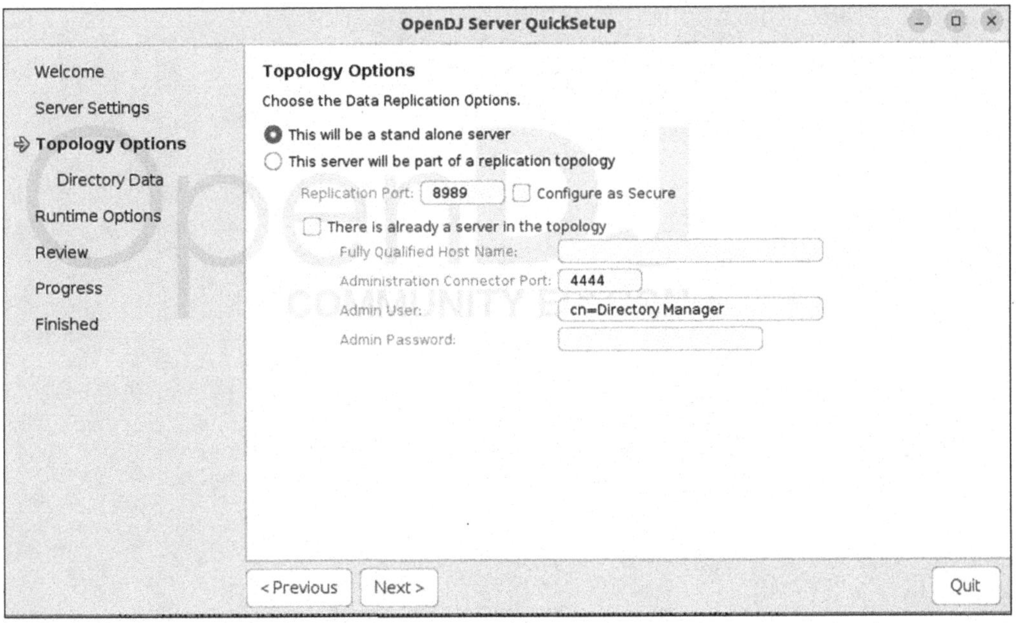

**Figure C-3.** *LDAP topology*

4. In the Directory Data screen, enter "dc=inflinx,dc=com" as the Directory Base DN, leave the other options untouched, and continue (see Figure C-4).

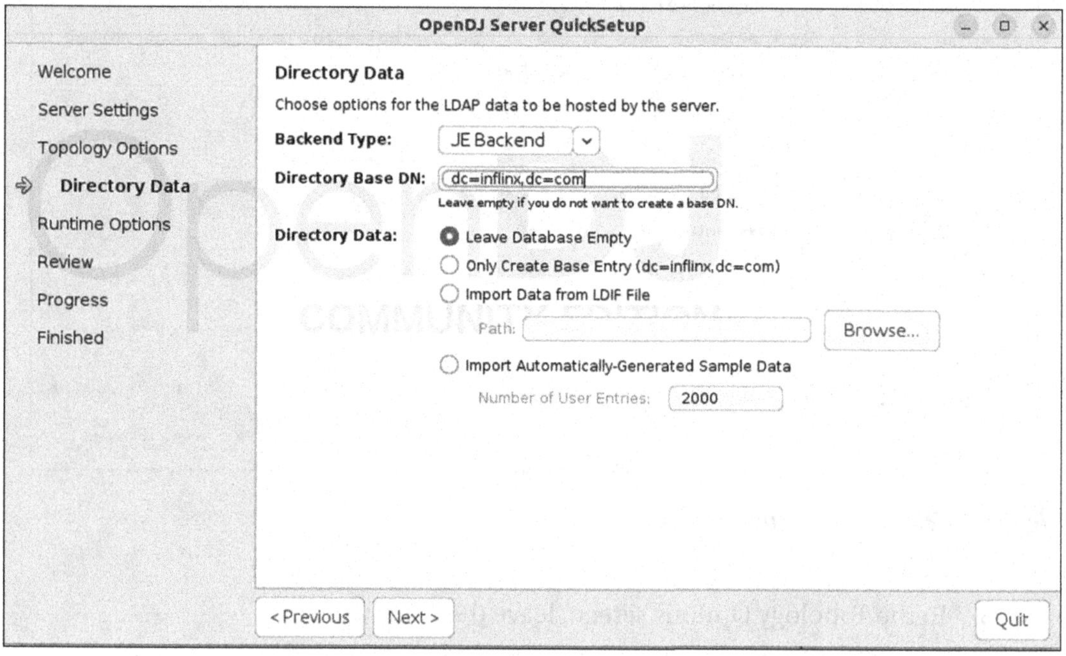

***Figure C-4.*** *LDAP directory information and the base DN*

5.  In the Review screen, confirm that "Run the server as a Windows Service" or "Start Server when Configuration has completed" option is checked and click the Finish button (see Figure C-5).

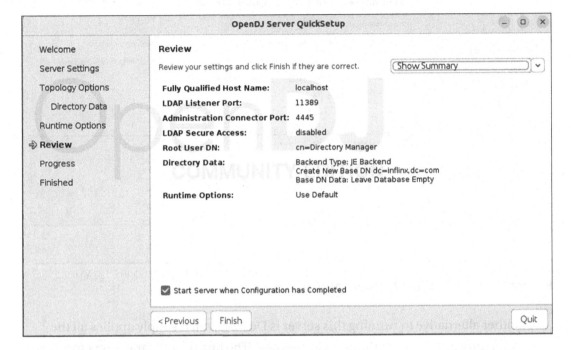

***Figure C-5.*** *LDAP reviews all the configurations*

6.  A confirmation indicates a successful installation (see Figure C-6).

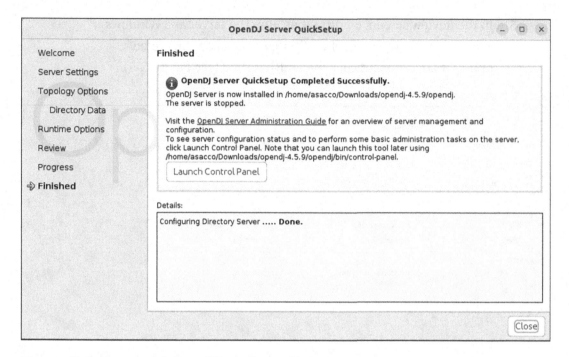

**Figure C-6.** *Successful OpenDJ confirmation*

Another alternative to running this server is Docker, which simply applies all the installation processes to the minimum expression. The image and parameters that support configuring the server are well documented on the Docker Hub web page.[3]

To do the same process; you can run using this command:

**Listing C-1.** How to run LDAP using docker

```
$ docker run -p 11389:1389  -p 4445:4444 --name opendj -e "ROOT_
USER_DN=cn=Directory Manager" -e "ROOT_PASSWORD=secret" -e "BASE_
DN=dc=inflinx,dc=com" openidentityplatform/opendj:4.5.9
```

Create a docker-compose file that simplifies the process to track or modify the configuration. The file with the same instructions as Listing C-1 but using docker-compose looks like Listing C-2.

---

[3] https://hub.docker.com/r/openidentityplatform/opendj

***Listing C-2.***  How to run the LDAP server using docker-compose

```
version: '3.0'
services:
  opendj:
    image: openidentityplatform/opendj:4.5.9
    container_name: opendj
    ports:
      - 11389:1389
      - 4445:4444
    environment:
      - ROOT_USER_DN=cn=Directory Manager
      - ROOT_PASSWORD=secret
      - BASE_DN=dc=inflinx,dc=com
    restart: always
```

If you run the previous listing using the command docker-compose up, you will obtain Listing C-3, which indicates that the server is running and you can start using it.

***Listing C-3.***  Output of LDAP server using docker-compose

```
$ docker-compose up
[+] Running 1/0
 ✔ Container opendj  Recreated                                     0.0s
Attaching to opendj
opendj  | Instance data Directory is empty. Creating new DJ instance
opendj  | BASE DN is dc=inflinx,dc=com
opendj  | Password set to secret
opendj  | Running /opt/opendj/bootstrap/setup.sh
opendj  | Setting up default OpenDJ instance
opendj  |
opendj  | Configuring Directory Server ..... Done.
opendj  | Configuring Certificates ..... Done.
opendj  | Creating Base Entry dc=inflinx,dc=com ..... Done.
opendj  |
opendj  | To see basic server configuration status and configuration, you
            can launch
```

```
opendj | /opt/opendj/bin/status
opendj |
opendj | [20/Jul/2023:12:01:22 +0000] category=com.forgerock.opendj.ldap.
          config.config severity=NOTICE msgID=571 msg=Loaded extension from
          file '/opt/opendj/lib/extensions/snmp-mib2605.jar' (build 4.5.9,
          revision d967673e1af894245300dc734496caf0a74701d4)
opendj | [20/Jul/2023:12:01:22 +0000] category=CORE severity=NOTICE
          msgID=134 msg=OpenDJ Server 4.5.9 (build 20221209101029, revision
          number d967673e1af894245300dc734496caf0a74701d4) starting up
opendj | [20/Jul/2023:12:01:22 +0000] category=JVM severity=NOTICE
          msgID=21 msg=Installation Directory:  /opt/opendj
opendj | [20/Jul/2023:12:01:22 +0000] category=JVM severity=NOTICE
          msgID=23 msg=Instance Directory:      /opt/opendj/data
opendj | [20/Jul/2023:12:01:22 +0000] category=JVM severity=NOTICE
          msgID=17 msg=JVM Information: 17.0.5+8 by Eclipse Adoptium, 64-
          bit architecture, 1988100096 bytes heap size
opendj | [20/Jul/2023:12:01:22 +0000] category=JVM severity=NOTICE
          msgID=18 msg=JVM Host: 63278e99ccd4, running Linux
          5.15.49-linuxkit amd64, 7947780096 bytes physical memory size,
          number of processors available 12
opendj | [20/Jul/2023:12:01:22 +0000] category=JVM severity=NOTICE
          msgID=19 msg=JVM Arguments: "--add-exports=java.base/sun.
          security.x509=ALL-UNNAMED", "--add-exports=java.base/sun.
          security.tools.keytool=ALL-UNNAMED", "-Dorg.opends.server.
          scriptName=start-ds"
opendj | [20/Jul/2023:12:01:23 +0000] category=BACKEND severity=NOTICE
          msgID=513 msg=The database backend userRoot containing 1 entries
          has started
opendj | [20/Jul/2023:12:01:23 +0000] category=EXTENSIONS severity=NOTICE
          msgID=221 msg=DIGEST-MD5 SASL mechanism using a server fully
          qualified domain name of: localhost
opendj | [20/Jul/2023:12:01:23 +0000] category=CORE severity=NOTICE
          msgID=135 msg=The Directory Server has started successfully
```

```
opendj  | [20/Jul/2023:12:01:23 +0000] category=CORE severity=NOTICE
           msgID=139 msg=The Directory Server has sent an alert notification
           generated by class org.opends.server.core.DirectoryServer (alert
           type org.opends.server.DirectoryServerStarted, alert ID org.
           opends.messages.core-135): The Directory Server has started
           successfully
opendj  | [20/Jul/2023:12:01:23 +0000] category=PROTOCOL severity=NOTICE
           msgID=276 msg=Started listening for new connections on LDAP
           Connection Handler 0.0.0.0 port 1389
opendj  | [20/Jul/2023:12:01:23 +0000] category=PROTOCOL severity=NOTICE
           msgID=276 msg=Started listening for new connections on
           Administration Connector 0.0.0.0 port 4444
opendj  | [20/Jul/2023:12:01:23 +0000] category=PROTOCOL severity=NOTICE
           msgID=276 msg=Started listening for new connections on LDAPS
           Connection Handler 0.0.0.0 port 1636
opendj  | Server Run Status:        Started
opendj  | OpenDJ is started
```

You will obtain the same result on the console using docker run or docker-compose approaches.

# Installing Apache Directory Studio

The Apache Directory Studio is a popular, open source LDAP browser that can help you browse LDAP directories very easily. To install Apache Directory Studio, download the installer file from the official website;[4] just consider that the brew option was unavailable when this book was written. In this book, the version of Apache Directory Studio used is V2.0.0-M17.

The installation depends on your operating system; for example, if you have macOS or Linux, you only need to download the tool from the web page and run it on the bash *./ApacheDirectoryStudio*. If you have Windows, follow the instructions to indicate where to install the tool.

---

[4]https://directory.apache.org/studio/downloads.html

Once the installation is complete, the next step is to create a connection to the newly installed OpenDJ LDAP server. Before you can proceed, make sure your OpenDJ server is running. Now it's time to configure your Apache Directory Studio; you can do it by following the next steps:

1.  Launch the Apache Directory Server (see Figure C-7).

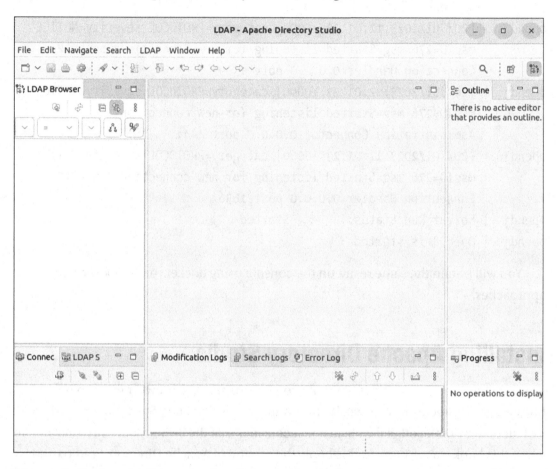

***Figure C-7.*** *Apache Directory Studio welcome page*

2.  Launch the New Connection wizard by right-clicking in the "Connections" section and selecting "New Connection" (see Figure C-8).

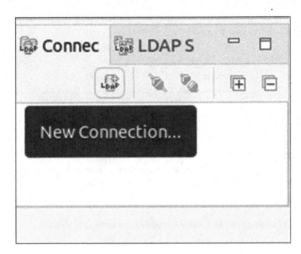

**Figure C-8.**   *Creating a new connection*

3.  On the Network Parameter screen, enter the information displayed in Figure C-9. This should match the OpenDJ information you entered during OpenDJ installation.

***Figure C-9.*** *LDAP connection network parameters*

4.  On the Authentication screen, enter "cn=Directory Manager" as Bind DN or user and "opendj" as password (see Figure C-10).

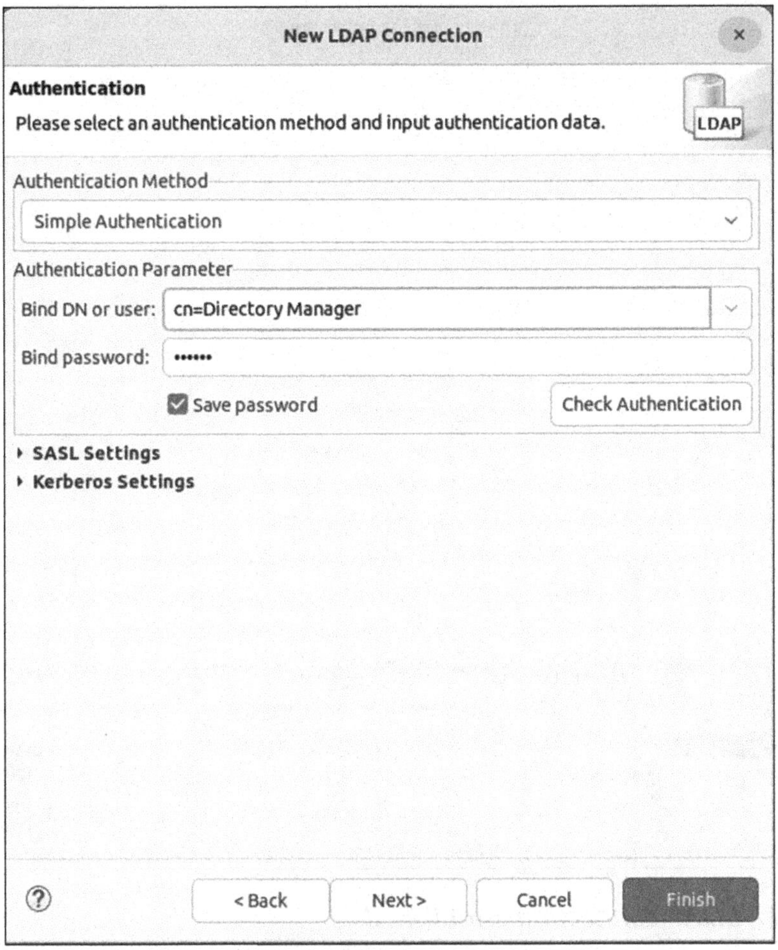

*Figure C-10.*  *LDAP connection authentication*

5. Accept the defaults in the Browser Options section and click the Finish button.

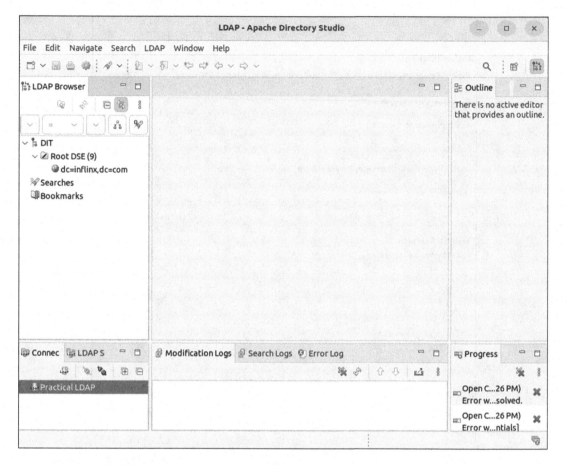

***Figure C-11.*** *LDAP connection established*

Another option to do this without installing anything on your machine is using an image of Docker,[5] which a particular user achieves by running the application on the docker image and using VNC;[6] you can access the application like a web page. To do this, just add the content of Listing C-4 to the previous docker-compose file.

---

[5] https://hub.docker.com/r/clickbg/apache-directory-studio
[6] https://es.wikipedia.org/wiki/VNC

**Listing C-4.** How to run Apache Directory Studio using Docker

```
version: '3.0'
services:
  //previous content
  apache-directory-studio:
    container_name: apache-directory-studio
    image: clickbg/apache-directory-studio:latest
    ports:
      - 5901:5901
```

After you execute the command docker-compose up, you need to open your VNC client and enter the URL 127.0.0.1:5901, which is shown in Figure C-12.

**Figure C-12.** *VNC client to access Apache Directory Studio*

If everything is okay, you will see Figure C-13 containing the same interface you have if you install it on your machine.

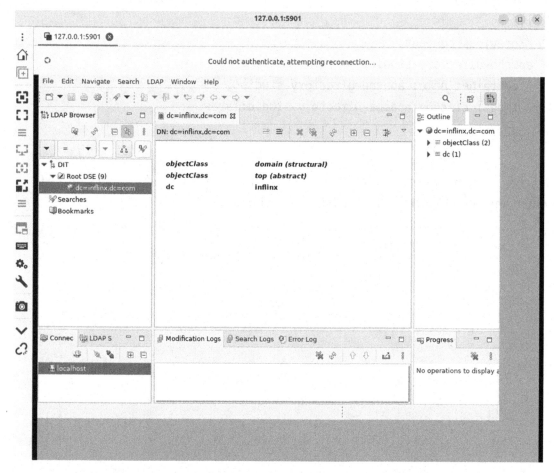

***Figure C-13.*** *VNC client with the interface Apache Directory Studio*

The configuration using the Docker image or installing the tool on your machine is the same because the Docker image emulates the application.

# Loading Test Data

In the previous sections, you installed the OpenDJ LDAP server and Apache Directory Studio for accessing the LDAP server. The final step in setting up your development/test environment is to load the LDAP server with test data.

---

**Note**    The accompanying source code/downloads contain two LDIF files, `patrons.ldif` and `employees.ldif`. The `patrons.ldif` file contains test data that mimics your library's patrons. The `employees.ldif` file contains test data that mimics your library's employees. These two files are heavily used for testing the code used in this book. Please download these files before moving forward if you have not already done.

---

Here are the steps for loading the test data.

1.  Right-click "Root DSE" in the LDAP browser pane and select Import ➤ LDIF Import (see Figure C-14).

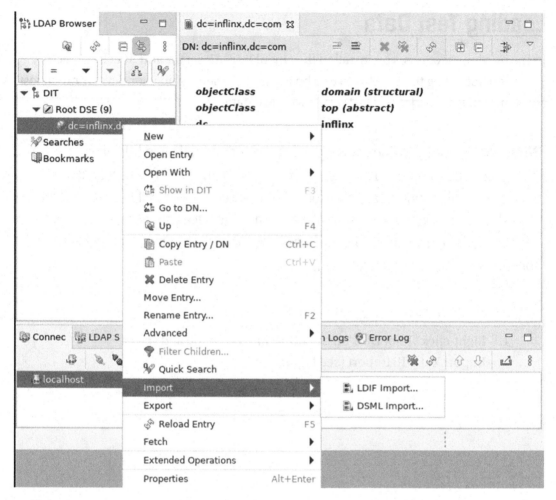

***Figure C-14.*** *LDIF import*

2.   Browse for this `patrons.ldif` file (see Figure C-15) and click
the Finish button. Make sure that the "Update existing entries"
checkbox is selected.

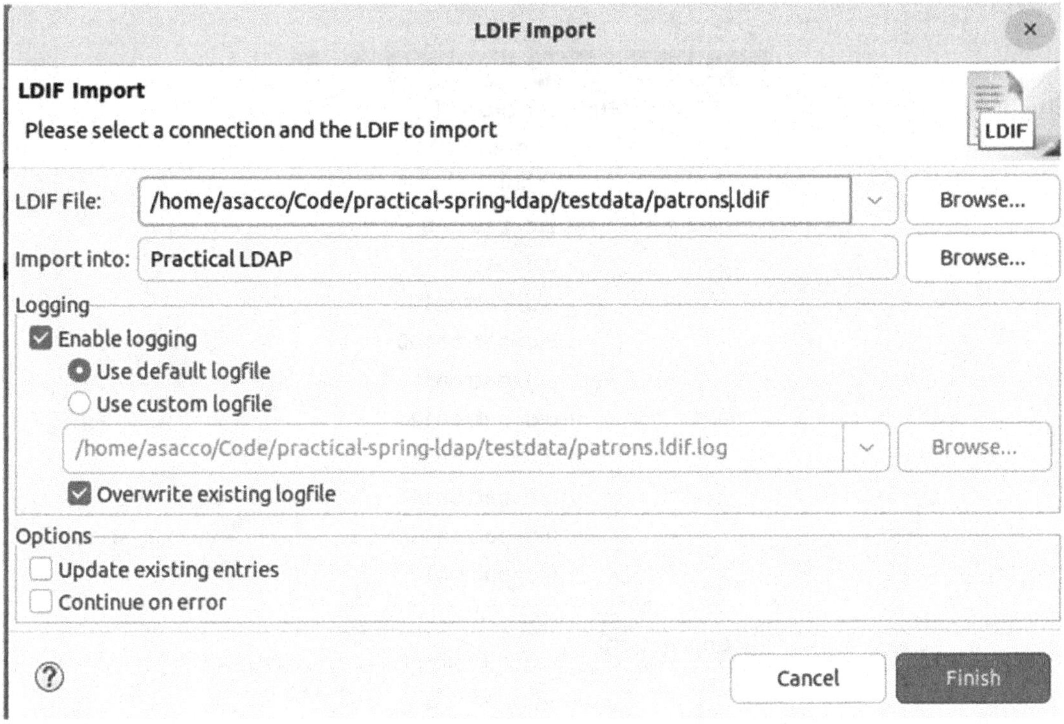

**Figure C-15.** *LDIF import settings*

3. Upon a successful import, you will see the data loaded under the dc=inflinx,dc=com entry (see Figure C-16).

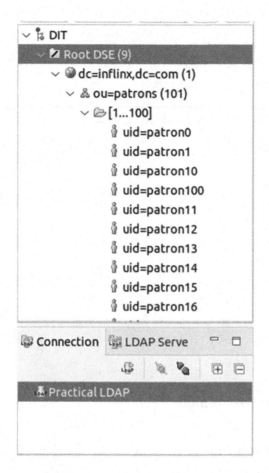

*Figure C-16.* *LDIF successful import*

# APPENDIX D

# Opening a Project

In this book, you will see some examples of projects that explain different LDAP features. You can create it following the instructions in the different chapters or download it from the official source code; if you want to download and import it on your IDE, you can follow the instructions in this appendix.

---

**Note**   Consider that the IDE suggested for this book is IntelliJ, so all the instructions are related to this IDE.

---

To run all the projects in this book, you need to have them installed on your machine JDK 17 or up; there is no restriction about which distribution you need. In Appendix A, you will find more information about the tools you need to install.

Figure D-1 shows how to open a file or an existing project in IntelliJ IDEA. To select the project you want to open, choose **File ➤ Open**.

© Balaji Varanasi and Andres Sacco 2023
B. Varanasi and A. Sacco, *Practical Spring LDAP*, https://doi.org/10.1007/979-8-8688-0002-3

***Figure D-1.*** *Menu option to open a project*

When you click Open, a pop-up will appear, so you can select the project's location to import on the IDE. Figure D-2 shows the modal that appears on the IDE, where you need to select the location of the files to import.

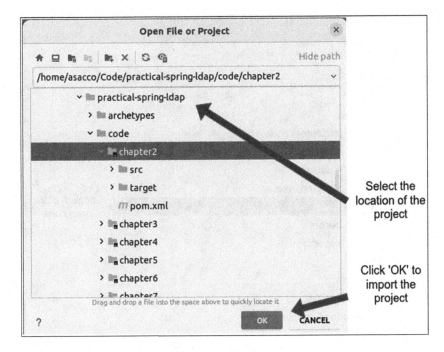

***Figure D-2.*** *Pop-up window to select the project to import*

After you import the project on your IDE, you can open the different packages to find the main class, usually located in the root package. Figure D-3 shows all the project structures appearing in Chapter 2.

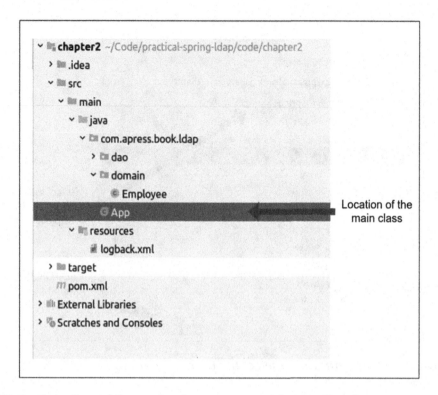

**Figure D-3.** *Location of the main class to execute the application*

To run the application, you only need to click the main class and choose the option Run Application or run it using the terminal.

# APPENDIX E

# Further Reading

In this book, you will see different libraries, technologies, and vendors of LDAP that do not cover some advanced topics because they are out of the book's scope, so you can have a list of books or resources to check to learn more in depth. There are three groups of resources. Each covers a specific type, like general resources about Docker, Spring Boot, some topics about the IDE, and others connected with LDAP.

## General

- *Mastering OpenLDAP* by Matt Butcher (Packt Publishing):[1] In this book, you will see different aspects of using OpenLDAP without using any technology, which is an excellent way to go more in depth on how LDAP works behind the scenes.

- *LDAP System Administration* by Gerald Carter (O'Reilly):[2] This book shows you different aspects related to the administration of LDAP, which are not part of this book but are essential if you want to use it on a productive application.

- *Beginning IntelliJ IDEA* by Ted Hagos (Apress):[3] This book covers all the aspects of using IntelliJ, like the installation process, how you can debug the application, and the most relevant elements to acquiring the basic skills of the IDE.

---

[1] https://www.packtpub.com/product/mastering-openldap-configuring-securing-and-integrating-directory-services/9781847191021

[2] https://www.oreilly.com/library/view/ldap-system-administration/1565924916/

[3] https://link.springer.com/book/10.1007/978-1-4842-7446-0

311

© Balaji Varanasi and Andres Sacco 2023
B. Varanasi and A. Sacco, *Practical Spring LDAP*, https://doi.org/10.1007/979-8-8688-0002-3

- *Docker in Action* by Jeff Nickoloff and Stephen Kuenzli (Manning):[4] In this book, you will find an extensive explanation of Docker's aspects and how it interacts with the different layers of the operating system. Also, you will learn how to create an image or run an existing one.

- *Learn Microservices with Spring Boot* by Moisés Macero García (Apress):[5] Suppose you want to understand all the aspects of a microservice, like how to create a new one, or the philosophy of using microservices instead of monoliths. In that case, this book will help you to understand these concepts and how to implement them using Spring Boot.

- *Learning Spring Boot 3.0* by Greg L. Turnquis (Packt Publishing):[6] This book covers most of the relevant topics in the new version of Spring Boot, like messaging and reactive applications.

- *Laurentiu Spilca's channel on YouTube:*[7] You will find different videos about most of the relevant topics of Spring-like security, performance, and some basic tutorials. Laurentiu is one of the most recognized speakers about different topics related to Spring; he published many books, some covering specific topics like Spring Security and others covering more general topics.

---

[4] https://www.manning.com/books/docker-in-action-second-edition?query=Docker%20in%20Action

[5] https://link.springer.com/book/10.1007/978-1-4842-6131-6

[6] https://www.packtpub.com/product/learning-spring-boot-30-third-edition/9781803233307

[7] https://www.youtube.com/c/laurentiuspilca

# Index

## A

AbstractFallbackRequestAndResponse
ControlDirContext
Processor, 163, 171–173
AbstractFilter, 133
AbstractRequestControl
DirContextProcessor, 163
AbstractRequestDir
ContextProcessor, 163
Acceptance testing, 77
ACID properties, 214, 215, 224
ADD_ATTRIBUTE code, 71
ADD REQ command, 235
afterPropertiesSet, 64
AndFilter, 144, 145
Apache Directory Studio, 285
   create connection, 297
   install, 295
   LDAP connection, 299, 300
   network parameters, 298
   VNC client, 301, 302
   welcome page, 296
ApacheDS, 15, 99, 100, 103, 224
Apache Maven
   archetypes, 43
   declarative dependency
     management, 43
   definition, 42
   plug-ins, 43
   standardized directory structure, 43
   tools support, 43
applicationContext.xml file, 65, 68

Archetypes
   command line, 56
   directory structure, 48
   group id, 54
   local repository, 44, 45
   logs, 44
   maven install commands, 45
   plug-ins, 54
   pom.xml file, 48, 54
   practical-ldap-archetype, 44
   practical-ldap-empty-archetype, 43
   practical-spring-ldap/code directory, 47
   values, 54
Aspect-Oriented Programming (AOP),
   223, 224
assertTrue method, 255
@Attribute annotation, 194
AttributesMapper implementation, 63
Authenticate method, 247, 249, 250, 252
Authentication
   basic implementation, 246
   configuration, 248
   DAO interface, 246
   DN, 250
   JUnit test, 250
   operations, 12
   Spring LDAP, 245
   working, 247
AuthenticationDao
   implementation, 253
Automated integration tests, 77, 81
@Autowired annotation, 67

313

© Balaji Varanasi and Andres Sacco 2023
B. Varanasi and A. Sacco, *Practical Spring LDAP*, https://doi.org/10.1007/979-8-8688-0002-3

Printed in the United States
by Baker & Taylor Publisher Services